Other Books by Edmund Keeley

INVENTING PARADISE

INVENTING PARADISE

•

THE GREEK JOURNEY
1937–47

•

EDMUND KEELEY

Farrar, Straus and Giroux

NEW YORK

Farrar, Straus and Giroux
19 Union Square West, New York 10003

Copyright © 1999 by Edmund Keeley
Distributed in Canada by Douglas & McIntyre Ltd.
Printed in the United States of America
Designed by Abby Kagan
First edition, 1999

Library of Congress Cataloging-in-Publication Data
Keeley, Edmund.
    Inventing paradise : the Greek journey, 1937–47 / by Edmund
Keeley.
        p.   cm.
    Includes bibliographical references and index.
    ISBN 0-374-17717-1 (alk. paper)
    1. Miller, Henry, 1891–   —Journeys—Greece.   2. Americans—
Travel—Greece—History—20th century.   3. Authors, American—20th
century—Biography.   4. Greece—Description and Travel.   I. Title.
PS3525.I5454Z713   1999
818'.5203—dc21
[B]   98–51340

Permissions appear on pages 275–77.

remember me, . . .
heap my mound by the churning gray surf
so even men to come will learn my story.
　　　　　　—Homer, *Odyssey*, 11
　　　　　(translated by Robert Fagles)

ACKNOWLEDGMENTS

*A*long with the several American and British writers in this book who made Greece the focus of their work for the better part of their lives, I feel that my first debt of gratitude is owed to the country itself: the generosity of its landscape, its poetry, its people. And I am especially grateful to the informal and uncompensated teachers who early on taught me how to know and love its riches: Theodore Litsas and Charles House in Salonika before the war; Bruce Lansdale, George Savidis, George Seferis, George Katsimbalis, and Nikos Gatsos in Athens and elsewhere during the decade after the war. There have been other teachers since, as well as the lessons that have come to me from the continuing rediscovery of things once thought to be lost or to have changed so as to be unrecoverable, only to shine forth once again in some new form of wonder. For helping me to try to capture in this book both the early and later manifestations of the recurring poetry in Greece, whether in actual or literary forms, I thank those who were good enough to read the manuscript and to offer their advice and encouragement: my wife, Mary; my agent, Georges Borchardt; my friends Carolyn Kizer, Robert Fagles, John Chioles, Peter Bien, Daniel Halpern, Chrysa Tsalikidou, Dimitris Gondicas, and Ian MacNiven. I was also helped by good talk with David Roessel and Avi Sharon, both scholars working with sensitivity and enthusiasm in some of the same territory covered by this book. And my learned friends Zissimos Lorenzatos and Dimitri Daskalopoulos provided, with charm and grace, the benefit of their personal knowledge of Henry Miller's "little band of friends" in Greece. Finally, I have had the immense good luck to work with Elisabeth Sifton, whose shrewd, subtle, and knowledgeable suggestions proved essential in preparing the final text—the kind of patient and intelligent editing that any writer longs for and has to be in the gods' favor to find.

CONTENTS

Weave a circle round him thrice,
And close your eyes with holy dread,
For he on honey-dew hath fed,
And drunk the milk of Paradise.
　　　　—Samuel Taylor Coleridge, "Kubla Khan"

Keep Ithaka always in your mind.
Arriving there is what you are destined for.
But do not hurry the journey at all.
Better if it lasts for years,
so you are old by the time you reach the island,
wealthy with all you have gained on the way,
not expecting Ithaka to make you rich.
　　　　　　—C. P. Cavafy, "Ithaka"

INVENTING PARADISE

THE FIRST EDEN

In the spring of 1939, Henry Miller was restless in Paris. *Tropic of Capricorn* had just come out, but, as he wrote his young friend Lawrence Durrell, people were not buying books—in fact, they were not even living, just "holding their breath for the expected catastrophe" of a world war. Miller tried to believe that the war wasn't imminent, but the possibility remained firmly in his mind. If it were to come, he would choose life over war. Some months earlier he had made his position clear in the hundred-page letter dated October 17, 1938, that concluded his voluble correspondence with Michael Fraenkel published under the title *Hamlet*: "War is not just war: it is a universe which each one explores to a different end. Myself, I am terrified of it . . . As long as I have two legs to run with I shall run from it, and if necessary, crawl away on all fours . . . Even if what I see about me is Hell, it is Life just the same, and I prefer this life of hell to the gamble of war. I love life above truth, above honor, above friends, country, God or anything." The politics of what was happening did not really interest him. Once things began to go to pot, he wrote Durrell, the jackals must reign.

Though Miller told his English friend that, despite the expected catastrophe, he was enjoying a completely solitary life after the publication of *Capricorn*, his imagery gave him away: every night, he concluded, he mounted the guillotine and had his head chopped off only to grow a new head "like that!" He was reading the proofs of Anaïs Nin's latest book to weed out "dinosaurian errata," a way, maybe, of avoiding the growing conviction that would soon become fact: after all these years of their sexual and literary intimacy in Paris, she would not go along with his plans to escape to some other world but would stay in Paris, for better or worse, with her husband. Miller ended up calling his solitude "the paradise of the over-driven scribes who write their way into Purgatory." The time had surely come for him to look for another kind of paradise.

For his part, Lawrence Durrell was in the doldrums, as he wrote Miller to say, working only fitfully, with no real impetus. He had been to Stratford, where Shakespeare had become an American industry, but one that charmed him into a sense of kinship with all the boys and girls drawn to the place by "the dim alarm in their own lives, to try and find a meaning in the life of the great unknown national man." The meaning he himself found was the secret of silence buried in New Place, where Shakespeare had lived in seclusion for the last five years of his life, now a trim English garden with a commemorative stone marking the spot that the retired bard's house had once occupied. Clearly, Durrell, too, was restless, eager for a change. He told his American friend that he had planned on spending a year sailing between cheap ports with his wife Nancy, say in Spain, Greece, Turkey, but things now looked so bad that he didn't know what to do.

Miller had written recently that he wished he could say he would see Durrell in Greece soon, but that his escape route was turning him toward America and the grandiose empty spaces "where man is nil and silence reigns." Durrell picked up that theme but hesitated. "Return to Corfu with the Italians outside our house? Spend the summer in Cornwall? OR GO TO AMERICA." That would be a big uprooting, he thought, a "big turn in the meridian." Sooner or later, surely, but . . . In the end he chose Corfu, and by late May so had Miller, as the first stop in an itinerary that he believed would take him through much of continental Europe, England, Ireland, America, and back to the Middle East and the Far East. Neither Miller nor Durrell could know that together and with the help of a few Greek friends they were about to create a country that would keep the war at a safe distance and give both of them, at least for a while, all the new life they longed for.

One of those friends was the Greek poet George Seferis, thirty-nine, born with the century on February 29 of a leap year, which allowed him to tell Miller that according to the calendar he was approaching his tenth birthday when they met. Though younger than Miller by any calculation, he was the less boyish of the two and more learned, an ardent student of the long Greek tradition in poetry from Homer and the classical dramatists to Vitzentzos Kornaros of the seventeenth-century Cretan renaissance and Dionysios Solomos of the modern demotic movement. This tradition, and the history of his people that it embodied, were both a resource and a burden that added weight to his ample body. Miller was to recognize a crucial vitality in Seferis long before the poet became, in 1963, the first of his countrymen to win a Nobel Prize. In *The Colossus of Maroussi*, the luminous book Miller wrote about his journey to Greece and his friendship with the group of local pleasure-loving mythmakers who changed his life, he tells us that Seferis was "passionate about his own country, his own people, not in a hidebound chauvinistic way but as a result of patient discovery following upon years of absence abroad." Miller goes on to say an essential, if seemingly paradoxical, truth about the source of the poet's strength: Seferis "had begun to ripen into a universal poet—by passionately rooting himself into the soil of his people." Some thirty years later, a few months before Seferis's death in 1971, Miller wrote his old friend to say that even after all the years that had separated them he could still hear Seferis's voice in his ears and could still remember "how much I envied your patriotism—rather, your love of Greece—something I have never been able to feel for my own country."

Yet, in the spring of 1939, George Seferis was tormented by what surrounded him on his return home from service as Greek consul in Koritsa, Albania. Three years earlier, before heading north, he had opened a poem with a declaration that in subsequent years was to become the one line of his poetry any Greek intellectual, whether or not a reader of Seferis's work, could quote in public: "Wherever I travel Greece wounds me." But the poem was written at a time when the wounding was caused first of all by nostalgia, and even that was colored by the self-irony implicit in the poem's title: "In the Manner of G.S." By 1939 Seferis's state of mind left little room for either nostalgia or irony, and in his comments recorded in the journal he kept from 1925 into his late years, he showed himself almost in tune with Miller's mood regarding the international crisis some months before the two met for the first time. A March 1939 entry defines the "Situation in Europe" by way of a passage from Homer's description of the land of the Cyclopes (as translated here by Robert Fagles):

> *They have no meeting place for council, no laws either,*
> *no, up on the mountain peaks they live in arching caverns—*
> *each a law to himself, ruling his wives and children,*
> *not a care in the world for any neighbor.*

Seferis's comment: "Exactly: the era of the Cyclopes."

A month later his journal reports that "we are living in a time of pervasive sleepwalking," and he predicts that when the moment arrives for us to wake up, nothing will remain in place—

though the only hope is for that moment to come, since humanity inscribes great circles consisting of generation after generation, and it is our fate to be dwelling along an infinitesimal arc of this trajectory "embedded in deepest night." The cause for this dark view of things had become specific. That very day, April 7, the Italians had invaded Albania, including some of those towns with a long Greek history such as Avlona, Saint John, The Saints Saranda, while Great Britain slept and the French wrote "bright articles about politics in general: the rich man looking through the needle's eye." They knew not what they did, nor what they would have to pay, Seferis added.

Approaching war wasn't the only thing on Seferis's mind. After his return from Koritsa, he had been given the unpalatable assignment of press officer to the Department of Press and Information. From the start of his diplomatic career, he had measured the cost of having to serve two masters, but the continuing conflict between his official duties as a civil servant and his obligations to his muse became acute under the Metaxas dictatorship, then in its third year. In August 1936 General Ioannis Metaxas, leader of the highly marginal ultra-right-wing Freethinkers' Party, after being appointed caretaker Prime Minister by King George II, had suspended key articles of the Constitution as a prelude to establishing a reactionary, paternalistic, and puritanical regime under the banner "Third Hellenic Civilization," designating himself "First Peasant" and "First Worker" and disciplining his countrymen with "quazi-fascist rhetoric" and enterprising police surveillance. By the spring of 1939 Seferis could see increasing evidence of the Greek dictator's sympathy for Germany and its totalitarian modes. Friends deemed to be critical of the regime had been arrested and sent into exile. The dictator's militaristic youth organization, modeled on Hitler's, was marching in the streets. And though decrees such as one censoring Thucydides' famous rendering of Pericles' funeral oration honoring those Athenians who died in the first year of the Peloponnesian War were a source of comedy, the stilted language of officialdom was a dangerously mixed mess, anathema to any serious writer.

In May, Seferis's journal tells his imagined reader that, after finishing what he thought an unsatisfactory essay on poetry, "we have to face the fact that in these days we cannot choose either the hours when we work or the way in which we express ourselves—at least in prose." By August, returning to his journal after a two-month hiatus, he asks himself how one can possibly move ahead "in this fog." Poetry remained his only recourse, but even that was a struggle. What was to become his most celebrated prewar poem, "The King of Asini," had been in progress almost two years by that spring and was worrying him still. Like Miller and Durrell, he seemed to need rejuvenation, open air, stimulating companions. That prospect was given him a month later at the home of his friend George Katsimbalis, in Maroussi, where he was introduced to "the first Anglo-Saxon writers I have known," Henry Miller and Lawrence Durrell, who had come to hear Katsimbalis read a selection of Seferis's poems in English translation.

George Katsimbalis had been Seferis's intimate friend for years, a champion of his first volume, *Strophi* (*Turning Point*) (1931), and a regular correspondent during Seferis's years abroad in the diplomatic service, giving his friend news of the literary life in Athens and mailing him current periodicals. He was as ample in girth as Seferis but with a tougher body, the shoulders never stooped, his stance as he surveyed the world around him and his vibrant voice, even his ever-present cane, still bearing news of his military service in the First World War. Seferis considered him a companion like no other. Early on he remarked to Miller "with deep feeling" that Katsimbalis, who soon became the "colossal" figure at the center of Miller's book on Greece, was a great fellow, no doubt about it, something extraordinary: "a human phenomenon, I should say."

Seferis, softer than Katsimbalis, subtler, also more forgiving, did not allow Katsimbalis's uncompromising and sometimes wrongheaded critical sensibility to compromise their friendship, at least not until much later on, when some difference of opinion led to a break in their correspondence. For now, the poet took Katsimbalis's criticism in his stride. When his second volume appeared—a long, strictly rhymed post-symbolist poem entitled *I Sterna* (*The Cistern*; 1932) that he considered a new departure—he wrote to his sister, Ioanna (Jeanne) Tsatsos, from London, "Katsimbalis, who is brilliant and loves me as few do, wrote me in a recent letter [about *The Cistern*]: 'you have betrayed all of us who believe in you' "—to which Seferis responded, "I think I would have betrayed them if I had done the opposite of what I did." Throughout his life Katsimbalis thought the prolific and highly influential Kostis Palamas was the greatest of contemporary Greek poets, and during his later years was dismayed to see Palamas gradually lose his dominance while the Alexandrian Greek C. P. Cavafy slowly rose to legendary stature, first abroad and then in Greece: "That, that—you know what," he would mumble. "How can you read him?" Typically, the question was only half-serious, meant to be provocative, because the fact is that Katsimbalis prepared and published the first substantial bibliography of Cavafy's work as early as 1943.

In the 1930s and even later, Katsimbalis was the best champion a young Greek writer could have because he showed the most passionate commitment to serious new writing—at least that which he liked of it—and he had the loudest voice in its defense, even if he rarely put his passion down on the page. Except for his various bibliographies and several translations, Katsimbalis published very little during his lifetime. Seferis was among the first to see what a good literary editor his friend would make, and he told his sister so in 1931. Four years later, Katsimbalis, working anonymously with another friend and fellow critic of his age named Andreas Karandonis, launched and financed what was to be the most important Athenian literary journal to emerge between the wars, *Ta Nea Grammata* (*The New Letters*), publishing new work by the best poet of the older generation, Angelos Sikelianos, and by the two future Nobel laureates Seferis and Odysseus Elytis, among other important writers who made up the now famous "Generation of the Thirties."

By the summer of 1939 that noble enterprise was becoming a casualty of the times—after the spring issue of 1940 there was a hiatus until its final offerings in 1944–45—and George Katsimbalis had begun to put his passion less into editing and bibliographical collecting and more into his greatest talent, talking, along with another consuming enterprise, guiding friends to the treasures of Greece, both ancient and modern, both actual and imagined. Durrell had discovered Katsimbalis sometime before Miller arrived in Greece in July 1939, and soon he introduced Miller to the Katsimbalis circle: along with Seferis, there was Niko Hadjikyriako-Ghika, the most celebrated painter of his day; D. I. Antoniou, a soft-spoken sea-captain poet; Theodore Stephanides, a doctor, botanist, poet, and translator described by Miller as "the most learned man I have ever met and a saint to boot"; Seferis's sister, Ioanna, also an occasional poet and diarist who was memorable to Miller for her "queenliness"; and her husband, Constantine Tsatsos. Tsatsos was a professor-statesman who was sent into exile for challenging the Metaxas dictatorship and who subsequently defied the German and Italian occupiers of his country in 1941 by openly honoring October 28—the first anniversary of the Italian invasion—at Athens University in commemoration of the Greek resistance. These two challenges to totalitarian regimes were recognized by his countrymen as courageous acts of conscience, eventually rewarded by his election as the first President of his country after the fall of the 1967–74 Colonels' dictatorship.

All these people—but especially Seferis and Katsimbalis—became the companions of Miller and Durrell on their prewar journey toward a partial understanding and uninhibited love of contemporary Greece, a country each ended up creating in his own image. The story of that creation in the case of Durrell began on Corfu several years before Miller reached Greece, and in the case of Miller it began not with his September visit to Maroussi to hear Katsimbalis read Seferis's poetry but in Piraeus, where he arrived for his first and only visit to the country during a July heat wave in 1939, aboard the good ship *Théophile Gautier*, out of Marseilles.

Before the Second World War and even immediately after the war, that is how you usually reached Athens: by ship landing at the port of Piraeus. In recent years you would normally reach Athens by plane, which makes it difficult to see just what it is that gives the modern city precise definition. From the air, what you are likely to take in first is the great valley filled with off-white apartment buildings, all seemingly the same in design and height, stretching from the sea at the edge of the airport to what appear to be haze-shrouded mountains outlining a bowl-shaped horizon. You can find a certain definition in the few open spaces—sometimes green, sometimes brown, sometimes bald—that interrupt the spread of concrete to offer now and then a thing suddenly remarkable: a high hill with a shaved crown like a monk's tonsure capped by a whitewashed church with a flag on a pole beside it for the cap's feather, the hill called Lycabettus; or a smaller hill, the more familiar Acropolis, with temples under scaffolding and not one but two open-air theaters of weathered marble; and just beyond the green oasis that used to be the Royal Garden, a narrow horseshoe of a stadium in the ancient style, restored at the turn of the century in pure white marble to serve the first of the modern Olympic Games.

What really gives the postwar cement city a lighter definition is something invisible from either sea or air: an underground life that still belongs to the neighborhoods, each bearing remnants of the village life that came to Athens during this century with the millions who moved there from the provinces and places abroad for a share of the action. And almost all Greeks south of Salonika believe that Athens is where the action is, whether your pleasure is business, entertainment, culture, politics, or simply an escape from boredom. The great migration to the city has done much to form the split character of the contemporary Athenian: intensely individualistic, charming with both men and women, arrogant (anybody is clever enough to be a tycoon or a prime minister), as much on the make as the citizen of any other city, but at the same time as filled with domestic pride as any villager and almost as traditional.

The Athenian has little concern for public enterprise or communal responsibility and much cynicism about politics, even if politics, and the quality of the local soccer and basketball teams, are still the principal subjects of debate wherever two or three men are gathered together over coffee. But along with this cynicism about communal activity, Athenian men and women are still passionately devoted to the family circle and the home territory. They normally identify their origins first by the villages of their parents, then by their Athens neighborhood, and though these latter are endless—Alimos, Faliron, Nea Smyrni, Imitos, Kaisariani, Chalandri, Maroussi, Filothei, Psychico, Pangrati, Metz, Patission, Exarchia, Hilton, and more—their names can rouse, in those who have lived the best part of their lives in one or another, all the nostalgia and chauvinism of a provincial hometown. And like other Greeks, the Athenian is generally hospitable to foreigners once they are brought into the home, whatever the national prejudice against the latest country to attempt to insert its finger—as the expression goes—into their affairs.

From the close-to-earth view of things, one Athens neighborhood resembles its neighbor. One grid of apartment buildings, one grid of streets, merges with the grid next door, and there is little evidence of the border between them. Yet this lack of distinction in architecture and city planning has the advantage of keeping life at a human level, the level of sentiment and rumor. All those in an Athenian apartment building—unlike their counterparts in New York City, say—eventually come to recognize and even sometimes address one another, especially in the older buildings where there now seems to be continual communal argument over what is and what isn't an essential repair. And you get to recognize the neighbors in the buildings next door by patronizing the same local kiosk or bakery or neighborhood café, where your needs and theirs are usually anticipated before the asking. The doorman and his wife, ever vigilant, ever ready to break the boredom by gossip with the doorman and his wife down the street, become part of a network of people who know more than is necessary to know about life in this row of apartment buildings and the next and sometimes the next beyond that. Along with this chummy curiosity about the trespasses of others, you find as much tolerance of the neighborhood's walking eccentrics as a Greek village shows toward its roving idiots, the "naturals" who are God's special children.

One neighborhood that most every Athenian knows to a degree is Kolonaki, or Little Column, named for the column once standing alone on the edge of town but now in a busy square close to the city center. Kolonaki used to be regarded as the ritziest if most conservative part of Athens to live in, until too much traffic and polluted air began to tarnish its upper-class image, though it always had a bohemian fringe around the slope of Lycabettus, where writers and artists, both foreign and domestic, could find fairly cheap, congenial homes in the few two- and three-story houses left over from the early days when the streets were unpaved. The square that used to provide open-air tea and coffee for the elite in a paved figure-of-eight island known affectionately as "the Kolo Bidet" (the Ass Bidet) has now been cleared away to make room for the young who cruise in on motorcycles to eat pizza at the new mall or hang out over a drink to see who else may show up for a revved-up move into serious nightlife elsewhere. And very recently some Athenians on the rise who chose to live in the distant suburbs where the air is cleaner and the parking easy have begun to come back into Kolonaki because they miss the sidewalk cafés and restaurants, however upgraded, where the talk about politics and films and trips to the islands still has some wit in it, and where the boutiques that have taken over the ground-floor apartments on street after street are as classy as any in Europe.

But Kolonaki still has its village aura. The pharmacist will know your recurring ailments and sometimes give you unsolicited advice, the small bookstore around the corner will help to shape your taste in local literature, the taverna up on the hill will know your preference for barreled wine and a grilled porgy. The neighborhood has a Friday open-air market for those who like bargains and banter, along with several tiny "supermarkets" for those who prefer more expensive packaged goods and imports. It also has a relatively high-class brothel on the ground floor of an apartment building too old to do for boutique rental though only a block above the local embassy row. This brothel has a limited life ahead, it seems, given the way business has slowed down in the wake of the belated sexual revolution and the expanding liberation of both young and not so young. And it has a persistent, peripatetic enemy in Kolonaki's God-forgiven madman.

They say the madman is a carpenter by profession, but no one seems to know where his workbench is. He first came into the neighborhood during the Colonels' dictatorship, marching up the hill into the Lycabettus forest at the head of an imaginary platoon of reluctant soldiers. Muscular, handsome, grim-faced, he would start at the bottom of Loukianou Street at high noon, salute the flag outside the residence of the British ambassador—any flag would presumably do in a moment of peril—then start his climb in the middle of the street at a fast pace, swinging his arms like an evzone on parade, bellowing out a Greek military marching song full-throated, stopping only in front of the brothel to preach obscenely at the ladies of the late afternoon and night now withdrawn behind its closed doors, pausing once more at the main crossroads to curse at the vehicles trying to interfere with his onward progress against the invisible gun emplacement high up on the hill.

When the madman first appeared, some in the neighborhood took him to be a symbol of resistance against the political oppression that was then trying to crush the free Greek spirit, and after the dictatorship fell, others saw him as a lunatic soldier of the Church militant fighting to reestablish a lost moral center, but now that he is white-haired and thinner and less triumphantly vocal, showing up infrequently but still a strong climber when he does, people say that his history goes back to the Korean War and that his obscenities are directed more at his own imaginary troops than at the world outside his head. The cursing is to urge his men to leave their friendly camp followers behind and fight on gallantly uphill against a vital but tenacious North Korean emplacement, to prove that the valor of the Greeks is at least equal to that of the Turks, who were, for the brief period of the Korean War, Greece's fighting ally rather than enemy.

Whatever the madman's history and significance, no one confronts him during his march these days, no one takes his cursing personally, no one does more than give him a passing glance, as though he has as much right in his madness to the center of the street as the saner jaywalkers and arm-in-arm lovers who take to the center to avoid the narrow rutted sidewalks and their unattended defecations. The casual attitude of the residents toward their madman over so many years makes him as much a part of the expected scene as the gray-haired former prime minister who always had a reserved table waiting for him and his wife during the lunch hour at Philipous Taverna on Xenokratous Street. And for a few of the remnant literary bohemians in the neighborhood, the march of the madman past his tolerant onlookers recalls George Seferis's narration about a presentable weeping man in a poem he wrote about the time of Henry Miller's arrival in Greece in the summer of 1939:

That man walks along weeping
no one can say why
sometimes they think he's weeping for lost loves
like those that torture us so much
on summer beaches with the gramophones.

Other people go about their business
endless paper, children growing up, women
ageing awkwardly.
He has two eyes like poppies
like cut spring poppies
and two trickles in the corners of his eyes.

He walks along the streets, never lies down
striding small squares on the earth's back
instrument of a boundless pain
that's finally lost all significance.

Some have heard him speak
to himself as he passed by
about mirrors broken years ago
about broken forms in the mirrors
that no one can ever put together again.
Others have heard him talk about sleep
images of horror on the threshold of sleep
faces unbearable in their tenderness.

We've grown used to him, he's presentable and quiet
only that he walks along weeping continually
like willows on a river-bank you see from the train
as you wake uncomfortably some clouded dawn.

We've grown used to him; like everything else you're used to
he doesn't stand for anything
and I talk to you about him because I can't find
anything that you're not used to;
I pay my respects.

Seferis's 1939 man of sorrows and those who take him so for granted are surely a metaphor for the silent anxiety of those who were sleepwalking in the prewar days that Seferis recorded in his journal, but the difference between that story and the Kolonaki madman's is the essential one of the shifting distance between fiction and reality, between poetry and history. The madman's continual battle with imaginary presences appears to be the product of cruel wartime history, a reality that extended through the harsh German occupation of the Second World War and the devastating civil war that followed, to the Korean War and its aftermath in the political turmoil that ended in the Colonels' dictatorship. The strongest perception our madman evokes is that of historical victim rather than poetic symbol or metaphor.

Seferis's man of sorrows is finally more moving. His "boundless pain," however meaningless to his prewar onlookers, seems to extend far back into Greek history, beginning with that of Odysseus' pitiable companion Elpenor and of his captain's compassion for him (these identified by Seferis himself) and ending with what can be seen as a representation of the sensibility that the poet often called the "*kaimo tis Romiosinis,*" freely translated as the bitter yearning of modern Hellenism. That yearning has a general meaning and a continuity. Though the pain in it appears to be in some part a personal matter—suggested by those lost loves and broken forms in broken mirrors—the images of horror that torment the weeping man on the threshold of sleep carry a warning of things to come for those who take him for granted, even—as the last lines imply—for you the reader, "*hypocrite lecteur!—mon semblable,—mon frère!*" His coming into the neighborhood to walk the streets with those eyes like cut spring poppies is for the purpose of bearing witness to threatening times, which proved all too real in late 1939 and beyond.

Of course, within the world of poetry, the actual has its shifting realities depending on your point of view. Even during times of local crisis or anxiety, the foreign writer who has fallen in love with Greece will, at least early in the affair, see the country with all the distorting passion that a lover should, and if he is forced to go elsewhere, he will look back with an intensely lyrical nostalgia on what he has left behind. Bernard Spencer, a superb English poet who is known these days to only a faithful few and who (along with his friend Lawrence Durrell and the Greek poet Nanos Valaoritis) became Seferis's first translator into English, was haunted by the radiant prewar Greece he knew, and he made it the subject of poem after poem during his expatriation in Cairo and later in London after the war. Yet he wrote about it not as soul-wounded Seferis did but as a lover still touched by the first flush of his passion:

> *Spring shakes the windows; doors whang to,*
> *the sky moves half in dark and half*
> *shining like knives: upon this table Elytis' poems lie*
> *uttering the tangle of sea, the "breathing caves"*
> *and the fling of Aegean waves.*
>
> *I am caught here in this scattering, vagrant season*
> *where telephones ring;*
> *and all Greece goes through me*
> *as the wind goes searching through the city streets.*

Greece, I have so much loved you
out of all reason;
that this unquiet time
its budding and its pride
the news and the nostalgia of Spring
swing towards you their tide:

Towards the windmills on the islands;
Alefkandra loved by winds,
luminous with foam and morning, Athens
her blinded marble heads,
her pepper-trees, the bare heels of her girls,
old songs that bubble up from where thought starts,
Greek music treading like the beat of hearts;
haunted Seferis, smiling, playing with beads.

And since especially at this time
statues and blossoms, birth and death require
we give account of manhood and youth,
the wind that whirls through London also rings
with the bang and echo of the Easter gun,
as in days gone,
from where the pilgrims' torches climb
over a darkening town
to set the bony peak of Lykahvetoss,
Athens, and all the opening year on fire.

This evocation of springtime Athens and the torch-lit climb up Lycabettus hill at Easter is brought to us with something of the same uncompromising emotion, if softer rhetoric, that Henry Miller delivers to us in the account of his arrival in Athens by way of Piraeus on a boiling day in July. He tells us at the start of *The Colossus of Maroussi* that he had found Durrell's letters about Greece poetic but confusing in their blend of dream and reality, of history and myth, and he had thought that his young English friend was "laying it on" as his way of coaxing him to make the trip, but the reality proves to be "a world of light such as I had never dreamed of and never hoped to see." In any case it soon becomes clear in the book that the American was quite prepared when so moved to take up dream and myth for his own mode of laying it on.

Despite his caution about Durrell's "poetic" introduction to Greece, Miller appears to have been more than well disposed toward his new country before he reached its shores. Aboard ship on the voyage to Piraeus, he had an illuminating conversation with the second Greek he'd ever met. (The first was a painter in Paris named Malliarakis, who had told him, "Miller, you will like Greece. I am sure of it.") This second conversation, with a medical student returning to the homeland from Paris, taught him that the Greeks were not only an enthusiastic, curious, and passionate people but rich with the sterling human qualities of "contradictoriness, confusion, and chaos." Miller admits that he was already enamored of Greece and its people before actually seeing the country; he could tell in advance that the Greeks were a friendly, hospitable people, "easy to reach, easy to deal with." And nothing that he encountered during his first few days in this brave new world could change his mind, not the arid, desolate, finally terrifying ride from Piraeus to Athens that made him wonder for a moment why he had decided to come to Greece, not the taxi driver who was "like an animal who had been miraculously taught to operate a crazy machine," not the wily guide who tried to charge him an arm and a leg but who finally settled, after much amicable bargaining, for a price that didn't insult him, not even the heat, which had become so intense that Miller had to retreat to a cool place and never got beyond the gate of the Acropolis or to the Theseum or to any of the other places on the morning's itinerary.

Within a matter of hours, Miller became a typical Athenian, first of all by not visiting the Acropolis—an activity most local citizens would consider to be reserved for schoolchildren and moonlight lovers—and then by giving himself over to a series of strategies for avoiding the heat: eating ice cream, drinking ice water, lying down naked in a pool of sweat through the late afternoon and into the early evening, heading for the nearest park to sit at a table and drink more water. The park Miller encounters that evening, by the Zapion, is his first glimpse of the Greek Eden: "It remains in my memory like no other park I have known. It is the quintessence of park, the thing one feels sometimes in looking at a canvas or dreaming of a place one would like to be in and never finds." And it is in this park that he first falls in love with the Greek people:

> Seeing lovers sitting there in the dark drinking water, sitting there in peace and quiet talking in low tones, gave me a wonderful feeling about the Greek character. The dust, the heat, the poverty, the bareness, the containedness of the people, and the water everywhere in little tumblers standing between the quiet, peaceful couples, gave me the feeling that there was something holy about the place, something nourishing and sustaining.

What he finds especially magical is that the place is filled, he thinks, with the poorest people in the world, and the gentlest. He concludes that he is glad he arrived in Athens during an incredible heat wave, because seeing it under what appear to him as the worst of conditions, he feels "the naked strength of the people, their purity, their nobility, their resignation," this especially visible that hot night because "the Greek knows how to live with his rags: they don't utterly degrade and befoul him" as they do people in other countries Miller had visited.

There is something both touching and curious in this quick generalization about the Greek character and its focus on poverty, especially in the public areas of central Athens, where you will find Athenians of all stripes and ages but less than a broad selection of people in rags. Miller was himself walking the poverty line in those days, which may in part explain the singleness of his perspective and the abundance of his sympathy, but it also has roots in a romanticism about the nobility of those who manage to live the simple life of the rural poor, what foreigners—including Miller himself—used to call the peasant life. On the voyage to Piraeus, Miller had found his companions other than the Greek (a Turk, a Syrian, some Lebanese students, an Argentinian of Italian extraction) all devoted to progress and the machine, to efficiency, capital, and comforts, all devoted to America. But even the Greek he spoke to on board wanted to go to America too someday, since, according to the author, "every Greek dreams of going to America and making a nest egg." So Miller lectured all of them about America, where there were millions unemployed yet where the American people, "with all their machine-made luxuries and comforts," were "empty, restless and miserable."

Miller's romanticism about the simple life in Greece as against the presumed life of comfort in America (despite all those millions of unemployed) remained resolute. Twenty-five years later, in 1964, never having returned to Greece, he wrote in a text accompanying a selection of drawings of the country by Anne Poor that the more we (presumably we in the West) advance technologically and the more we become robotized, sterilized, and stultified, "the more nostalgic we grow over the simple way of life," and this is represented by a stroll through the countryside of his remembered Greece where you would encounter mules and donkeys rather than speeding motor cars, people carrying loads on their heads instead of in their heads, and men, women, and children "gathering roots, herbs, even weeds, to round out their meager repast," in short, the "timeless, tireless routine of the peasant." Miller worries that things may now have changed in Greece and that the simple folk may yearn to roll about in a Rolls-Royce or a Cadillac and eat caviar or smoked sturgeon, but "most likely all these simple folk pray for is that their donkey will last yet another season, that the crops won't be ruined by frost or blight, the fishing boats will return in safety from a long and perilous voyage." He declares that the threat for the future comes from the West, not the East, and he fears that what "we are offering them, even with the best intentions, may prove their undoing."

Alas, when Miller wrote in this mode, the worst had already happened—at least from his perspective, if not necessarily that of the villager who had somehow survived the German occupation, the postwar devastation, the civil war, and the American aid program. By that time the so-called peasant probably had a tractor in place of his prewar donkey or at least belonged to a cooperative that did, and the fisherman, if still fishing at all, faced not the usual perils of the sea but that of losing an arm when he dropped dynamite illegally to kill a reasonable quota of fish or that of facing fishing grounds made barren by the illegal dynamiting done by other fishermen. The earthen floors of village houses that so appealed to Miller in 1939 were by now more often than not replaced by a concrete slab, the mud bricks of the houses by red brick or cinder block (especially in those many villages that the Wehrmacht burned to the ground), and rural life was less bucolic, if more comfortable, because of the introduction of electricity, a program that was soon expanded under the 1967–74 dictatorship with the anticipated result of the junta's gaining in popularity among the former peasant class. With the later advent of European Community aid, a farmer in the more fertile areas could look forward to becoming rich enough to put money in a bank or into an apartment building and to sending his daughters to one of the new universities, thereby relieving them of not only having to work in the fields and carry heavy loads on their heads but, for some of them, the inner burden of ignorance, superstition, and tedium.

Twenty-five years after Miller's visit the simple folk in the cities had become less simple and the city much more crowded, as the great migration from rural areas continued. Access to the sea became more and more difficult, so that a citizen's first savings were inevitably spent on a second- or third-hand car or a motorcycle of some kind to allow for escape from the increasingly air-polluted neighborhoods, at the same time increasing that pollution and making transport more and more complicated. In the days before the war, Seferis had celebrated what was then the broadest escape route to the sea in a poem called "Syngrou Avenue," the four-lane toll road lined by pepper trees that took you past "columns whose burden makes them more narrow" so that you could leave behind "the bodies deliberately carved for counting and for hoarding riches" and emerge suddenly to see "the blue body of the mermaid." In the postwar decades, that avenue, lined less by pepper trees than by new concrete habitations for commerce and tourism, would eventually overflow on any weekend with fast-moving cars and motorcycles—some of these with mother and child clinging to the driver—in a relentless exodus to find that blue mermaid as she swam farther and farther away from the city's yearning heart.

As Miller himself says at one point, you have to learn to take the bad with the good. And if what is good for you gradually proves to be bad for you—or anyway less good—while becoming something better for others, that is the cost of time going by, a fact of life that can be confronted only by what most approaches the timeless. Beyond the virtues of the simple peasant life, Miller found at the very start of his Greek journey—so we learn in *The Colossus of Maroussi*—something timeless in the landscape and seascape of Greece: something essentially different about the sea, the sky, the light of his newly discovered country. On leaving

Athens for Corfu to meet Durrell, he had his first encounter with what still transforms the foreign visitor: "Out of the sea, as if Homer himself had arranged it for me, the islands bobbed up, lonely, deserted, mysterious in the fading light." And after the light vanished, there was the brilliant night sky, clear as no other. Then, approaching the harbor at Patras, the lights strung across the waterfront like Japanese lanterns gave him the impression of an impending festival. And finally, there is the exotic touch that comes in with the men rowing out to meet the passenger ship, pushing the oars in front of them instead of pulling on them, curiously "moving their heavy burdens about at will with deft and almost imperceptible movements of the wrist."

Miller alludes here to Homer, whom he claims not to have read at all, and he mentions that Missolonghi is opposite Patras, but unlike his predecessors in the nineteenth and early twentieth centuries, his thoughts are not conventionally Byronic, concerned neither with the remnants of classical landscape nor with the long-gone struggle for the liberation of modern Greece. His eyes at this time are on the literal landscape in front of him and the access it gives to his strictly contemporary search for personal freedom and for the roots of the divine in himself. The scene before him rouses a moment of epiphany. Though he still senses that the war is getting closer every day, the hope is there that peace will stay for a while and that men "might still behave like human beings." He feels himself "completely detached from Europe," having "entered a new realm as a free man." And for the first time in his life, at the age of forty-eight, he is happy "with the full consciousness of being happy"—bliss enough for him to tell himself that if he had any sense he ought to kill himself on the spot and be done with it. He decides after the fact that it was a good thing he didn't have the power or the courage to give in to that impulse because there were even greater moments to come, something beyond bliss. Marvelous good things happen to one in Greece, he concluded, things that happen to one nowhere else in the world, because in Greece "God's magic is still at work and, no matter what the race of man may do or try to do, Greece is still a sacred precinct." By morning he moved on from these first perceptions of his new Eden to Corfu, an island with its own particular definitions of both an earthly and an otherworldly paradise.

ISLAND OF
THE ALMOST BLEST

*C*orfu, called Kerkira by the Greeks, provided Lawrence Durrell his first access to modern Greece and its language, though for a while he preferred to call the island by an Anglicized rendering of its ancient Greek name, Corcyra. Even so, it did not take this expatriate English writer long to become a celebrant of both the contemporary landscape and the contemporary language of what he eventually came to look upon for a time as his adopted country—more than simply his second country. Durrell first arrived in Corfu in 1935, when he was twenty-three. He was accompanied by his first wife, Nancy, and the couple were soon joined on the island by his widowed mother and three siblings, sister Margo and younger brothers Leslie and Gerald, this ménage in due course brilliantly caricatured by Gerald in his best-selling book *My Family and Other Animals.* Early on, Durrell and Nancy settled into their own whitewashed house in the hamlet of Kalami on the northeast coast, and that is where they eventually received Henry Miller as their guest in the summer of 1939. Durrell wrote his first substantial novel on Corfu, *The Black Book,* what he himself called, in a 1937 letter to Miller, a "goodish beginning" but a "not quite adult" work, and what he acknowledged, in a preface to its reprinting some twenty years after the first 1938 Paris edition, was a book written much under the influence of *Tropic of Cancer.* At the same time, that novel, brooded over during his early days on Corfu and the occasion for ample correspondence with his older and more self-assured American friend, who helped him get it published, became the means for Durrell's discovering what he felt to be his own voice, "lame and halting perhaps, but nevertheless my very own."

A clear image of Durrell's Corfu does not emerge out of the book's blackness, its "spiritual and sexual etiolation," as the author himself put it—that clarity had to wait for *Prospero's Cell,* first published in 1945. But his sense of having found his first true voice in that particular Mediterranean climate is consistent with what he describes, in *Prospero's Cell,* as a change in the heart of things when out of desolate Calabria he crossed the sea to encounter Ionian islands coming out of the darkness to meet him: "You enter Greece as one might enter a dark crystal; the form of things becomes irregular, refracted . . . Other countries may offer you discoveries in manners or lore or landscape; Greece offers you something harder—the discovery of yourself."

Some twenty years later, Henry Miller gave this perception his own characteristic twist: "To know [Greece] thoroughly is impossible; to understand it requires genius; to fall in love with it is the easiest thing in the world. It is like falling in love with one's own divine image reflected in a thousand dazzling facets." By way of Corfu, Greece afforded both Durrell and Miller a particular insight into what the country had to offer the Anglo-American visitor. To discover yourself or to recognize your own divine image in what you see before you requires that you confront new possibilities nakedly on your own, with a certain innocence and with a heart open to recognition, uncluttered by prejudice or arrogance or snobbery. You must approach what is before you as a free spirit or quickly learn how to become one. In this way both Durrell and Miller found they could be nourished by the purely contemporary landscape as much as by remnants of the ancient world, by the unadulterated personal response instead of by the trained expectation, by the passions aroused in the company of human presences as much as by ghosts from the distant past. They also found in those contemporary presences and their natural habitat vital resources for their art.

Close to a century before Durrell arrived in Corfu, another English writer, Edward Lear, discovered the island and stayed long enough to perfect several enduring ways of representing the many dazzling facets of his divine image. He did so without giving in to the dominant post-Byronic mode of his times—adoration of the ancients and their sites, dubiety toward the moderns and their unfamiliar ways—and he thereby provided an early model for the new perspective that Durrell and Miller brought to philhellenism in the late 1930s. In the spring of 1848 Lear—poet, painter, faithful keeper of journals, and relentless correspondent—came to Greece for the first time as Durrell did, by way of the island closest to Italy, the country that in those days was the usual terminus of the Grand Tour. He was thirty-five at the time, a man who lived and traveled alone, tormented all his life by epileptic fits that he kept secret and by recurring depression, what he called his Demon and the Morbids, yet a brilliant humorist who ended up one of the most celebrated "nonsense" poets of his time and of ours. He was a gentle man who made friends easily though he thought himself ugly and therefore always drew himself with a elongated brow and nose, a huge balloon of a belly, and birdlike feet. In due course he became the greatest painter of Greek landscapes in the nineteenth century.

Though Lear's first visit to Corfu was brief, the island immediately captured his fancy: "About 3 this morning we anchored in the beautiful paradise of Corfu bay, & here I am," he writes his sister Ann, who had served for years as his only teacher. "This afternoon I have been wandering all about & nothing can be more lovely than the views . . . The extreme gardeny verdure, the fine olives, cypresses, almonds, & oranges, make the landscape so rich, & the Albanian mountains are wonderfully fine. All the villages seem clean & white, with here & there a palm tree overtopping them . . . I wish I could give you any idea of the beauty of this island—it really is a Paradise." He was able to create more than an idea of the place after returning to Corfu in 1855 for the first in a series of longer visits. Everywhere he went, day in day out, he drew and colored the landscape before him after it had passed through the filter of his delicate yet cunning imagination. Lear had no formal education to speak of, though he was thoroughly read in Byron and the other Romantics, in classical mythology, and in the Bible under the guidance of his sister. As was also at least partly true of both Miller and Durrell, his informal approach to learning appears to have given him unusual freedom to discover new things and to be rejuvenated creatively by what he discovered. At the age of forty-seven he remarks: "I am almost thanking God that I was never educated, for it seems to me that 999 [out of 1,000] of those who are so, expensively and laboriously, have lost all before they arrive at my age . . . whereas I seem to be on the threshold of knowledge."

One thing Lear learned in Greece was not to be intimidated or overwhelmed by the classical landscape as he had come to it through literature, though what remained of the antiquities that his eyes saw before him were a part of what his hand drew. His casual attitude toward the ancient presences that his reading had placed in the Greek landscape can be seen in his first trip through Attica in the company of the classical scholar Charles Marcus Church, who tells us that as the two journeyed along, Lear would sing an Italian air or chant Tennyson's "The Lotos-Eaters" with deep feeling while "sitting on the yellow shore of Aulis"—no verses by Homer or Aeschylus or even Byron here—

or he would "throw off some nonsense ditty, as in the mid-day halt by the hot sulphur-springs of Thermopylae: 'There was an old man of Thermopylae / who never did anything properly.' " Lear's focus was first of all on the poetry he could find in the living landscape in front of him, whether the settings he painted were home to the churches and monasteries of Byzantium, the remnants of Venetian citadels, mosques and minarets left over from the Turkish empire, or the broken columns of antiquity. More often than not, his painted and sketched landscapes included figures in modern dress: shepherds on the mountainside, fishermen in the coves, women spinning or washing on the shore beside purple seas.

When Lear settled in Corfu for his extended stays during the decade 1856–66, it was at least in part because he found a British community there that could serve in some degree as patron of his art. But that community of upper-class British colonizers was not really one he could belong to, being a self-educated artist who preferred to travel on his own and to see things as they really were (even if he did refer to himself on one occasion as "an English gentleman"). As Philip Sherrard remarks in his introduction to *Edward Lear: The Corfu Years*, one thing this self-engrossed British society would not do "was to demean itself by any attempt to understand the people over whom it exercised its unsolicited guardianship: as one British observer succinctly put it, between the British and the Greeks 'no love . . . is lost: they hold us in utter contempt, and we look on them as removed but one degree from donkeys.' " Lear may have been dependent on this society for his livelihood, but it is clear not only from his letters and journal entries but from the subjects of his art that he felt increasingly alienated from the society life of Corfu and found his escape in drawing and painting the natural life that most satisfied his poetic sensibility: the valleys and mountains and high bluffs of the island and the local people who made these their habitation. The retreat into the countryside would become urgent whenever his Morbids grew intolerable. During a second long stay in Corfu from the winter of 1861 to the spring of 1862, Lear starts out with euphoria: "the island is, if possible, lovelier than ever, & I cannot conceive more fairy-like scenery, or more perfect Greek landscape"—so he writes Alfred, Lord Tennyson's wife, Emily; but as the winter wears on, despite a hard schedule of work that begins surprisingly by his studying modern Greek from five or six until eight in the morning, his journal entries show an increasing despondency. The day before Christmas is "a weary day—but when have I not been weary in winter time, or indeed anywhere when settled." By mid-March, the noise from his neighbors—"shrieky shrieky music" and a dog howling all the time—is enough to drive him mad, and he tells his journal that "it is *certain* that *this* sort of life will not do." He puts his despair into nonsense verse:

> There was an Old Man of Corfu,
>   Who never knew what he should do;
> So he rushed up and down, till the sun made him brown,
>   That bewildered Old Man of Corfu.

As usual, the only solution was to get out of town and into the countryside to paint: a grove sketched at Analipsis, the village of Potamos with its white campanile in the distance and two straw-hatted villagers in the foreground leaning against a terraced hillside, and, best of all, Palaiokastritsa on the island's western coast. It is here that he found the kind of poetry and serenity in the landscape which brought immediate relief, as he wrote his friend Chichester Fortescue: "there is just now perfect quiet, excepting only a dim hum of myriad ripples 550 feet below me, all round the giant rocks which rise perpendicularly from the sea: which sea, perfectly calm and blue, stretches right out westward unbrokenly to the sky, cloudless that, save a streak of lilac cloud on the horizon . . . to my left is one of the many peacocktail-hued bays here, reflecting the vast red cliffs & their crowning roofs of *pinari* [holm oak], myrtle & sage. Far above them, higher & higher, the immense rock of St Angelo rising into the air, on whose summit the old castle still is seen a ruin, just 1,400 feet above the water. It half seems to me that such life as this must be wholly another from the drum-beating bothery frivolity of the town of Corfu, & I seem to grow a year younger every hour." And it is this wholly "other" life that he paints from one angle and another in browns, purples, and dark greens, with the care for detail and the tender shading of an artist thoroughly in love with his subject yet committed to an unsentimental, if imaginative, rendering of it.

Lear was wise enough to know that the landscape would change and that the euphoria it engendered would be short-lived. Already "accursed picnic parties with miserable scores of asses male and female are coming tomorrow, & peace flies." What he didn't know, though he may have hoped for it, was that Palaiokastritsa was now fixed not only in his memory—to live as long as he lives, his journal says—but in the record of his perception that he would pass on to others. In any case, before he returned to the frivolity of the town, what he had seen and recorded in this countryside served to conjure up a half-serious image of the afterlife he longed for: if he ends up in some kind of heaven, his journal tells us, he wants no creeds or "moony miracles" but a plain worship of God, and if he is surrounded by thousands of polite angels he will tell them, "Please leave me alone . . . Let me have a park & a beautiful view of sea & hill, mountain & river, valley & plain, with no end of tropical foliage, a few well-behaved small cherubs to cook & keep the place clean, & after I am quite established—say for a million or two of years—an angel of a wife."

The quiet, the solitude, the expansive beauty that Lear found in Palaiokastritsa are mirrored in the seascapes he painted there: the beaches deserted, the bluffs high and seemingly inaccessible, what man-made structures they hold kept at a distance, and the sea opening out to boundless space. It is this kind of island landscape—a "dream world," if you will—that travelers to Greece have longed to discover in recent centuries, and it is what many travelers actually succeeded in finding, not least of all in the prewar decade that saw Durrell and Miller in Greece. But as Philip Sherrard—himself a devoted apostle of island solitude and open-ended spaces—has pointed out, what was once possible to see and imagine in the place Lear called paradise is no longer there in anything like the same measure; and this is true of many of the most beautiful Greek islands. Sherrard writes that every stretch of the Corfu coastline that is accessible by road or path has been butchered, bartered, drawn and quartered, and "so immersed and desolated beneath the ferro-concrete hideosity of hotel and boarding-house, discotheque, bar, cafeteria and chop-house, and the wave after wave of pink-faced, white-bodied neo-Visigoths that summer-long blotch and bespatter its beaches, with the accompanying raucousness of motorcar, motorbike, motorscooter, transistor radio, motorboat, and the other gimcrackery and detritus (plastic and mineral) of mass tourism, that one searches in vain, across the wreckage of this dishallowed world, for the virginal loveliness that confronted Lear at virtually every footstep. His beloved Palaiokastritsa, for example, is a total disaster, but it is absolutely no exception. And this contagion is gradually creeping inland and up the hills . . ." Alas, poor Lear. Now, late in the last decade of this century, an even more ominous contagion is creeping into his once isolated bays from the Albanian coast that Corfu almost touches at its northern extremity: armed scavengers, sometimes desperate, sometimes merely criminal, who, after the collapse of the Albanian pyramid schemes, the riots in the cities, and the emptying of the jails, began to cross the narrow strait between the two countries to steal what they could on the run and return home again.

Still, the threat from the unjustly dispossessed of Albania and their criminal compatriots is surely a passing bit of history, and if

Corfu and other Ionian islands such as Cephalonia and Lefkada have no harbor and few accessible stretches of beach that have not been invaded by inflatable craft from Italy and yachts from Piraeus or elsewhere, there are still hidden places inland for those in search of the way things were in more serene days. And there are pockets of relatively uncluttered space even among the island towns. Famous Ithaka, for example, however crowded its small bays with transient craft, still has at this writing only one postwar hotel—and that modest—for those who arrive by car ferry in search of Homer or those who have learned by way of Cavafy's poem evoking the island that in any case the secret pleasure of these Ithakas, whatever your mode of transport and accommodation, is in the journey getting there.

The 1937–38 diary entries that are the form and substance of Durrell's book on Corfu, *Prospero's Cell* (even if the dates are not historically accurate) show us that the author came to the island knowing his Homer—as he came to know his Cavafy thoroughly while writing the book some seven years later in Alexandria—but his primary impulse was, as Lear's was, not to search out literary presences, ancient or modern, but rather to discover a contemporary landscape that would serve the personal mythology of his art. Durrell's image of Corfu is well rooted in the contours of the island and in the actual habits of the people who live there, and at the same time that image has its mythic dimension: the deliberate evocation of a land where the real and the imaginary can exist in tandem, a land that inspires a poetic re-creation of itself. In his very first diary entry, Durrell tells us that he and his wife found it difficult from the start to imagine any strict dividing line in Corfu between "the waking world and the world of dreams." Like Lear, he immediately discovered the poetry that came with living out of town, where the views were unobstructed and the routine of life open to one's own devising. In his third diary entry he describes his "old fisherman's house" at Kalami, ten miles from the town by sea and thirty miles by road, set on a rock that "offers all the charms of seclusion" and a prospect that Lear would have envied. On first entering the house, a day when the sky lies above in "a heroic blue arc," Nancy remarked that "the quietness alone makes it another country." And Durrell's description of the place shows that from his first moments there he had entered into a new world where what he sees is transformed into striking metaphor: "The hill runs clear up into the sky behind it, so that the cypresses and olives overhang this room in which I sit and write. We are upon a bare promontory with its beautiful clean surface of metamorphic stone covered in olive and ilex: in the shape of a *mons pubis*. This is become our unregretted home. A world. Corcyra."

There are also companions who visit regularly to ensure that the seclusion does not become oppressive, and Durrell tells us that two of them "seem of almost mythological quality," which makes them essential figures in his new literary landscape. The first is a writer named Ivan (actually Gostan or, in Greek, Constan) Zarian, a man with an imposing mane of hair and the habit of conducting—presumably an imaginary orchestra—as he intones his latest love song or recites a soliloquy from Hamlet in French, Armenian, Russian, Italian, German, and Spanish (Durrell adds that "he scorns to learn English properly"). He claims to be Armenia's greatest poet—something that would be hard to challenge on the island of Corfu—but Durrell tells us that he makes the claim with "a firmness and modesty that completely charm." He is at work on an exhaustive study of the wines of the island, pausing to relish a glass now and then, but from his manuscript-littered workroom on the top floor of the St. George Hotel he manages to send Durrell a note to say that he has immortalized him this week in his literary column for "some new world Armenian newspapers." And a month later, Durrell receives a poem about Corfu in Armenian, with an English version appended to it: "The gold and moving blue have stained our thoughts so that the darkness is opaque, and we see in our

dreams the world as if in some great Aquarium. Exiles and shar-
ers, we have found a new love. This is Corcyra, the chimney-
corner of the world."

The other companion described by Durrell as having an almost mythological quality was Theodore Stephanides, at that
time also a close companion of Durrell's much younger brother
Gerald and one of those in the group of Katsimbalis's friends who
later devoted themselves to entertaining and educating Miller and
Durrell during their visits to Athens. In *Prospero's Cell*, Durrell
portrays Stephanides as having a fine head and a golden beard
and the perfect manners of an Edwardian professor, incredibly
erudite about the island, "possessor of the dryest and most fastidious style of exposition ever seen," given to stalking across the
countryside with a "massive bug-hunting apparatus on his back,"
all of which suggested to the author that Stephanides was probably the "reincarnation of the comic professor invented by Edward
Lear" during the one of his stays on the island those many years
before.

However subtly or elaborately Durrell may have invented
Stephanides for his own literary purposes, the man in the flesh
taught his English friend much of value about Corfu in particular
and Greece in general. From less creative sources one gathers that
the learned gentleman was a complicated mix: born in India, his
mother English and his father Greek, a British-trained doctor and
radiologist, botanist, poet and translator, companion of Katsimbalis in the Greek army during the Smyrna campaign following
the First World War and his collaborator in early translations of
selected modern Greek poems, including amply those of Kostis
Palamas, at that time Greece's poet laureate (without portfolio).
Stephanides, who served as a medical officer in the British Army
during the Second World War, was said to speak Greek with a
strong English accent, and he wrote in English more than in
Greek: three volumes of poems, a battle memoir called *Climax in
Crete*, a book on the microscope and the practical principles of

observation, and an English version of the Cretan Renaissance epic-romance *Erotokritos* in heroic couplets—all 1,550 verses of it—briefly prefaced by Lawrence Durrell. An early photograph of Stephanides shows him standing with Katsimbalis, both in uniform, both at ease, Stephanides not only leaner than his friend but dapper enough with his trimmed beard and even his casual stance to do for a royal aspirant, Edwardian or otherwise.

Gerald Durrell's image of Stephanides in *My Family and Other Animals* is at least as elaborate as his brother's, and colored by a stronger affection. What Gerald found instantly attractive in Theodore (as he was always called) was the doctor's capacity for treating him as his equal when Gerald was but ten years old, not only as grownup but as equally knowledgeable in zoology. Theodore endeared himself to the ten-year-old immediately: after their first meeting he mailed him a package with a pocket microscope in it and a note saying that though the instrument was not of high magnification, he hoped Gerry would find it at least "sufficient for *field* work" in his "investigation of local natural history." They subsequently had tea every Thursday in Theodore's study, among jars and bottles containing minute fauna, a telescope, microphotographs, X-ray plates, diaries, notebooks, and a table of microscopes each under a glass dome. There they would explore together, among other exciting items, the mouth parts of the rat flea, a sprinneret from the garden, and the *cyclops viridis*—the last maybe leading to a further discussion of the mythological cyclops who forged iron for Hephaestus, and a Salonika peasant superstition that was reminiscent of an account of vampires in Bosnia, and finally the pros and cons of life on Mars.

Theodore's special talent outside his laboratory perhaps explains his enduring friendship with George Katsimbalis: the telling of seemingly tall stories that he insisted were factual, whether about technical matters such as the Egyptian practice of embalming people by the ingenious method of extracting the brain through the nose or more personal matters such as his triumphal entry into Smyrna riding a white horse at the head of a column of soldiers, which ended in havoc after a too enthusiastic woman patriot suddenly threw eau de cologne in his horse's eye. When the stories focused on Corfu, the Lawrence Durrell of Gerald's *My Family and Other Animals*—seen by his younger brother as often preciously literary or pedantically full of himself—surprisingly declared Theodore's stories obvious fabrications. Among other tales having to do with life as usual on the island, Gerald has Stephanides tell Larry and the rest of the family about the *"well developed"* but unfortunate opera singer who arrived in town to sing the heroine's role in *Tosca* and who, during the suicide scene that ended her first performance, messily injured herself when she threw herself from the set's castle battlements onto a stage that had not been prepared for her landing; and then, during her second performance, after the embarrassed stagehands had covered the stage by mattress upon springy mattress, the battered heroine, following her swan song, ended up mystifyingly bouncing into view thrice above the battlements when she was supposed to have been laid out dead. And there was the tale about the town's fire chief who returned from a mission to Athens with a sparkling red motorized fire engine that replaced the one drawn by horses but proved too wide for all but the main road in and out of town, and also a new fire alarm with a glass window that the chief decided to attach to the fire station door because nobody could predict in what part of town a fire was most likely to appear; then, when the owner of a flaming garage some streets away rushed to the fire station to sound the alarm, he was berated violently by the chief for having broken the glass on his brand-new alarm instead of simply knocking on the station door. Larry protests: "Really, Theodore, I'm sure you spend your spare time making up these stories." To which Theodore answers, smiling happily in his beard, "If it were anywhere else in the world, I would have to, but here in Corfu they . . . er . . . anticipate art, as it were."

The Durrell of *Prospero's Cell* would give that perception no argument at all. By the time we are introduced to the third of his regular companions in that book, a sixty-year-old recluse called simply Count D, the island of Corfu is well on its way to becoming a sublime work of art, not merely an "Eden" between "two great ribs of mountain," as Durrell first describes it, but a never-never land shaped by Shakespeare's most mature imagination, Prospero's isle of "fresh springs, brine-pits, barren place, and fertile." It is Count D who makes the case for this association during the gathering of competing talkers that takes place one weekend a month at his invitation, bringing him together with Durrell, Theodore, and Zarian in his country house, full of Venetian family portraits, tarnished silver, and terra-cotta Greek relics plowed up in his fertile valley. Durrell's biographer, Ian MacNiven, reports that Durrell told him Count D was a construct of some four originals, including, probably, Palatiano, a prominent Corfiot intellectual reputed to have kept the skull of his mistress on his writing desk. In his book Durrell tells us that Count D is the "possessor of a literary mind completely uncontaminated by the struggle to achieve a technique . . . a mind with the pollen still fresh upon it." Zarian describes him as a philosopher filled with a speculative calm, much admired by him for "the gravity and charm of his address." And Count D describes himself as having arrived at the kind of detachment that now allows him to be after "not the *interpretation* of the Principle of *x*, as I call it . . . but to interpret the ordinary world of prescribed loyalties and little acts like shooting or lying or sleeping through the Principle"—one of his "remarkable flights," in Durrell's view.

Another flight that Durrell must have found equally remarkable is Count D's argument for viewing their island as Prospero's. The Count's "chain of reasoning," challenged for a while by Zarian's skepticism, begins with the suggestion that the Greek custom of having the hostess or maid bring in glasses of water holding spoons filled with some kind of preserve—in this instance a "dark viscous raisin jam" called Visino—is the source of Caliban's "wouldst give me / Water with berries in 't." Caliban's exchange with Prospero at that point in *The Tempest* holds all the clues. His curse: "a south-west blow on ye, / And blister you all o'er!" presumably has an Ionian ring to it, since no evil could befall a Corfiot worse than the hot sirocco weather out of North Africa. And the name of Caliban's mother, the mysterious blue-eyed hag, Sycorax, is "almost too obvious an anagram for Corcyra." Then there is the speech by the spirit Iris in Act IV, with its inescapable Mediterranean coloring: "And thy broom-groves, / Whose shadow the dismissed bachelor loves, / Being lass-lorn; thy pole-clipt vineyard; / And thy sea-marge, sterile and rocky-hard . . ." Count D concludes that it is even possible Shakespeare visited Corfu: note the "well-wishing adventurer" described as "setting forth" in the dedication to the sonnets, signed by T.T., the printer Thomas Thorpe, who may have had the courage to publish the sonnets in 1609 as a pirated edition only if famous Shakespeare "were *out of the country*" at that time, presumably visiting Corfu two years before he wrote *The Tempest*. Durrell tells us that at this point in the Count's reasoning, Theodore, already having given up the talk and gone to bed on the floor above, puts down his massive volume of medical lore, receives Zarian's news about Shakespeare's visit with "skeptical good humour," blows out his candle, and walks over to his bedroom window to sniff the jasmine and to look out on the fishermen setting out from Palaiokastritsa in their coracles of straw and wood.

It is Lear's beloved Palaiokastritsa that allows Durrell a fanciful flight of his own, first of all back to Homer. If Corfu/Corcyra is, as some historians would have it, the home of the ancient oar-loving Phaecians (Durrell's spelling), then, according to Durrell, the likeliest place for the meeting between Odysseus and Nausicaa, daughter of the Phaeacian king Alcinous, is surely Palaiokastritsa, "drenched in the silver of olives," its little bay lying in a trance "drugged with its own extraordinary perfection—a conspiracy of light, air, blue sea, and cypresses." But Durrell is not one to press the case made by historians whose "peculiar sentimentalities," as he puts it, drive them to trace places and origins "by the shallow facts of romance," or the case made by those archaeologists who, "like earnest mastodons petrified in the forests of their own apparatus," come and go, each with his pocket *Odyssey* and each with "his lack of modern Greek."

As though to establish his credentials as a new kind of Greek-speaking philhellene, while at Palaiokastritsa Durrell quickly leaves Homer behind and sails off in a little white boat to explore the sea caves of the contemporary landscape opening out before him. His wife Nancy is aboard, sitting forward with her "head thrown back, lips parted, long fair hair blown back over the ears—the doe's pointed ears," maybe or maybe not hearing the woman's voice singing on the cliff above, anyway "drinking the wind like some imagined figurehead on a prehistoric prow," the author's simile here suddenly restoring the balance between the Greek past of his learning and the modern country he has come to love. A year later, sailing south of Palaiokastritsa in a fair wind, he will confirm his sense of a certain continuity in Greek history by swimming ashore at the Ermones beach just before dawn to "build in the gleaming sand the figure of a gigantic recumbent Aphrodite," pebbles for pearls, a belt from withes of sapling, mouth open with the shriek of being born, left there where the sea gnaws at her long fingers to amaze "the wide-eyed fisher-boys" who may or may not recognize the goddess of love who has risen from the foam.

Along with teaching Durrell how Corfu creates its own artistic image of itself, his companions—especially Theodore Stephanides and Zarian—gave him access to both the modern history of the place and the particular character of its daily life and entertainment, from the antics of Karaghiosis in the local shadow theater to the miracles of the island's patron St. Spyridon, and from there to the practical rituals of walking the grapes barefoot at vintage time. When Durrell finally left the island in the winter of 1940 for mainland Greece, where he lived until he was evacuated to Egypt just ahead of the invading German army in April 1941, the epilogue to *Prospero's Cell*, parts of which appeared originally in an open letter to Seferis published in the October 1941 issue of *La Semaine Egyptienne*, reveals that his nostalgia for Corfu and for Greece more generally was focused first of all on the human, earthly, non-literary dimensions of what he had left behind: the fate of his island companions—Theodore now with the British forces in Italy, Zarian in Geneva, the Count somewhere in the mountains of Epirus—then other figures in the landscape of his days in Greece, then the landscape itself, so rich with possibilities for innocent hedonism. It is "Greece as a living body" that in Egypt Durrell misses most, a "landscape lying up close against the sky, suspended on the blue lion-pads of mountains," with its "summers of indolence and deduction on the northern beaches of our island—beaches incessantly washed and sponged by the green Ionian," a landscape he finally recognizes as "conforming so marvellously to the dimensions of a human existence," made for lovers in their Edenic days of innocence, as his poem of this period called "Summer" suggests:

> . . . *Prodigals of leisure and brown skins,*
> *Wine mixed with kisses and the old*
> *Dreamless summer sleeps they once enjoyed*
> *In Adam's Eden long before the Fall.*

It was the washed and sponged beaches of Corfu that initiated Henry Miller into certain essential island mysteries of modern Greece in the summer of 1939. High noon, within an hour of his arrival on the island, he was in Kalami with the Durrells and down to the sea in front of their house before lunch for his first swim in almost twenty years. He thought Larry and Nancy a couple of dolphins who practically lived in the water. As soon as they were done with the afternoon siesta that first day, off they rowed to another cove with a tiny white shrine where they "baptized [themselves] anew in the raw." They go to town only once a week by caique, and that doesn't please Miller much more than it did Lear. The American finds that the town has "a desultory air which by evening becomes a quiet, irritating sort of dementia," a typical place of exile where you are always sitting down to drink something, everything ridiculously cheap—you can get a shave and haircut for three and a half cents—but also the home of kings, one of whom lived in a dreary and lugubrious palace that Miller believes would make an excellent surrealist museum. Back in Kalami, the Durrells are visited by Theodore, whose knowledge of plants, flowers, trees, rocks, animal life, microbes, diseases, comets, etc., overwhelms their American guest, and it is from Theodore that he first hears about Seferis and Katsimbalis. Miller tells us that, for some strange reason, the latter name made an impression on him immediately, and after hearing Theodore's "hallucinating descriptions" of his life with Katsimbalis in the trenches during the Great War, he began to employ the name Katsimbalis familiarly, as though he had known the man all his life. The next day he joins Durrell in writing Katsimbalis "an enthusiastic letter" expressing their hope of meeting with him shortly in Athens. It seems the Colossus was already on his way to becoming a larger-than-life figure in the landscape before Miller actually came under the aura of his ample presence.

But well before the return to Athens, Miller had other new things to discover, beginning with the old Edward Lear pleasures of rural solitude, first of all while camping out with the Durrells on an isolated stretch of sandy beach where time was "completely blotted out" and where the only intrusion was by a crazy shepherd who woke them of a morning by guiding his sheep over their prone bodies under the gaze of a "demented witch" who would suddenly appear on the cliff above to curse the shepherd out. A week goes by and they see no one but the mayor of a mountain village some distance away who arrives to look them over and finds Miller alone, dozing under a rock. According to the author, he and the mayor shared about three words of English and maybe ten of Greek, but that is enough for a "remarkable colloquy" during which Miller imitates movie actors, a bronco, a high diver, and finally a Chinese mandarin, which leads to a dialogue in Chinese, neither knowing the language, and after the mayor somehow produces an interpreter, they exchange a number of lies about China and then about Pygmies, followed by much drinking of wine, and after a flute is produced by somebody, interminable dancing in the style of St. Vitus, ending up in the sea, "where we bit one another like crabs and screamed and bellowed in all the tongues of the earth." Some of this is good training for future encounters, real and imaginary, with George Katsimbalis as the Colossus. And had the episode been witnessed by Durrell's Count D, he would surely have taken it for evidence of a contemporary reincarnation of Caliban and his drunken companions, even if Miller and his new village friends were obviously slave to no man. In any case, the American is soon transported out of this world of wild earthly delights and incoherent free expression into a region more metaphysical and visionary.

Miller and the Durrells broke camp at the seaside on a "strange sultry day" and crossed the scorching sand to begin their climb up to a pass that would bring them out to the mountain village where Spiro the driver was waiting to take them back to Kalami by car. They trekked up a dry riverbed beside their loaded "mountain ponies," clambered up a gully that was meant to be a path, suddenly reached a clearing and heard "a weird melody" sung by young women stirring a poisonous liquid insecticide for the nearby olive trees. Miller calls their song a song of death that blended in well with the mist-covered landscape. But the fog suddenly broke to reveal "a great blue area of sea," not at the expected level but "in some middle realm between heaven and earth." The atmosphere had a "Biblical splendor" now, punctuated by the bells from the ponies, the poison song, a faint boom of distant surf, and "an indefinable mountain murmuring" that Miller feels may be nothing more than "the hammering of the temples in the high and sultry haze of an Ionian morning." In this "operatic realm," he has a moment of illumination: as he smokes a light Greek cigarette, his palate itself becomes "metaphysically attuned," and the drama now "was of the airs, of the upper regions, of the eternal conflict between the soul and the spirit."

In the light-headed other-worldly mood inspired by this episode, it is not surprising that the writer's mind begins to travel from images of earthbound history to cosmic—if still subjective—perceptions. He sees the mountain pass they now enter as, first of all, a crossroads through the ages of "meaningless butcheries" and "vengeful massacres," a death trap "devised by Nature herself for man's undoing" like other such death traps in Greece. And this leads him to declare that the ancient Greek "lived amidst brutal clarities which tormented and maddened the spirit," and these urged him to war with everyone, including himself. Yet out of this "fiery anarchy" Miller perceives the emerging of "lucid, healing metaphysical speculations which even today enthrall the world." And though he feels, maneuvering his way through the pass, that he is "wading through phantom seas of blood," the crossing finally transports him to a vision of man's brotherhood that is to a degree reminiscent of his favorite poet Walt Whitman's "all the men ever born are also my brothers," and of Wallace Stevens's "heavenly fellowship / Of men that perish and of summer morn" who have formed a ring to chant "Their boisterous devotion to the sun" in a "chant of paradise." Here is

Miller's prose chant of a less heavenly paradise before he comes out into the bright "work-a-day world" of the village up ahead:

In this mountain pass there must also have been moments of clear vision when men of distant races stood holding hands and looking into one another's eyes with sympathy and understanding. Here too men of the Pythagorean stripe must have stopped to meditate in silence and solitude, gaining fresh clarity, fresh vision, from the dust-strewn place of carnage. All Greece is diademed with such antinomian spots; it is perhaps the explanation of the fact that Greece has emancipated itself as a country, a nation, a people, in order to continue as the luminous *carrefour* of a changing humanity.

The reference to Pythagoras surprises until one remembers that, along with being an ascetic philosopher who taught the transmigration of souls, he was the founder of a brotherhood. But what emerges as the personal emphasis here is Miller's effort to accommodate his antipathy to war and his search for a complete emancipation, motives that first compelled him to leave Paris and travel to an unknown country. And it is a new rumor of war that now shatters the serenity of Kalami, where his days of reading and meditation had been rolling by "like a song." Ominously, the King of Greece has returned suddenly to Athens, and panic has spread through the town of Corfu. Durrell, to Miller's dismay, speaks more than half-seriously of enlisting in the Greek army to serve on the Albanian frontier, as does Spiro the driver, though he is past the age limit. Miller finds himself boarding a boat to Athens with his friends at four in the morning amid a "shameful scramble" of those who had been sitting on the quay trying to look unconcerned "but actually quaking with fear" and who now struggle to get their possessions on board. Yet, in all the panic and confusion, like Cavafy's distressed Phernazis, who still works on his epic poem as he waits for the Roman legions to advance on his hometown, Miller's "poetic idea comes and goes insistently." He wakes to go up on deck and watch the boat glide through a narrow strait: "on either side of us were low barren hills, soft, violet-studded hummocks of earth of such intimate human proportions as to make one weep with joy. The sun was almost at zenith and the glare was dazzlingly intense . . . There was something phenomenal about the luminous immediacy of these two violet-colored shores . . . It was more than a Greek atmosphere—it was poetic, and of no time or place actually known to man."

In the midst of women in rags with breasts bared to nurse "their howling brats," the deck a mess of vomit and blood, Miller rejoices that he is "free of possessions, free of all ties, free of fear and envy and malice." He feels that he could have "passed quietly from one dream to another, owning nothing, regretting nothing, wishing nothing." His passage from the sea's solitude through the mountain pass of massacres and its imagined history and on to his vision of brotherhood and emancipation has served to convince him that life and death are one, that "neither can be enjoyed or embraced if the other be absent." What Corfu has given Miller, as it did Lear, is not simply a new image of Eden but an inner serenity that makes it possible for him to put the threat of war and its fear of death to one side as others around him cannot, and to approach what lies ahead of him with some of the fresh clarity and insight that he felt men of ancient Greece must have gained in that "dust-strewn place of carnage" he had crossed the previous day. He now goes on to Athens as a freer spirit to cross into a different region of discovery for a short time; then, after war is actually declared, he returns to Corfu to live on his own (Durrell's sister Margaret [Margo] cooking for him) until the autumn rains set in.

Now that the war had begun in earnest elsewhere and the Greek army was mobilized at the Albanian frontier, Miller found that he had to get a pass every time he went into the town of Corfu, yet it was a "wonderful period of solitude" for him: silence the whole day long, no newspaper, no radio, no gossip, "thoroughly and completely lazy, thoroughly and completely indifferent to the fate of the world," the "finest medicine a man can give himself." For the moment, his accommodation of the antipathy that had been working on his spirit was as complete as his solitude: "You know there is a war on but you haven't the faintest idea what it's about or why people should enjoy killing one another . . . When you're right with yourself it doesn't matter what flag is flying over your head or who owns what or whether you speak English or Monongahela." What we need, he declares, is not the truth dished up in the daily papers and all the machines of destruction, the explosives, battleships, politicians, lawyers, the gadgets and canned goods and razor blades, even the cigarettes and money of our tormented existence; what we need is "peace and solitude and idleness." He realizes that of course this is "a pipe dream," that people want better working conditions, better wages, better opportunities "to become something other than they are," and he soon finds it impossible, even on Corfu, to withdraw totally and indefinitely. With the rains come roads washed out and landslides that block free passage with the debris of rocks and trees. He is marooned for days on end. When Nancy arrives unexpectedly to collect some of the belongings that the Durrells had left behind in their quick exodus, Miller decides "impulsively" to return to Athens with her. What he returns to are those Greek friends of Larry and Nancy's—Katsimbalis, Seferis, Stephanides, Antoniou, Ghika—who eventually show him ways other than withdrawal for challenging the demons that torment his kind of spirit in time of war.

3

THE MYTHMAKERS

*O*n the way to Athens during the first panic caused by threatening news from the world beyond Corfu—this before Miller returned briefly to the island alone—he and the Durrells stopped overnight in Patras at the Hotel Cecil, described by Miller as the best hotel he'd ever been in. Be that as it may, the setting was hardly idyllic. You could hear the drums of war far in the distance, and closer at hand, at Missolonghi on the shore opposite, you could apparently make out the hovering presence of Byron's ghost, source of a mythology that had not yet gone dry, even so far into the twentieth century. Breakfasting at noon, Miller decided that the thought of war drives people frantic, makes them cuckoo, even "intelligent and far-seeing" people like his friend Larry, who again spoke of wanting to go off to join the Greek forces on the Albanian border, clearly a mad Byronic gesture that resulted in a "terrible wrangle" with Nancy—the war talk, according to Miller, camouflage for a private dispute that left him feeling helpless. War had actually not yet been declared in

Greece, and after a brief conversation with the "far more clear-headed" British consul in Patras, Miller himself relaxed enough to think it possible that war would never be declared.

It was in any case a more amiable madness and a more productive mythology that greeted Miller when he and Durrell reached Athens. The American and British mythmakers from Corfu met their match there, mythmakers who were also free-wheeling individualists, eccentric in their way but in a different style, their capacity for standing at a slight angle to the universe, whether in their person or in their work, made possible because they were firmly grounded in the soil of Greece. The first of these was a man who could turn almost any event in his life into a story of mythic dimensions but who, even given all his talent for seducing an audience, could hardly have suspected that one of his ardent new listeners from another world would one day turn him into the grand figure at the mythical center of a book called *The Colossus of Maroussi*.

George Katsimbalis was born into the third generation of a wealthy family that ended up owning, along with a hundred acres of land in the Athens suburb called Maroussi, a segment of the richest real estate in Greece: a corner of Syntagma (Constitution) Square in the heart of the city. His grandfather was a simple man but—as the Greek expression goes—cunning enough to catch birds in the air. He made his fortune by providing horse-drawn carriages (two for a start, then four, then who knows how many) for both passengers and goods moving between Tripolis, capital of the Peloponnese, and the other important towns in the region. Katsimbalis's father inherited enough leisure to become a major Athenian dilettante, described by his son's friend Thanasis Diomidis as a "classic Belle Epoque aesthete" who collected books, art, and other aesthetes like no one else in the city, and who had a lust for the good life that included massive eating—as many as 150 meatballs at one sitting, his son insisted, no exaggeration.

Katsimbalis himself was a more than avid eater, but he would never have settled for stuffing himself with meatballs. Miller has him pounding his chest like a gorilla between "great carnivorous gulps of food" and washing it all down with "a hogshead of retsina," and he suggests that the son may not have had his gourmet father's "sensual refinements and accomplishments." The truth is, Katsimbalis was at least as discriminating as his father when it came to food, and he always knew where the best of the local tavernas could be found in Athens, whether Vasilena's place in Pireaus that served some seventeen different kinds of hors d'oeuvres or the garden taverna called Svingous off Patission Street that featured two delicacies only: suckling pig cooked on the spit so the crackle dissolved in your mouth like brittle, followed by giant deep-fried puff balls soaked in honey syrup. And on the road outside Athens, Katsimbalis, cane in hand to point out oddities along the way or to slice the air for emphasis, would lead his companions however many kilometers might be needed to follow up a rumor of some food or drink in the neighborhood that was just waiting to be made legendary. He knew no pleasure equal to that of finding the best there was to eat wherever he might land, sharing it with somebody close by, whether friend or stranger, and storing the pleasure of it so that he could brag about the experience the first chance he got, with or without the benefit of witnesses. Departing Athens for a "cure" at the sulfur-spring spa at Methana on the Peloponnesian coast, he writes Seferis about his difficulty in finding enough rhymes for the word *Methana*, to write him "a commemorative and . . . bon voyage sonnet," that rhyme word presumably meant to play on the Greek for intoxication, *methi*. In place of the sonnet, Katsimbalis explains to his friend, he accomplished the word's first nuance in a most unexpected and startling way: having barely disembarked he came across a man "who happened to know the best taverna, the subtlest (supposedly) retsina, the most select hors d'oeuvres, and had already ambushed an octopus (my God!) marinated in wine, some garlic-potato sauce for eggplant to blow your head off, and more." He reports that the result of this gourmet outing was that he stayed too long that evening at some vice president's table, completely plastered. "This is how I started my cure. This is how I continued it yesterday. This is how—do you doubt it?—today and tomorrow, and heaven help me!"

Along with suggesting that Katsimbalis's devotion to the good life exceeded his father's cruder example, this letter to Seferis pinpoints the paradox at the heart of Katsimbalis's role as a leading man of letters in Greece both well before and well after the Second World War. Though the most thorough bibliographer of his day and one of the earliest translators of modern Greek poetry—as his father was a translator of Omar Khayyám—and though in his younger days a prolific and entertaining writer of letters (more than a hundred to Seferis alone), Katsimbalis never wrote a sonnet, or a play, or a work of fiction, or a collection of essays, yet he was crucial to the development of the best writing in Greece in the first half of this century. The first images of Katsimbalis that Miller provides us in *The Colossus of Maroussi* would lead the reader to believe that his hero's genius went into storytelling as a performance, his creative energy expended on monologues, listening to which was like watching a man write a book expressly for the listener: "he writes it, reads it aloud, acts it, revises, savors it, enjoys it, enjoys your enjoyment of it, and then tears it up and throws it to the winds . . . a sublime performance, because while he's going through with it you are God for him—unless you happen to be an insensitive and impatient dolt." Anybody who knew Katsimbalis and was lucky enough to have the right kind of noonday or night in his company would be unlikely to challenge this insight about the man's talent, but it is not the whole story.

For some forty years, beginning in the late 1920s, Katsimbalis gave generously of his time and his fortune to promote those writers in a variety of styles—traditional Greek, symbolist, realist, surrealist, modernist—whom he considered the most gifted of both the established and the new generations, and he did so with more than mere talk and without taking public credit. As the actual but undesignated editor of *Ta Nea Grammata,* which he financed out of his pocket and supervised from solicitations for material to final proofreading, and later as editor of the *Angloelliniki Epitheorisi* (*Anglo-Hellenic Review*), he published over a period of some twenty years those Greek writers who are now recognized as among the likeliest to endure into the next century. Katsimbalis was also the presence who was the most hospitable to foreign writers, both as personal host to those who passed through Athens and as an editor interested in exploring the kinship between modern Greek writing and work in other languages.

Henry Miller had little chance to see it during his time in Greece, but the truth is that the sober, productive, punctilious side to Katsimbalis led to accomplishments that matched those he exhibited as a hedonist, gourmet, and imaginative talker. And what allowed the two sides of his active self to coexist without conflict was his passionate commitment to Hellenism, to the Greek tradition in language, literature, food, myth, politics, to the country's culture, both high and low, and to its natural beauty— in short, whatever he felt best characterized the spirit of modern Greece. This commitment is obvious in his passionate engagement with its literature and in his relentless promotion of Greek writers. It is less obvious in his role as a giant oral mythmaker, though Miller caught something of this essential element. When he tells us that there was "a great element of the tragic" in the man "which his adroit mimicry only enhanced," we are reminded of Seferis's representative man with "trickles in the corner of his eyes" who seems to carry within him that bitter yearning, the "*kaimo tis Romiosinis,*" which Seferis found characteristic of modern Hellenism. Katsimbalis embodied this yearning in the core of his person, however flamboyantly or silently he chose to reveal it.

Miller tells us at one point that Katsimbalis "always talked against a landscape, like the protagonist of a lost world," a specifically Attic landscape containing characteristics that the American listed in a free-ranging recipe of what "spiced and flavored" Katsimbalis's talk, the concoction again emphatically Greek: "thyme, sage, tufa, asphodel, honey, red clay, blue roofs, acanthus trimmings, violet light, hot rocks, dry winds, *rezina*, arthritis and the electrical crackle that plays over the low hills like a swift serpent with a broken spine." During his first visit to Katsimbalis's home in Maroussi, Miller listens to his hero winding up his monologue on the veranda until he was in full flight, in "a spread eagle performance" that celebrated the clear atmosphere and blue-violet hues that came in with the twilight, then opened out to include talk of special herbs and trees, exotic fruit, inland voyages, talk of thyme and honey and the sap of the arbutus that can make you drunk, of islanders and highlanders and men of the Peloponnese, and on and on—until Miller is transported into a vision of "the true splendor of the Attic landscape" which in turn leads to a recognition that "there is no old or new, only Greece, a world conceived and created in perpetuity," while the man talking to him "had ceased to be of human size or proportion, but had become a Colossus . . . a figure who had outgrown his human frame, a silhouette whose reverberations rumbled in the depths of the distant mountainside."

That this is the moment when Katsimbalis is transformed into the mythic figure at the center of the book is only the first implication of the epiphany Miller here describes. Though he was aware from the start that Katsimbalis had the power to cast a spell over him, one that could only be broken by "a power and a magic almost equal to [Katsimbalis's] own," Miller doesn't appear to recognize fully that, along with exercising a spellbinding creative impulse, Katsimbalis meant his monologue to implant an indelible image of Greece in his foreign listener that would lead in time to adoration. This intention worked on the American from the start, whether or not Miller knew it, as it had on other visitors from abroad. Returning from his first evening with Katsimbalis, after a "succulent repast at the *taverna* in Piraeus" (Vasilena's?), he followed his host to Syntagma Square to be introduced to the poets George Seferis and Captain D. I. Antoniou, who by the early hours of the morning had become his "stalwart friends."

When Miller retires to his room in the Grand Hotel opposite, he goes out on the balcony of his room to look down on the deserted square below and to catalogue all the Greek friends he has made in the short time he has been in the country. This leads to a number of quick generalizations and comparisons, to the immense benefit of the Greeks and to the disadvantage of the English, at least the "sorry lot" he came across in Athens and elsewhere: "The Greek has no walls around him: he gives and takes without stint . . . Everywhere you go in Greece the atmosphere is pregnant with heroic deeds. I am speaking of modern Greece, not ancient Greece." And this is followed by a eulogy to Greek women, in his view not only as heroic as the men but, along with Orthodox priests, responsible for sustaining the Greek fighting spirit through modern Greek history: "For stubbornness, courage, recklessness, daring, there are no greater examples anywhere. No wonder Durrell wanted to fight with the Greeks. Who wouldn't prefer to fight beside a Bouboulina [the celebrated War of Independence heroine], for example, than with a gang of sickly, effeminate recruits from Oxford or Cambridge." The Katsimbalis monologue, his generosity as host, and the new friends he had introduced to his American visitor clearly began to do their good work for Greece early on. Unfortunately, the stalwart English philhellenes who would eventually join the Katsimbalis entourage—Rex Warner, Patrick Leigh Fermor, Philip Sherrard, among others—arrived too late to contribute their sense of poetic reality to broaden Miller's pleasure and mute his anti-British prejudices, which at this time were shared in large measure by his

English friend Lawrence Durrell (Durrell's biographer, Ian Mac-Niven, considers the young "Mediterranean hand" Xan Fielding the one exception to Miller's distaste for the British expatriates he encountered in Durrell's company).

Miller's encounter with the poets Seferis and Antoniou in Syntagma Square was followed by a second meeting at Katsimbalis's home in Maroussi which included Theodore Stephanides, who "had made a translation of some Greek poems" that the group was to hear in English. Though Miller was lucky enough that evening to have for companions two of the best Greek poets of the time and the doctor-poet he himself described as the most learned man he had ever met, his casual failure to tell us what poems he heard by whom on that occasion seems to reinforce the impression he gives his reader of having left his interest in what he calls "book-learning" back in Paris, an interest that in any case "gradually dribbles away" a few days later when he returns to total silence and solitude on Corfu. But the mythmaker in him was fully enchanted by the human dimensions of the poets, and though he claimed that Seferis and Antoniou knew more about American literature than he ever would, their presence in the house of the Colossus apparently inspired Miller to begin an elaborate monologue about Sherwood Anderson that finally led him to identify himself with "the man who can make even the egg triumphant" but who would "probably have been astounded had he heard of the exploits I was crediting him with." By this point in the evening, Katsimbalis must have been more than sufficiently impressed by the mythmaking talent of his new disciple.

Miller's image of Antoniou also reveals creative energy. He sees the poet as a man with weather in his blood and traces of it in his countenance, a captain who battles the elements while sailing from one island to another, "writing his poems as he walks about strange cities at night." The image has a touch of the heroic, which no doubt would have amused the quiet, self-effacing, sensitive man, all his life a bachelor, at sea some forty years without a break, whose one link to the heroic, by the testimony of his own poetry, was the name of the cruise ship he captained after the war, the SS *Achilles*. Antoniou was an early champion of free verse in Greece, learned in his own tradition and better read than most in foreign literature, a sympathetic, even enthusiastic listener who rarely entered into a dialogue, especially when his dear friend Katsimbalis was next to him to do the talking. His gift was in his poems, with their laconic, understated images of voyages to distant places and exotic harbors, lines that are occasionally reminiscent of Cavafy's "Ithaka," though they do not suggest, as the Alexandrian does, that the voyages themselves have offered proper recompense, even by way of memory, for the loneliness of exile or the mixed agony and joy of the return. What remains of the voyages is the stories and the words that render them memorable:

> *Obstacle to what?*
>
> *You recognized the ship*
> *with the blond hero's name—*
> *seed of the sea with a landsman's fate—.*
>
> *We brought you no more than stories*
> *of distant places, memories*
> *of precious things, of perfumes.*
>
> *Do not seek their weight upon your hands;*
> *your hands should be less human*
> *for all we held in exile;*
> *the experience of touch, the struggle of weight,*
> *exotic colors*
> *you should feel in our words only*
> *this night of our return.*

Obstacle to what
the mast that told you
of our return?

The nostalgia in Antoniou's poetry, described in another poem as that which "left us useless / for life," brings with it some of the wounding that Seferis knew well but that Miller was not likely to have discovered in his free-floating Athenian gatherings, where all such wounds of the spirit were washed clean by watered ouzo or raw retsina. And it is not likely that he had the time or the occasion while Antoniou was ashore to see deeply into either the countenance or the poetry of a man so reticent in his person and in the promotion of his work. Seferis, who knew both the poetry and the man intimately, comes nearer than his American friend to capturing the essence of Antoniou when he sees in him a representation of the same bittersweet sensibility that is central to his own work of this period. In a review of Antoniou's first published volume (1936), he had spoken of his "seafaring friend" as a simple, circumspect man, with a look that was normally fixed "on an imaginary margin somehow to the left or the right of us," yet sure of himself when he really wanted something. What he carried inside him that was special, Seferis suggested, was "the rather vague feeling that we love in the very few who help us to go on living in our country and that differentiates us—if anything does—from other peoples of the world." Katsimbalis shared that feeling, that yearning, which Seferis again tried to define by what he calls "the dangerous expression," *kaimo tis Romiosinis.*

This quality which Seferis saw as characteristic of the man Antoniou he also finds emerging clearly in the voice of the poet traveling from one seaport to the next and back "to our bucolic Athens," the voice of a man who balances the scales of sentiment, placing his own fate in confrontation with other fates faraway and foreign. In Seferis's view, the poems written on empty cigarette boxes that fill up Antoniou's cabin, what he calls his "bottles in the sea," offer images of a sometimes colorful but more often tormented sense of life: days that are as endless as the coal he loads under leaden skies, days spent between sea and sky on the bridge as the ship rolls in its seaborne agony, "harbors with the bitterness of harbors, with the disenchantment of a desire at last realized after forty days and nights of cramped struggle, smiles of exotic countries, momentary, as the dawn that came up once upon a time on our island"—these, concludes Seferis, are the colors, whether we see them immediately or not at all, that are found in the poetry of "our seafaring friend." The man whom Miller knew lived more among these colors than those of the suburban landscape at Maroussi or of the early-twentieth-century poster-advertisements lining the walls of Apotsos, just off Stadiou Street, where he would meet Katsimbalis and maybe the latest visitor in town for noontime ouzo and an abundant spread of Greek hors d'oeuvres, *mezedes*, whenever his ship docked at Piraeus. Yet even there the captain's quiet voice could sometimes raise the ordinary to the level of myth as effectively as the voices of his louder companions, and it is this voice rather than the one in his poetry that Miller's portrait of him tells us he occasionally heard.

In the case of George Seferis, Miller—who saw him more often, and not only in Athens but during some of his travels around Greece—seems to have grasped both the particular qualities of the poet's personal charm and certain principal impulses of his work—apparently read to him by Katsimbalis in English translation—though again he sees this new "stalwart friend" transformed at moments into a curious mythic figure, a "wild boar which had broken its tusks in furious onslaughts born of love and ecstasy" and "a mellifluous Asiatic warbler who had more than once been floored by an unexpected thunderbolt." Miller comes closer to the amiable reality of Seferis when he speaks of the poet—a heavy man with slow but strong gestures—taking him by the arm to walk him back and forth in the dusk, wrapping his whole being around that arm with "warmth and tenderness," then walking him all the way back to his hotel as an act of friendship, demonstrating a quality of "enduring love" that Miller now found rare in men generally but in all his Greek friends. And the "queenliness" that he encountered in Seferis's sister, Ioanna Tsatsos, was a similarly pervasive quality that he felt was scarcely ever met with in modern women but that, like the warm friendliness of the men, "all Greek women share to a greater or a less degree." This generalization allows him to move on to an even broader view of what has so recently captured his heart: "Wherever you go in Greece the people open up like flowers," a thing that "cynical-minded people" would say was possible because Greece is a small country. But, Miller insists, Greece is not a small country: "it is impressively vast. No country I have visited has given me such a sense of grandeur . . . Greece is a little like China or India. It is a world of illusion."

A world of illusion, however enchanting, is open to many individual perspectives, some more grounded in reality than others, most of them opening out easily to myth. Seferis's perspective at the time has its overtly mythical dimension yet is more ominous, finally more tragic, than Miller's. It is a perspective that places the modern Greek in the mythological and historical contexts that still strongly influence his world of illusion. Here, for example, is a poem from the 1935 series with the revealing title of *Mythistorema* (literally, Novel, but with obvious connotations of Myth and History):

> Our country is closed in, all mountains
> that day and night have the low sky as their roof.
> We have no rivers, we have no wells, we have no springs,
> only a few cisterns—and these empty—that echo, and that
>   we worship.
> A stagnant hollow sound, the same as our loneliness
> the same as our love, the same as our bodies.

We find it strange that once we were able to build
our houses, huts and sheep-folds.
And our marriages, the cool coronals and the fingers,
become enigmas inexplicable to our soul.
How were our children born, how did they grow strong?

Our country is closed in. The two black Symplegades
close it in. When we go down
to the harbors on Sunday to breathe freely
we see, lit in the sunset,
the broken planks from voyages that never ended,
bodies that no longer know how to love.

The tone here appears to represent, in an unmistakably Greek setting, the "Waste Land feeling" that Seferis suggested (in a 1948 essay on T. S. Eliot) "runs through all the poetic expression of our times," a feeling that he tells us "an old man" called Cavafy was the first to bring into Greek poetry (certainly without any influence from Eliot). And though Seferis himself admits having learned from what he called Eliot's "dramatic manner of expression," what characterizes this poem is not Eliot's eclectic allusiveness but the subtle impregnation of a contemporary landscape with symbolic overtones that emerge naturally from the literal details of that landscape and, along with this, the plausible linking of present and distant past by way of a single allusion to a specifically Greek mythology: the dangerous clashing rocks called the Symplegades, which Jason and the ancient Argonauts had to pass through into the Bosporus. Their good ship *Argo*, the first longship made, returned safely from its voyage carrying the Golden Fleece. Here, in keeping with the poet's Waste Land feeling, our contemporary Greek Argonauts travel on broken planks, and their voyages never end.

When Seferis accepted the Nobel Prize in Stockholm in 1963, he gave an interview in which he quietly complained that the younger generation of writers in his country considered their long tradition a burden, while he continued to regard it not only as alive but as an essential resource for the writer. His poetry is the proof of this conviction, and it offers evidence that Miller was on to something when he said that Seferis had embedded in his poems "the spirit of eternality" that Miller saw everywhere in Greece and that whatever Seferis looked at "was Greek in a way that he had never known before leaving his country," the product of a passion for the homeland which, Miller thought, was a "special peculiarity of the intellectual Greek who has lived abroad." But Seferis's perspective extended well beyond the homeland. He often spoke of himself as sharing a "diaspora" point of view akin to Cavafy's, in part because of his upbringing in Smyrna, in part because of his service in Albania, Asia Minor, and the Near East. In a 1970 *Paris Review* interview he indicated that he was interested in everything that finds expression in the Greek language and the Greek lands—"I mean taking the Greek lands as a whole," and by "whole" he presumably meant wherever diaspora Greek communities had once thrived and had contributed to the Greek tradition (he mentions Moldavia and Wallachia specifically). When it came to touring the homeland, Miller reports, Seferis revealed an unusually keen grasp of Greek history and its haunting presence in his country's landscape: "He could look at a headland and read into it the history of the Medes, the Persians, the Dorians, the Minoans, the Atlanteans. He could also read into it some fragments of the poem which he would write in his head on the way home while plying me with questions about the New World. He was attracted by the Sibylline character of everything which met his eye."

What Miller's perception misses is that the prophetic aspect of Seferis's vision during these days in the late 1930s was motivated not only by a profound recognition of the link between the Greek present and its historic or mythic past but also by a deep sense of impending loss, of imminent catastrophe. We have seen this prophetic insight at work in Seferis's journal entries of spring and summer in 1939 where he speaks of the sleepwalkers who know not what they do, nor what they will have to pay. It is also there in the poems he wrote in 1939, beginning just before Miller's visit and extending into the weeks immediately after his departure. In the poem significantly called "The Last Day," what the speaker perceives is that on that day "by the following dawn / nothing would be left to us, neither the woman drinking sleep at our side / nor the memory that we were once men." The penetrating question the speaker raises is "How does a man die?" And to make the necessary tragic link between current prospects and the Greek past, he predicts that by the following dawn everything will be surrendered, "our women slaves at the springheads and our children in the quarries," a prophecy that has the contemporary Greek sharing the fate of the defeated Trojan women in the *Iliad* and those Athenians who Thucydides tells us were taken prisoner after the destruction of the Sicilian expedition in 413 B.C.

The poem that best represents the complexities of Seferis's mood during these months is "The King of Asini," a work he had been carrying inside him with some agony since the summer of 1938 and continued to carry during the days when he, along with his perhaps less prescient companions, was doing what he could to be a carefree host to his Anglo-Saxon friends. It is now his most famous prewar poem, celebrated as "a very great work" in a postwar letter Durrell wrote to Seferis while he was preparing (along with Bernard Spencer and Nanos Valaoritis) the first selection of Seferis in English translation, published in 1948 under the title *The King of Asine* [sic] *and Other Poems*. The poem was completed a little more than a month after Miller left Greece, the final draft written—according to what Seferis told Eliot some years later—during the course of a single night, 10:00 p.m. to 3:00 a.m., without the poet's having any notes in front of him. But his agonizing over it for more than a year and a half is demonstrated by his having written six drafts in two groupings, with a hiatus of some months between the two. The early drafts, almost totally discarded after the hiatus, are in the form of a dramatic monologue by the King of Asini, who is known to us only by the single mention of his name in the *Iliad*'s catalogue of those who went to Troy. The King tries to account for his having been ignored by literary history, for having been the victim of a sentence to oblivion (the title Seferis gave to another poem of this period). He tells us that the rhapsodists who recited epic poems never got as far as his citadel at Asini, the tragedians simply forgot him and anyway preferred the bloody tales of Mycenae and Argos, he was out of date for pastorals and idylls, and besides, he was a man who denied himself the angry hands, the wet lips, the tears and the fury of life to the point of ending up spreading his soul across a great empty circle. The monologue tells us that the King was left with nothing human, only the sea throbbing around his flesh, the void that nature abhors, but exactly why this was so or what larger significance it has does not emerge from the fragmentary text.

A second and third draft elaborate on the same theme, with a few new images that will be carried over into the later drafts, but these and the published text show a startling difference that is characteristic of Seferis's best poems. The voice we hear in these versions is no longer that of the King of Asini but that of the poet's persona, speaking in the first person plural because his narration has a listener: the woman who is his companion during a two-year search for the King (and presumably for his final significance in the poem) in the ruins of his Mycenean citadel on a bluff protected from the sea by great blocks of stone near the contemporary coastal town of Tolon. The narration begins with a beautiful description of the King's acropolis and leads us to the sudden apparition of the King as a void under a gold burial mask, remnant emblem of a vanished life:

All morning long we looked around the citadel
starting from the shaded side there where the sea
green and without luster—breast of a slain peacock—
received us like time without an opening in it.
Veins of rock dropped down from high above,
twisted vines, naked, many-branched, coming alive
at the water's touch, while the eye following them
struggled to escape the monotonous see-saw motion,
growing weaker and weaker.

On the sunny side a long empty beach
and the light striking diamonds on the huge walls.
No living thing, the wild doves gone
and the king of Asini, whom we've been trying to find for two
    years now,
unknown, forgotten by all, even by Homer,
only one word in the Iliad and that uncertain,
thrown here like the gold burial mask.
You touched it, remember its sound? Hollow in the light
like a dry jar in dug earth:
the same sound that our oars make in the sea.
The king of Asini a void under the mask
everywhere with us everywhere with us, under a name:
" 'Ασίνην τε . . . 'Ασίνην τε . . ."
                  and his children statues
and his desires the fluttering of birds, and the wind
in the gaps between his thoughts, and his ships
anchored in a vanished port:
under the mask a void.

The poet's strategy—shifting from a dramatic monologue with
the King as speaker to the poet-persona narrating the adventure
of searching for the King in his ancient citadel—presents the

reader from the start with a human drama in the world we know instead of that early series of literary allusions offered by an unknown, undefined voice out of the ancient past. The change also allows the poet to open the poem with the description of a literal contemporary setting (anyway the way it was before the tourist invasion) and to move on from there without strain to the symbolic and mythic nuances that lie buried in that setting. The stanza that follows carries us forward another step: the void under the gold mask comes to represent a general void that appears to have taken into its empty circle vital things that have disappeared or descended to the lower world or come under the shadow of a present sorrow, including the very country itself:

> *Behind the large eyes the curved lips the curls*
> *carved in relief on the gold cover of our existence*
> *a dark spot that you see traveling like a fish*
> *in the dawn calm of the sea:*
> *a void everywhere with us.*
> *And the bird, a wing broken,*
> *that flew away last winter*
> *—tabernacle of life—*
> *and the young woman who left to play*
> *with the dog-teeth of summer*
> *and the soul that sought the lower world gibbering*
> *and the country like a large plane-leaf swept along by the*
>   *torrent of the sun*
> *with the ancient monuments and the contemporary sorrow.*

The poem now focuses on the poet's rumination over his having found, in the King of Asini's fate and in the ruins of his citadel, a metaphor for the inescapable losses of our human existence and the bitterness that comes with a sense of inevitably being forgotten, especially for those creative artists with "the power for carving a few signs on the stones," as Seferis put it in "The Sentence to Oblivion," the poem that precedes this one in his *Logbook I* volume. The theme had haunted him for some years, expressed in his prose as a conviction that poetry in his day is merely a kind of holding action for a time in the future when great poetry will again be possible. But in these months immediately before the advent of war, this conviction gave a despairing resonance to certain moments in the poetry as well, in this case not entirely relieved by the poem's rather ambiguous ending (at least in the Greek), which has the speaker either asking if, or wishing that, a startled bat emerging from a cave among the ruins, as the sun climbs toward the heart of midday, could be the reincarnate presence of the forgotten King's soul.

> *And the poet lingers, looking at the stones, and asks himself*
> *does there really exist*
> *among these ruined lines, edges, points, hollows and curves*
> *does there really exist*
> *here where one meets the path of rain, wind and ruin*
> *does there exist the movement of the face, shape of the*
>   *tenderness*
> *of those who've waned so strangely in our lives,*
> *those who remained the shadow of waves and thoughts with*
>   *the sea's boundlessness*
> *or perhaps no, nothing is left but the weight*
> *the nostalgia for the weight of a living existence*
> *there where we now remain unsubstantial, bending*
> *like the branches of a terrible willow tree heaped in unremitting*
>   *despair*
> *while the yellow current carries down rushes uprooted in*
>   *the mud*
> *image of a form that the sentence to everlasting bitterness has*
>   *turned to stone:*
> *the poet a void.*

Shieldbearer, the sun climbed warring,
and from the depths of the cave a startled bat
hit the light as an arrow hits a shield:
" Ἀσίνην τε . . . Ἀσίνην τε . . ." If only that could be the
  king of Asini
we've been searching for so carefully on this acropolis
sometimes touching with our fingers his touch upon the stones.

Whatever poems in translation Henry Miller heard Theodore
Stephanides or Katsimbalis read during his evenings in Maroussi,
this beautiful evocation of the ghosts of past and present that
haunted Seferis's mythmaking sensibility, with "his way of looking forwards and backwards" at once (to use Miller's own terms),
was not among them, though the poem was close to birth by the
time Miller left Greece. It proved to be the last poem included
in the last volume that the poet readied for publication before
he left Greece for Egypt and South Africa with the Greek
government-in-exile, one step ahead of the advancing German
army. But other poems Miller heard, and his friendship with Seferis, apparently enabled him to grasp some of the positive implications of what he justly saw as Seferis's love for his country, so
different from his own disdain for all that he felt his own homeland represented during these prewar days. Yet Seferis's feeling
for Greece, during this time of broadening threat and imminent
sorrow, was more complicated than the sentiment Miller dis-
cerned, because it carried within it both the adoration and the
bitterness of loss that are alive in the long-term lover. Seferis's
forward-and-backward vision had as much darkness in it as light,
and there is a dark side to his image of the essential Greek sun, a
source that can illuminate a day which is both angelic and black,
as his first postwar poem, "*Thrush*," movingly dramatizes. Something of this ambivalence regarding the homeland appears to
have its place in most educated modern Greeks, though the dark
side of their perception emerges most often on a less cosmic and

metaphoric level as unrestrained irony about their fellow citizens and about Greek politics, while their glowing pride in their country can sometimes slide into what others less committed might see as irrational chauvinism.

Katsimbalis is the Athenian intellectual who sings the full range of possibilities within the ambivalent light and dark of the Greeks' passion for Greece. His best aria in this mode, as directed for us by Henry Miller, comes when Miller suggests that Katsimbalis should write down the stories he tells so well. "I'm not a writer, I'm an extemporaneous fellow," he declares. And then he adds, "What good would it do to be a writer, a Greek writer? Nobody reads Greek . . . The educated Greeks don't read their own writers; they prefer to read German, English, French books." And after this thrust of his cane at the belly of his contemporaries, he goes into another key to celebrate the flavor and beauty of modern Greek beside wooden French—inflexible, logic-ridden, too precise—and then beside too flat, too prosaic, too businesslike English, a language that he insists doesn't allow you to make verbs. Flourishing his cane, he tells Miller that the language his American friend uses "doesn't have any guts today. You're all castrated. You've become business men, engineers, technicians. [Your language] sounds like wooden money dropping into a sewer." And then he recites some Seferis in the original for "the sheer beauty of its resonance," and then some Sikelianos, and finally some Yannopoulos, who was "greater than your Walt Whitman and all the American poets combined."

Pericles Yannopoulos was in fact mad. Katsimbalis says so himself, though he insists that he was mad rather than crazy: "there's a difference." According to the Colossus, Yannopoulos was madly in love with the Greek language, with Greek nature, with the Greek islands and mountains and vegetables even, so madly in love that he committed suicide. He was a man "out of proportion," without the French *sens de mesure*, because, Katsimbalis announces, "the true Greek is a god, not a cautious, precise, calculating being with the soul of an engineer." Katsimbalis doesn't tell Miller exactly what Yannopoulos wrote except to say that he could write about rocks for pages and pages, and when he couldn't find any more rocks to rave about, he would invent new rocks. Katsimbalis adds that critics of Yannopoulos said he wrote about the wrong things, but as far as he is concerned, these critics were rabbits while Yannopoulos was an eagle, soaring too high, like Icarus—though the truth is that his death by suicide seems to have had a more earthbound impulse and a less numinous style, a consummation Katsimbalis passes over as a story for another time.

Pericles Yannopoulos, as Miller creates him by way of Katsimbalis, is clearly a mythmaker in Katsimbalis's image, even if this larger-than-life figure, who made up his own myth of a modern Greek paradise, was in fact less literary than Katsimbalis, as well as less rational, less generous, less earthy, and, though given to dramatic gestures, finally less colorful, at least on the page. What Yannopoulos wrote was almost totally in relentless polemic prose that extolled the virtues of Neohellenism in various forms—climate, landscape, attitude—and that denigrated everything that he considered foreign to Greece, especially English and European civilization, which in his view has had a life of only ten centuries on the planet and is anyway barbarous because totally ignorant of modern Greek history and culture. He defined the Greek Way for artists and ordinary citizens as one that rejected all outside influence and exploited what he saw as the glories of his native soil and the beautiful forms and colors it engendered, obvious to anyone who gazed out at the landscape and those who inhabited it under the cleanest air in the world. The climate and landscape abroad, especially in England and Germany, was responsible for the unimaginative character of their people, the earth black, wet, fat, heavy, given to fog, frost, cloud cover, rain, snow, and cold, the giant mountains angrily one on top of the other, the forests darkly thick, and every house burning coke, every body burning alcohol, while Greece had all the gifts of nature: the sun, the mountains, the sea, the islands, the trees, plants, birds, and beasts, most of all the divine light to illuminate the Greek earth, home of the longest history in the world, from the beginning of humanity to the present.

But the unlimited rhetorical pleasure of celebrating this paradise on earth, let alone the delight of the paradise itself, was apparently too much for a single life of such devotion to bear very long. In 1910, at the age of forty, notoriously handsome Pericles Yannopoulos, who had told friends that the only way to travel from this life to the next was on horseback, hired a carriage and went down to the sea near the section of Athenian coast called Skaramanga, unhitched one of the carriage horses, and, dressed in his best, with a crown of wildflowers on his head and a sack of lead weights around his neck, mounted the unhitched horse and rode into the sea until he could safely drown. It is said that the horse, in a state of intense anxiety, vaulted free of its rider at the last moment and reached the shore to live out its given term in peace.

Katsimbalis doesn't mention that it was his father, Yannopoulos's best friend, who arrived to identify the corpse that washed up several days later farther along the coast, near Eleusis, home of the Mysteries—some say with the crown of wildflowers still in place. Katsimbalis *père* and Yannopoulos's brother-in-law arranged the burial in the Eleusis cemetery, and the story of the suicide brought the name of Yannopoulos back into public attention for a while after years of decline. Yet he was considered too eccentric, too maniacal, both in person and in print, to have much lasting influence on others, and though he was taken up for a while by the Generation of the Thirties (Katsimbalis devoted a special issue of *Ta Nea Grammata* to his essays in 1938), the excesses of his chauvinism eventually scattered dust on all but the story of his suicide. It remained as the source of an enduring nostalgia for those few in postwar Greece who could still manage to believe, after a world war and a civil war, in mad gestures by the ardently nationalist young.

There was another suicide that haunted some members of the Generation of the Thirties, that of the poet and translator Kostas Karyotakis in August 1928. Karyotakis was a writer of larger talent and influence than Yannopoulos, with a darker vision that proved, for better or worse, to be significantly representative of the generation that emerged from the First World War and that came to know what Seferis called the then current "Waste Land feeling" of "thirsting despair." Karyotakis drew heavily on the modern French tradition that was dominant in his time, in particular on Baudelaire and on one of T. S. Eliot's masters, Jules Laforgue. His best-known collection was called *Elegies and Satires*, and his principal mode was to find possible harmonies between the elegiac and satiric modes within tightly rhymed forms. He was a poet of urban life, like Cavafy, and, out of tune with Yannopoulos, he found ways to turn the local patterns of nature into a bitter elegiac metaphor, as we see in Rachel Hadas's brilliant version of Karyotakis's "Autumn, What Can I Say to You?":

*Autumn, what can I say to you? Your earliest breath is drawn
from city lights; you reach as far as heaven's cloudy air.
Hymns, symbols, early drafts of poems, all of them well known—
the mind's cold blossoms—fall like withered leaves in your long
    hair.*

*Imperious, gigantic apparition, as you walk
along the path of bitterness, of sudden snatchings up,
your lofty forehead strikes the stars; the hem of your gold cloak
drives dead leaves along the ground with its relentless sweep.*

You are destruction's angel, master of the death you bring,
the shadow which with nightmare pace advances on its way;
from time to time deliberately you flap a fearful wing,
and sketch unending questions, questions all across the sky.

O autumn, I was full of longing for your chilly weather,
those trees, that forest, even the deserted pedestal;
and as back down to clammy earth both fruit and branches fall,
I've come, a captive of your passion: let us die together.

One of Karyotakis's earliest supporters, Telos Agras, writing a long critical commentary on the poet's work for the first annual collection of essays in *Ta Nea Grammata* (1935), provides us with an image of Karyotakis at the other extreme from the image of Yannopoulos that we get from the *Colossus*. Agras first encountered Karyotakis as a civil servant in the Ministry of Welfare, a man of small build, impeccably dressed, articulate, obliging, attentive, prudent, his talk simple and direct, yet a man who was hardly free and easy, his eyes restless, often downcast, his recurrent smile not at all simple: it seemed to Agras to belong to only half of his face. Karyotakis could apparently wear the mask of a gregarious person, but his inner life was dominated by a kind of quiet cynicism—the result of a failed search for faith both in and beyond himself—that often led to despair. The inner life came to the surface not only in his ingeniously crafted poems but in his inability to find any peace in the public life he led as a civil servant and emerging poet, especially when he was transferred to the provincial town of Preveza at the age of thirty-two in 1928. Some stanzas from the late poem invoking that town in its title serve to tell the hidden story (again in Rachel Hadas's version):

Ah, Preveza, fortress and garrison!
On Sunday we'll go listen to the band.
I got a savings booklet from the bank.
First deposit: thirty drachmas down.

Strolling slowly up and down the quay,
"Do I exist?" you say. "You're not alive!"
Here comes the steamer, and her flag flies high.
His Excellency the Governor may arrive.

If at least one person from this place
from horror, boredom, and disgust would drop,
silent and solemn, each with a long face,
at the funeral we'd all live it up.

After a little over a month in Preveza, Karyotakis dropped. He made a valiant effort to follow in the footsteps of Yannopoulos by drowning himself—though not on horseback—yet the effort failed: his suicide note advises those who can swim never to attempt suicide by sea, since in his experience you thrash about for some ten hours and drink plenty of water only to find that your body keeps rising to the surface. What proved effective in the end was a pistol pressed to his heart after he had chain-smoked a few cigarettes under a eucalyptus tree. His poetry hardly offers evidence that he expected to discover something beyond the grave to make up for the barren earthly garden he left behind; in fact, one late poem ends with an image of the dead rising on tiptoe to look out from their tomb over the "terrain of Paradise" only to see the Lord's "followers" playing cricket there.

In a talk on the poetry of Captain Antoniou and Odysseus Elytis that Seferis gave to Greek high school students in Alexandria during the Second World War, he introduced the name of Karyotakis by way of a prologue to his comments on his two younger friends: in Seferis's view Karyotakis was the most important, perhaps the only substantial, representative of the "big city" poetry in Greece that prevailed in the ten years after the First World War; a poet of exquisite sensitivity, who, though dying young, had left behind him a body of work that was a landmark in Greek literature. The trouble, according to Seferis, was that

Karyotakis engendered "karyotakism," a confining development. Seferis wraps his perception in a metaphor: Karyotakis, with his enchanting imagination, sings of the tragic plaster in his room, but his imitators lock themselves in the room and even within the plaster itself out of "a whining condescension." Seferis sees things beginning to change around 1930: the younger poets—Antoniou and Elytis in particular—soon turned to broader horizons: the islands of the Aegean, the mythology of the sea, voyages in new directions. And, though he doesn't say so, Seferis himself was the guiding voice in those years, especially after the publication of *Mythistorema* in 1935. That voice, the voice of a humanist with an ardent devotion to both the ancient and the modern Greek traditions, challenged not only "karyotakism" but, to some degree, even the remnant of Yannopoulos's influence on Greek writers who turned to the East rather than to the West—to the Byzantine and Greek Orthodox traditions rather than to the Enlightenment—for what Elytis called "the true face of Greece." While Katsimbalis was singing his madman's praises in the late summer of 1939, some of those who heard him—Seferis, surely, and no doubt Miller under his influence—still honored the enlightened, humanist vision that Greece had inspired among thinkers in the West and many in Greece itself. In fact, the poem that Seferis dedicated to Miller in November 1939, "Les Anges Sont Blancs," links this humanist preoccupation to the poet's portrait of his American friend, who appears as a figure with "the teethmarks of the tropics in his skin, / putting on his dark glasses as if he were going to work with a blowlamp." The poem's concluding lines, spoken by this figure, tell us that a man has to turn to stone if he chooses the company of angels, and when searching for the miracle, he must look inside himself:

> "The angels are white flaming white and the eye that would confront them shrivels

and there's no other way you've got to become like stone if you
     want their company
and when you look for the miracle you've got to scatter your
     blood to the eight points of the wind
because the miracle is nowhere but circulates in the veins
     of man."

This is the message that Seferis appears to have received from
Miller in return for his gift of myths rooted in the soil of Greece,
dark as they are light, emerging in poems that the American
found gem-like, scintillating, revelatory, with lines that made "the
encircling movement of embrace."

VOYAGING INTO THE LIGHT

*O*ne episode in Homer's *Odyssey* haunts the landscape of contemporary Greek culture, as it has literature elsewhere in the West: Odysseus' descent into the underworld. In Greece, it is not merely a literary phenomenon, though it is often present in the work of poets and dreamers. There is an actual site near the coast of Epirus, east of Parga, which is called the Oracle of the Dead and which a Greek archaeologist has spent years celebrating as the true source for Odysseus' voyage "down the dank / moldering paths and . . . past / the Land of Dreams" to the fields of asphodel "where the dead, the burnt-out wraiths of mortals, make their home." To reach the beginning of this underworld, the visitor descends a dank stairway into a labyrinth of corridors leading to a tall, cavelike enclosure free of light with a hole in it made for offerings of wheat and honey to the oracle in the crypt below, reputed to be the uppermost level of the palace of Hades and Persephone. The amiable and learned archaeologist, his face lined by a history of exile in the islands as an unrepentant Communist, will explain that the shades Odysseus talked to, after animal sacrifices and a libation of blood, were subsequently made available to visitors as shapes created by an elaborate mechanism of pulleys and mirrors, whose wheels alone have managed to survive the hungry maw of time. What has also survived, he will proudly show you, is black grain, ancient staff of life, a handful of which he carries in his pocket for the visitor to feel a second and then return to him carefully, as one might a handful of fine gold nuggets. His site appears small at first—walls of piled stones that could pass for a modern sheepfold—but with his monologue on the history of the place and its secret recesses, the setting comes to life not only with ghosts of the dead in misty fields but with gods and goddesses still enraptured by the smell of the now distant sea, still so in love with their vanished playground that they sometimes emerge into the sunlit air and wing in rapid flight across the drained Akherousia lake and its cultivated rice fields to the neighboring hills.

From the start of the Greek story, the living visited the dark underworld of the dead only in order to learn from the shades there how better to find the way back to the world of the living, where light from the sun would signal the route to your earthly home. When Homer's Odysseus goes down the dank paths to the fields of asphodel to seek guidance from the prophet Tiresias for the return journey to Ithaka, it is his mother's ghost who gives him essential advice: Hurry back to the light of day! And the ghost of his old war buddy Achilles reaffirms this sentiment when Odysseus tries to tell him how lucky he is to be as honored among the dead as he was among men on earth. Achilles calls such talk nonsense: he, at least, would rather be slave to the humblest of living men than rule over all these ghostly presences who have lost the breath of life.

Many centuries later, Dante picks up the theme in subtle ways at the point in his *Divine Comedy* where he condemns Ulysses (Odysseus) to a Christian underworld in which the Greek hero is made to reside in a tall eternal flame for having thought up the stratagem of the Wooden Horse to defeat Dante's Trojan ancestors. But the poet has the grace to create a grand final voyage for the aged Ulysses, who returns to Ithaka only to sail away again from wife and heir on a last "vigil . . . / Of feeling life" to reach "the new experience / Of the uninhabited world behind the sun." Some centuries later, Tennyson, in his poem "Ulysses," picks up on Dante to show us a Ulysses back in Ithaka "Made weak by time and fate" but unwilling to pause, "To rust unburnished, . . . As though to breathe were life" when "Life piled on life" would not be enough for him. So he readies himself to leave his aged wife and dutiful son in order to sail "beyond the sunset, and the baths / Of all the western stars," until he dies. And less than a century later, James Joyce again picks up the theme at the point where his Ulysses figure, Leopold Bloom, descends into an Irish underworld, the cemetery in Dublin where Paddy Dignam is to be interred, and finally emerges, after a walk through the graves to the cemetery's open, glimmering gates, with this reaffirmation: "Enough of this place . . . Plenty to see and hear and feel yet. Feel live warm being near you. Let them sleep in their maggoty beds. They are not going to get me this innings. Warm beds: warm fullblooded life." And still later, when George Seferis discovers his underworld in a ship sunk by the Germans off the island of Poros during the Second World War, he has his contemporary Odysseus emerge from his dialogue with the dead on the "other side of the sun, the dark side," bringing a lyrical message of universal love embodied in Aphrodite rising into the light to dispel all past images of tyranny:

> the heart of the Scorpion has set,
> the tyrant in man has fled,
> and all the daughters of the sea, Nereids, Graeae,
> hurry toward the shimmering of the rising goddess:
> whoever has never loved will love,
> in the light.

The Greek way, at least among the poets, is to descend into the sunless mysteries of the lower world not only to learn that death has its unhappy dominion and the sun its dark side but to re-affirm the godly virtue of the light that illumines the world above. And as the underworld has both a literal and metaphoric presence for some of those who search it out, so the Greek light appears to become for some both an outer and an inner source. During the greater part of this century, the outer light, the work of the sun at its high point, had the power not only to light up the landscape with a precision that turned colors primary and contours sharply clean but to dazzle and bewilder those who were used to the sun's subtler energies. Foreign painters had to spend hours taking the measure of this Greek light, accommodating its demands, working to tame it, and some despaired of ever learning its secret dimensions.

That source for precision can still be found in parts of Greece surrounded by the seas that cars cross uncomfortably on ferries, or protected from industry by roads still meant to be shared with mules and sheep. Yet even in the polluted cities there are days and nights when the wind clears the air and you can actually see the islands or peninsulas in the distance, their rock configurations in mauve or dark purple, the light of day incandescent on bright waters or the starlight radiant across the full dome of the heavens. But it is in the islands, some within easy reach of Piraeus, where the best hope remains for learning from the light, as Henry Miller was privileged to know by the circumstance of finding Greek companions so ready to show him the way there.

He tells us that Seferis and Katsimbalis one day introduced him to Niko Hadjikyriako-Ghika, called Ghika for short, a painter whose canvases are "as fresh and clean, as pure and naked of all pretense, as the sea and light which bathes the dazzling islands," and a week later, Miller and his two mythmaking friends, "jubilant" because they had not had a vacation in ages, board a ship in Piraeus to sail for Ghika's ancestral home on the island of Hydra. It is the beginning of what Miller calls a "voyage into the light" which, over the next two months, with a break here and there, will take him to the islands of Poros, Hydra, Spetses, and Crete, and finally end in Tripolis on the mainland. It is a voyage during which "the earth became illuminated by her own inner light," and by the time it reached the heart of the Peloponnese, it had revealed mysteries that changed Miller's life.

Early in his book he gives us a glimpse of what he later elaborates upon generously when he outlines some of what he came to see as he encountered newly discovered underworld figures that gave him his particular access to the light: at Mycenae he walked over "the incandescent dead," at Epidaurus he heard "the great heart of the world" and thereby "understood the meaning of pain and sorrow," at Tiryns, in the shadow of the "Cyclopean man," he felt "the blaze of that inner eye which has now become a sickly gland," at Argos, where the plain was a "fiery mist," he came upon "the ghosts of our own American Indians" and greeted them silently as he moved about in a "detached way . . . , feet flooded with the earthly glow," and from there on to other unfamiliar places, in each opening "a new vein of experience," finally, like "a miner digging deeper into the earth," approaching "the heart of the star which is not yet extinguished," where "the sun is man struggling to emerge toward another light."

By the end of this trip, Henry Miller had clearly learned, along with much else, to travel freely into the world of illusion and to come out into the bright country of metaphor—some would say too freely. But the first illuminations of his long voyage began on the literal level, when he sailed for the island of Poros and Katsimbalis arranged an impromptu meal on deck of the kind he loved to preside over whatever the time of day or night, the wine flowing profusely, everyone talking at once, and the feeling of affectionate warmth so strong that Miller thought it unlikely he would ever feel that way again. He reports that the war had now actually begun, but it was forgotten. The veiled sun emerged into the open, the lemon trees on the shore opposite came into sight, and with the madness induced by their fragrance, Miller found the group drawn together "in a frenzy of self-surrender."

Under the influence of that frenzy, Miller moved easily to a metaphoric level. As the ship sailed through the narrow passage between Poros and the Peloponnesian mainland, what first appeared to him as a dream image of sailing on land through the town streets, men and women hanging out of their windows just above his head, was soon transformed by the narcotic perfume from the lemon groves into a joyous passing through the neck of the womb—a "joy too deep almost to be remembered." Years later, one of his companions, George Seferis, took the literal and metaphoric nuances of Poros in another direction. In his journal he tells us that during the years immediately before the war, he saw the island as a "cocotte's bedroom," its narrow passage as a kind of Venetian canal between the houses, its "hothouse atmosphere"—lemon-scented, luxurious, sensually provocative—a trough of voluptuousness which might do as a "place for eminent international lovers." On returning to Poros after the war to write his famous poem *"Thrush,"* the international lovers he chose to put on the island were the eminent mythical lovers Odysseus and Circe, and a mythical lover manqué, Odysseus's poor companion Elpenor, transformed into *"l'homme moyen sensuel"* who makes a failed attempt to seduce Circe with words that finally suggest "the look of a worm that is in the fruit of sensual pleasure" (as Seferis himself put it in a commentary). In the relevant section of the poem, it is the arrival of the Second World War by way of a radio news broadcast that interrupts the Odysseus-Circe romance and dramatically fragments the lovers' farewell song:

> —*"Athens. The public has heard*
> *the news with alarm; it is feared*

> *a crisis is near. The prime*
> *minister declared: 'There is no more time . . .'*
> *Take cyclamen . . . needles of pine . . .*
> *the lily . . . needles of pine . . .*
> *O woman . . .*
> *— . . . is overwhelmingly stronger.*
> *The war . . ."*
> SOULMONGER.

Miller's prewar illumination on Poros highlights the joy of re-birth while Seferis's image highlights an unredeemed sensuality, but the principal difference between the two is the latter's harsh recollection of the climate of war that not only had begun to heat up during those days of free-flowing wine but would soon occasion the selling of souls. Seferis wrote his poem seven years after that late summer of 1939, yet, given his journal entries of the prewar time, one can't help wondering if thoughts of war were as easily dismissed by Miller's Greek companions as *The Colossus of Maroussi* suggests they were during the passage from Poros to Hydra, however seductive Seferis and Katsimbalis may have found Henry Miller's exuberant mood that day. And one wonders how fully they could have participated in Miller's euphoric nostalgia when he wrote up the event some months later. He tells us in the *Colossus* (as I shall call it henceforth), "In point of truth it is eons since I passed through that narrow strait. It will never happen again. Ordinarily I would be sad at the thought, but I am not now . . . This is one of the lowest moments in the history of the human race. There is no sign of hope on the horizon. The whole world is involved in slaughter and bloodshed. I repeat—*I am not sad.* Let the world have its bath of blood—I will cling to Poros." Cling in memory, anyway. For better or worse, Seferis and Katsimbalis could not let go of the island so easily. Their return to it, after what Seferis's poem calls "war, destruction, exile," was inevitable and, in the case of Seferis, haunted by those bygone events that had broken into the hothouse hedonism and dispersed the sensual aromas of the Poros he once knew.

But the change in the landscape was nowhere in sight when the journey was recorded while the companions were still on the road in the prewar land of metaphor and Henry Miller was soaring, in flight to higher regions, or, more precisely, emerging into new life on Poros, with a vision of "the whole human race straining through the neck of the bottle here, searching for egress into the world of light and beauty." That world is out there, in the new islands to be discovered only a slight distance down the way—Hydra first of all, a great rock that rises out of the sea "like a huge loaf of petrified bread." We are told that it is the bread turned to stone which rewards the artist for his labors when he first sights the promised land, the ordeal of rock which follows on the "uterine illumination" and out of which is born the spark that will fire the world. Miller acknowledges that he is speaking in "broad, swift images" because "to move from place to place in Greece is to become aware of the stirring, fateful drama of the race as it circles from paradise to paradise," and the island of Hydra is but one stepping-stone "along a path marked out by the gods."

Exactly what illuminations came to Miller in this Edenic place of rest and meditation remains imprecise in the *Colossus*, but it seems likely that the painter Ghika was a principal source for what he learned on Hydra. We hear about houses cubistically arranged, the "very epitome of that flawless anarchy which supersedes, because it includes and goes beyond, all formal arrangements of the imagination," and this suggests a direct link to his host and the flawless anarchy of Ghika's cubistic, brilliantly colored, imaginatively architectonic images of Hydra in his paintings of this period. As one critic succinctly remarked, Ghika managed to invest Cubism with the transparency of Greek light. But the painter, thoroughly conscious of what he was up to and more capable than we are of translating his artistic perceptions into words, had this to say about the vision of Hydra that he attempted to capture in "silent symphonies of geometric patterns and bright pigments":

At the midday hour, at the sun's meridian, the white-washed walls mirror an unbearable brilliance. Reflections off the sharp-edged stones, the lanceolate leaves, the acute angles of buildings emitted an incandescent haze that made the air seem to dance like a flame, to shudder as if at the passing of the haunting spirit of mystical high noon. You would say that Pan could have been heard on his pipes, bringing all things to a standstill and causing nature to hold her breath. The cube-shaped houses, like almond cakes dusted with rose-scented sugar, the lozenge-shaped roofs, and the serpentine enclosure walls—all were stilled. The gloomy archways, the rocky outcrops, the caves, the windmills, the solitary trees . . .

The poetry of this description is there in the artist's work, in his drawings as well as his paintings, shaped not by metaphor but by the lines and colors of his transforming imagination, hinting of a reality beyond that of the actual world he knew but still rooted in the essential elements of his island's landscape and the quality of its light. The reader will find it difficult to discern from Miller's fast-moving account of his Hydra visit just how much of Ghika's artistic sensibility he came to know there or elsewhere, though it seems he recognized intuitively that he was in the presence of the kind of sui generis free spirit that he himself aspired to be and that Ghika evokes when defining a genius as an individual who owes nothing to anyone, who is not subject to external influence, who is self-willed and obstinate. All we are told in the *Colossus* is that after talk of the great heroes and emancipators born on Hydra, of admirals' houses that Miller visited and votive offerings he made to saints who helped to cure the dead, the halt, and the blind, what he discovered in Ghika's house were things that strike the reader as disconcertingly down to earth: Ping-Pong, champagne, cognac, more ouzo and retsina.

Though he ended up talking to Ghika about "the monks in Tibet," territory that Ghika had studied and contemplated for some years, perhaps the most important illumination that came to Miller on the island he did not mention in the *Colossus* at all but put in the journal he wrote there to give Seferis as a parting gift several months later. ("Can you imagine somebody doing a thing as generous as that?" Seferis once said to me in conversation, shaking his head. "The only manuscript of his notes for the book he will write given as a gift to a friend before he has written the book?") The journal, which Miller recovered from Seferis's wife, Maro, in a photocopy soon after the poet's death in 1971, was published in 1973 as "First Impressions of Greece." It begins on Hydra, which we are told is the "birth-place of the immaculate conception," where everything is "miraculously produced out of nothingness," everything "white as snow yet colorful" (Ghika's influence?), the whiskey "especially favorable for discussion about Blavatsky and Tibet." Yet we learn that in the fortress where Ghika resides, the talk—presumably mostly in French—"always seems to revolve about Byzance," which turns out to be "the cultural link."

As we know, the influence of Byzantium in the Greek tradition was a significant theme for a number of the Greek intellectuals and writers who belonged to the Generation of the Thirties, a theme often bypassed by Western observers, especially among post-Byronic travelers to Greece. Miller's journal does not tell us exactly how the talk on Hydra established the "link" that Byzantium can be said to have created between the ancient, the late antique, the medieval, and the modern Greek cultures, but we do get an image of the territory that the conversation covered in what the author calls its "pendulum" swing back and forth from ancient Mycenae to Periclean Greece, from Minoan times to the

Greek War of Independence, and, most revealing, from Hermes Trismegistus of the *Hermetica* to Yannopoulos, Palamas, and Sikelianos. The latter list was surely a rich addition to Miller's continually expanding menu of exotic men of letters past and present whom he had come across in his travels at one time or another (Yannopoulos and Palamas were most certainly Katsimbalis's contribution, Sikelianos probably Seferis's). But the journal moves on quickly to the rich Byzantine inheritance in the day's literal menu, the "Gargantuan" meals that began with hors d'oeuvres sufficient by themselves for normal human satiety and that ended with a variety of fruit and a "Turkish pastry" that Miller learned was not Turkish at all but Greek by way of Byzantium, these great meals eased on their way by a very traditional Greek retsina that "dissolves everything in gold dust and aerates the lungs by a sort of refined turpentine shellac which evaporates and creates well-being, joy, conversation."

The journal is a kind of shorthand record of Miller's voyage of discovery, adjectives serving for what will later be translated into metaphors ("Everything is legendary, fabulous, incredible, miraculous—yet true," he tells us as he leaves Hydra behind). And it records encounters with real if surprising island people who will later be transformed into mythical figures in the *Colossus*—for example, his passing mention in the journal of the maid "who is called, who is *baptized*, Demeter" will become, in the later work, the maid "of divine origin . . . descended directly from the Erectheum, though she bore the name of a sacred cereal." Miller must have used the act of recording in the journal as a means of storing memories that he would later draw on—without benefit of the early document—to carry the reader from the literal landscape with figures into the world of metaphor and myth that dominates and enriches the *Colossus*. At the time he generously handed his journal to Seferis, he may have felt that his actual recorded notes would only inhibit his effective manipulation of that crossing, once he began to cash in his memories of the Greek voyage. But there was a cost in this. We find a number of tantalizing references to legendary people and anecdotes that fell by the wayside when his memory took over and he started to write his book—specifically, in the case of his days on Hydra, this parenthetical bit of shorthand notation: "(The story of the banker who wrote bad verse. The imbecile who kept a 33-volume pornographic diary. The nymphomaniac who danced naked on the estate and seduced the guests. Etc., etc. Legends, fables, myths galore)." We can do without the banker, but the imbecile and the nymphomaniac are disheartening losses.

When both the journal and the *Colossus* move on from Hydra to the island of Spetses (or "Spetsai" in Miller's purist version of the Greek), a comparison between the two shows that the transformations of the literal into the fabulous are sometimes enriching, sometimes not. The passage between the two islands, with Katsimbalis urging Miller on despite the inclement weather (Seferis no longer with them to provide stability), is an example on the positive side, this leg of the voyage—called "Homeric" both by Katsimbalis and in the journal—really coming to life only in the *Colossus* when Miller gives his metaphoric imagination full play in an elaborate description. Now the waves loom like white-toothed monsters "waiting to fall on us belly first," the sky is like the back of a mirror "showing a dull molten glow," the boat "like a cork" under the command of a fearless helmsman who leaves the tiller at one point to pull down the sails and is, according to Katsimbalis, "probably mad." In the journal, the boat is simply called "a mythological animal," and the helmsman, acting recklessly, pulls down a tarpaulin over the heads of his passengers to gain time and save fuel—though this serves for a grand generalization that distinguishes the "heroic Greeks from the Vikings": the daring of the Greeks, we are told, is based on certitude, and the Greek sailor "has genius when he undertakes a dangerous task."

In contrast, a comparison of the two recordings shows that a surprising reticence apparently came over Miller when he took up his pen to write about Spetses itself in the *Colossus*, for the journal entry covering the same ground offers precision, even color, that the later work lacks. For a start, Miller tells us in the journal that Spetses "marks an important step in the longer journey I am making," and he cites his long walks by the sea with Seferis's brother-in-law, Constantine Tsatsos, as the occasion for "deep corroborations of the answers I had already given to certain inner problems." He feels that in Tsatsos he has met "a man of fine spirit" who is a link with others past and future whom it is his destiny to meet, and that what is "vitally important" about Tsatsos is his purity. Miller doesn't elaborate on this purity, but his passing comment that Tsatsos is "now in exile" at least provides a hint. In fact, this learned professor of law, who had recently been engaged in a public dialogue with Seferis about the nature of Hellenism in the art of modern Greece, was in exile on Spetses for having infuriated Metaxas by calling for the victory of the democracies then under threat. (So his wife, Ioanna, reported in her book *My Brother George Seferis*. Tsatsos's views were apparently picked up by the authorities from a letter he sent to another famous political exile, Panayotis Kanellopoulos, who, like Tsatsos, ended up elected to high office after the war, Kanellopoulos as Prime Minister, deposed by the Colonels' coup of 1967.)

In the *Colossus*, Miller, "to be discreet," transformed Tsatsos into one Kyrios Ypsilon (Mr. Y), and he tells us that what he likes about this character is not his purity or his fine spirit or even his counsel during long walks by the sea but his "keen, buoyant nature, his directness, his passion for flowers and for metaphysics." Then, in place of a metaphysical seaside stroll with deep corroborations (these no doubt justly bypassed), Miller offers us a scene that has this acutely intelligent if hapless political exile, short in stature but tall in courage, receiving him in the deserted house of the great War of Independence heroine Bouboulina while sitting in a tin tub "soaking and scrubbing himself vigorously" near his shelf of Dante, Goethe, Fielding, D. H. Lawrence, Aristotle, and Plato, announcing that he would like to read Walt Whitman to keep up his morale and declaring, unsolicited, that without regular habits such as taking a bath "you go to pieces." He adds: "The nights are long, you know, when you are not free." End of significant encounter.

On their way back to the hotel from this bathroom scene, Katsimbalis tells Miller that "women are crazy" about "the great fellow" they have just visited, and that Kyrios Ypsilon has "an interesting theory about love . . . get him to talk to you about it some time." It is hard to believe, but Miller lets that opportunity for either elaboration or invention pass him by. And when Bouboulina's name comes up beside that of Joan of Arc in this sudden erotic context, what might have served as an excuse for a bit of colorful history also evaporates into the Katsimbalis monologue on the virtues of being "an extemporaneous fellow." In the journal, Miller, less self-protective, offers the opinion that every female heroine and every female saint was endowed with tremendous sexual ardor, and adds the news that Bouboulina "fucked her way to fame" and died pregnant.

Along with this tantalizing bit of Spetses lore—further details available, Miller tells us, by addressing George Katsimbalis at Maroussi—the journal provides more harsh candor (and color) than the *Colossus* about two of Miller's encounters on the island that aroused strong sentiments in him, enough, anyway, to enter into his memory's record, though held there in significantly milder form. One is with the character called Nick in the *Colossus*, a "fat fellow" who claims to have been a bookie in America and who brags about having seven American suits hanging up in his Greek closet because "you can't get anything decent here [on Spetses]," a "dump" compared to Buffalo, New York. Miller lets this Nick off the hook by giving him a mild fade-out line: "Funny," he tells Miller, "you like it here and I like it there. I wish we could swap passports. I'd give anything to have an American passport now"—a point of view that was hardly eccentric on that island or anywhere else in Greece at the time. In Miller's journal, Nick appears as John Stefanakos, "a fat sow with gravy dripping from his lips," with a house that is like "a refined lunatic asylum" and a wife who is "a mental but agreeable defective," very handy with a needle, "which John appreciates." John was born on Spetses but has his heart in Buffalo, New York. He's seen nothing of Greece but this island he's returned to, and since he thinks the country needs more machinery and more money, Miller considers him the perfect specimen of the lost man "whom America takes to her bosom, castrates and fattens like a eunuch," or, in another metaphor, "a discarded tin can such as one sees on the shores of every country in the world, in the wake of progress." So much for the great melting pot.

The second encounter on Spetses that apparently stirred Miller's vitriolic juices, as recorded in the journal, was with the Anargyrios College (a private secondary school), though one would hardly think so from the swift and gentle mention of it in *Colossus*, where we learn simply that it has buildings which he admires at one point and that it was donated, along with "most everything else of importance" on the island, by a cigarette king who gave it his name. In the journal, that brief mention is the occasion for a grand philippic, first against the "meaningless babble between great convulsions of time and matter" that the college represents, presumably in contrast to "the individual man," even the individual man and philanthropist named Anargyrios, who had no illusions beyond that of creating this "colossal mistake." Why is that so? Because trying to teach the Greeks " 'team work' " is "a piece of sheer fatuity," and the "naif English professor" who suggested that this was the college's nonsensical educational purpose is an example of the English insensitivity to "what is other, different." Finally, we are told that our misdirected cigarette king, though thoroughly Greek, carried on the American millionaire tradition "of doing what one pleases in this life and trying to undo his work in the next life, by endowments." It seems that Anargyrios's truly substantive contribution to the world, though ephemeral, was his Helmar, Murad, and Turkish Trophies, cigarettes which Miller says he will smoke again as soon as he can afford that luxury and which he recommends to all Greeks with the cry: "Smoke a Murad!"

One suspects that the changes from the journal to the book were occasioned by Miller's reluctance, anyway in this light-flooded context, to let his prejudices hang out so openly, even if that meant sacrificing some of the entertaining sting in his venom, perhaps especially when his dislike of his own country's material progress, of Greeks who had a longing for it, and of the English for being English were themes he had already exploited with sufficient venom. In the case of the Anargyrios College, Miller was on ground fully shared by others. A number of Greek students have testified over the years to their hatred of it; despite its early reputation as the best of its elitist kind, it eventually lost its clientele and closed its gates. And at least one Englishman who taught there for two years after the war, the writer John Fowles, condemned it in language that would have thoroughly pleased Miller. Fowles has written that he thought this school for Greek boys "an absurd simulacrum of a British private school," and during his time there in the early 1950s "a sickening emblem of an *ancien regime* still trying to cling by its fingernails to a sort of power." Again, in a 1994 commentary on his novel *The Magus*, published in 1966, Fowles reports that he found the boys were more ebullient and spontaneous than their British counterparts, but given less opportunity to learn the right kind of discipline: no organized games, too much homework, too many hours in the classroom, where the teaching methods appeared "antiquated," the teachers perhaps knowing their subjects but with few outside interests beyond common gossip, "rather like village schoolmasters in England." But the island itself he called "a jewel, a paradise."

Fowles spoke out of the despair of someone who knew the school well enough to have come to hate it passionately, and that was by contrast to the passionate love he felt for Spetses itself, for the Greek landscape that it represented, for the particular quality of the Greek light that he discovered there and that inspired his writing. In *The Magus*, set on Spetses, his narrator speaks of the island's having taken his breath away when he first saw it, and, recollected in tranquillity, the vision of it emerges grandly into metaphor, "floating under Venus like a majestic black whale in an amethyst evening sea," its hills covered with pine trees "as light as greenfinch feathers." Once ashore and away from the port, he sees its distinguishing characteristic to be silence, as though it belonged to "the world before the machine, almost before man," where the few things that happened seemed "isolated, framed, magnified by solitude," a place haunted by nymphs rather than monsters. Yet, like Seferis, Fowles's narrator encounters an "ultimate Mediterranean light" that has both an angelic and a black aspect, "supremely beautiful" but also "hostile." This he ascribes at least in part to "the terror, the stripping-to-essentials, of love." And again like Seferis, he finds that the Greece he came to know has a Circe-like quality that makes it unique; the landscape and the light "so beautiful, so all-present, so intense, so wild, that the relationship is immediately love-hatred, one of passion"—which, the narrator tells us, it took him many months to understand and many years to accept.

For the foreign writer in search of paradise, the Greek islands and the radiant landscape more generally sometimes appear to rouse a passion that is too intense to bear for long, and though the memory of it, like that of first love, may linger as long as life itself, the writer's heart usually finds ways to turn elsewhere. John Fowles lived on Spetses for two years, then exiled himself from the island for more than forty years. Miller visited it for four days during his six months in Greece and never returned. Durrell was a touch more faithful to the influence of his island initiation. He opened his postwar book about Rhodes, *Reflections on a Marine Venus* (1953), with a chapter called "Of Paradise Terrestre" and an admission that he suffered from the disease of islomania (finding islands irresistible). There is evidence that, having succumbed to this tenacious passion, after some thirty years of living away from the Aegean he was still pressed by it to write a relatively short book called *The Greek Islands* (1978). But in this book, which fully participates in Miller's and Fowles's celebration of the Greek *phos* (light here described as the "naked eyeball of God, so to speak"), Durrell concludes his return voyage to the Saronic Gulf and beyond with an image of Spetses that seems pallid after those he offers of Poros and Hydra. He tells us that some find the island appealing and some find it appalling, the former perhaps Athenians "who like life easy," the latter those who find the island "un-Greek," more like what you might encounter in France or Italy, but not so good as either Ischia or Corsica. Durrell here takes a stance somewhere short of a lover's. "A most unstrenuous place," he calls Spetses, where you can ride in horse-drawn carriages (no cars allowed) along a coast road that takes you to coves and bays and headlands "that seem like diminished samples of some great original." He concludes that the island "has little to show beyond the bones of Bouboulina," and the visitor who wanders along its pretty beaches and pleasant pine glades will somehow feel that it "just escapes being a modern suburb of Athens." At least when it comes to Spetses, and especially in comparison to Fowles's evocation of the island's breathtaking majesty years after he lived there, what Durrell's long-delayed return suggests is passion spent and islomania close to finding a cure. In any case, at the time he wrote his belated survey of the Greek islands he was living in the South of France, where he remained the rest of his life.

One Athenian who found postwar Spetses the place to go for rejuvenation was Durrell's persevering companion George Katsimbalis, who regularly spent part of his summers there in the 1960s and early 1970s. He liked the island's simple ways, its solitude, its lack of cars, its green walks, and the postwar Xenia Hotel by a sea that was immediately accessible and still pristine (not the grandiose Hotel Poseidon near the harbor, preferred by an earlier generation). And though in his late years he suffered from severe arthritis and the remnants of a leg wound from the First World War, he would take up his cane and climb to the high point of the hill above the town whenever the gods gave him strength enough for it, because up that way there was a taverna that he would swear had the sweetest onions in Christendom and barreled retsina so good it would make you weep.

This, like any other opinion about food, was something that nobody who met up with Katsimbalis ever managed to challenge, any more than they could challenge his still-energetic and sometimes almost pointless storytelling. One visitor who tried was the novelist Kingsley Amis, who arrived on Spetses for a month one summer during the 1967–74 dictatorship with his tall and handsome novelist wife, Elizabeth Jane Howard, to join my wife, Mary, and me in renting a white cottage from a British expatriate in the quaint if increasingly polluted Old Harbor. Amis insisted that the cottage originally belonged to a family of malevolent midgets, since you couldn't move from one room to another without cracking your head on some picturesque antique lintel or beam ("I will just squat here and cry and never move again," poor Elizabeth Jane once whimpered when a beam struck her for the second time that day in exactly the same place on her forehead). After several encounters with Katsimbalis that inspired Amis to make valiant efforts to mimic the narrative style and culinary pedantry of the Colossus, he ended up succumbing to his charm: "You know, it's remarkable, I've never seen anything like it, the old boy somehow manages to transform a relentlessly boring story and a greasy fried onion into an epic experience simply by never giving up on it."

There are those who say that the islands most easily approachable from Athens, some now by air, will soon be overwhelmed by the tourist trade of one kind or another, including even Poros, Hydra, and Spetses, which once provided a perennial summer home for some of the oldest Athenian families but which after the war gradually gave away a significant part of their territory to eccentric or merely rich foreign transients. Though none of these islands yet has an airport, getting there, which Cavafy tells us is the essential adventure, usually takes too little time for serious sensual pleasures now that hydrofoils and fast ferries have captured the routes. And there are rumors that the narrow stone pathways of Hydra and the carriage roads of Spetses will soon be taken over entirely by imported scooters and Harley-Davidson motorcycles and even fast-track BMWs, all given equal access to solitary places by the laws of progress under the patronage of the European Union. But others say that whatever the changing mode of transport in the Aegean and whatever the provenance of current travelers on a voyage into the Greek light, the yearning may be enough to lead the contemporary Odysseus and his hedonistic companions through the dislocation, clamor, and insentience of the modern world to those beautiful islands just a bit farther but still within reach, if only . . . That, in any case, is one way of reading Seferis's durable 1935 poem about voyaging in the Greek waters that once gratified the thirsting hearts of Henry Miller and Lawrence Durrell:

> What are they after, our souls, traveling
> on the decks of decayed ships
> crowded in with sallow women and crying babies
> unable to forget themselves either with the flying fish
> or with the stars that the masts point out at their tips;
> grated by gramophone records
> committed to non-existent pilgrimages unwillingly
> murmuring broken thoughts from foreign languages.

What are they after, our souls, traveling
on rotten brine-soaked timbers
from harbor to harbor?

Shifting broken stones, breathing in
the pine's coolness with greater difficulty each day,
swimming in the waters of this sea
and of that sea,
without the sense of touch
without men
in a country that is no longer ours
nor yours.

We knew that the islands were beautiful
somewhere round about here where we grope,
slightly lower down or slightly higher up,
a tiny space.

It took Seferis the greater part of another decade of journeying through a landscape increasingly darkened by war, destruction, and exile before he could bring his contemporary Odysseus into the world of light that signaled his island homecoming, but that is a story for a later time.

5

OF GODS, DEMIGODS, AND DEMONS

In prewar days, there were two major roads leading out of Athens to the rest of the mainland, one to the northwest heading for Macedonia by way of Thessaly, and one to the southwest heading for the Peloponnese by way of a bridge across the Corinth Canal. The latter route was preferred by Athenians. Northern Greece, in particular the city of Salonika with its supposedly muddy streets and provincial ways, was considered another country by those who were themselves provincial, and this prejudice prevailed despite Salonika's well-established vitality in the arts, including the art of living the good life. But for those tired of any city, including Athens, one advantage of the escape route to the southwest was the proximity of an open stretch of shore called Kineta beside a usually quiet, aquamarine sea, where Lawrence Durrell reported, in a 1941 letter to his friend and editor Anne Ridler, that he "bathed naked . . . from a pure dazzling white shingle beach, every pebble perfectly oval as if sucked by generations of Chinese women: and twenty feet of water clear like heavy glass, slightly frosted over."

In those days the traveler reached this deserted white beach after emerging from a dusty road still called the Sacred Way, passing through the industrialized home of the Eleusinian Mysteries, and negotiating the hair-raising climb up and over the pass known to Greek motorists as the Evil Stairway. That pass was presumably the ancient home of the mythical highwayman Sciron, who would force travelers to stop, bend, and wash his feet and, while they were doing so, would kick them over the precipice into the open mouth of a monstrous turtle lurking below to devour them whole. In the immediate postwar years, before the national highway carved a wide avenue through this pass, those courageous enough to look down the sheer cliff at the unprotected margin of the road might see the Nazi-induced equivalent of Sciron's carnage: a series of railroad cars toppled over the edge from the rusted tracks on a level just below the road to lie at grotesque angles in the shallow waters of the Saronic Gulf.

The prewar route through Eleusis to Corinth was one grandly celebrated by Angelos Sikelianos, the poet whom Katsimbalis quoted to Miller while waiting out their departure from Spetses for the Peloponnese in the fall of 1939: *"We've got a language,"* Katsimbalis proclaimed, "we're still making it. It's a language for poets, not for shopkeepers. Listen to this [from Sikelianos] . . . I suppose you've never heard the name, what?"—and then recited by heart some Greek lines for his Greekless companion. Sikelianos touched the Colossus deeply not only because of his creative mastery of demotic modern Greek—the spoken language that Solomos had established in the early nineteenth century as proper for poetry rather than the artificially generated purist language called *katharevousa*—but because Sikelianos, perhaps more than any other writer (though like Pericles Yannopoulos, as Katsimbalis described him to Miller), extolled the superhuman possibilities of the human and readily believed in the continuing presence of the ancient gods as they appeared in shapes familiar to the landscape—if not immediately recognized by passing mortals. For example, in his superb narrative poem "The Sacred Way," Sikelianos tells the story, really a fable, of a gypsy and two dancing bears, mother and son, that he encounters at a time when his spirit had been wounded in some unexplained way and had brought him out "to milk life from the outside world" on the road to Eleusis, which he regarded as "the Soul's road." He stops to sit on a rock rooted at the roadside like a throne "long predestined" for him, and suddenly three shadows enter the stillness there: the gypsy with his tambourine and his two bears dragged along by their chains. The gypsy strikes his tambourine, tugs fiercely on the chains, and the two bears rise heavily on their hind legs. But when the mother bear is slow to dance, the gypsy gives a single violent jerk on the chain hanging from the young bear's nostril, which is still bloody from the ring that had pierced it only a few days before, succeeding with this gesture in rousing the mother bear, groaning with pain, to dance vigorously. The mother's act of compassion—whether or not the gypsy is complicit in it—makes the moment visionary: the poet is drawn "outside and far from time, free from forms / closed within time," and the mother bear, already part Demeter, part Holy Virgin, becomes the "huge testifying symbol / of all primeval suffering for which, throughout the human centuries, the soul's / tax has still not been paid. Because the soul / has been and still is in Hades." The poem then builds to a concluding question: "Will the time, the moment, ever come when the bear's soul / and the gypsy's and my own, which I call initiated, / will feast together?" Darkness brings the answer:

> *And as I moved on, night fell,*
> *and again through the wound that fate had opened in me*
> *I felt the darkness flood my heart as water*
> *rushes through a gash in a sinking ship.*

Yet when—as though it had been thirsting for that flood—
my heart sank down completely into the darkness,
sank completely as though to drown in the darkness,
a murmur spread through all the air above me,
a murmur,

          and it seemed to say:
                    "It will come."

In another poem that again takes us beyond the world of mortals, the poet, now on the road to Corinth at the point where the Evil Stairway comes out to the stretch of pebbled beach called Kineta, watches a herd of goats plummet headlong down the hillside to the deserted shore, where the pines and mastic trees were "a deep breath I drew inside me," and there, at the shepherd's whistle, the goats gather in close and are soon seized by a sweltering noon drowsiness, the sun's quick heat shimmering upward between their horns as from a tripod. Then, in the dead silence,

    . . . we saw the herd's lord and master, the he-goat,
          rise alone
   and move off, his tread slow and heavy,
          toward a rock

   wedged into the sea to shape a perfect lookout point;
          there he stopped,
   on the very edge where spray dissolves,
          and leaning motionless,

   upper lip pulled back so that his teeth shone,
          he stood
   huge, erect, smelling the white-crested sea
          until sunset.

The poem is called "Pan," and the godly presence in it, emerging from a landscape that the poet has made fit for mystery, needs no more than that title for identification. Sikelianos had the advantage, as did Seferis and other contemporary Greek poets, of working with a landscape that easily evokes the ancient divinities and their more celebrated heroic and not-so-heroic worshippers because they had resided there for centuries in myth, or sometimes in myth that archaeology eventually translated into history, as in some of the legends of Troy and the Argolid. Even these days in Greece the gods and demigods, kings, warriors, and athletes still live in the current name of a place—Eleusis, Corinth, Nemea, Asini—or can be brought forth by a poet anywhere along the remnant pathways that legend has made familiar. When Sikelianos's poetry takes us across the isthmus from the mainland into the Peloponnese to arrive, just beyond the Corinth canal, at the great rock mountain called Acrocorinth, we are offered a sonnet that again carries us into the country of myth by a description of an actual landscape made to seem ripe for mystery and otherworldly apparitions, in this case, as the speaker climbs on horseback to the rock's high point, the transformation of his stallion into the soaring winged horse that carried Zeus' thunderbolts to the god:

The sun set over Acrocorinth
burning the rock red. From the sea
a fragrant smell of seaweed now began
to intoxicate my slender stallion.

Foam on the bit, the white of his eye
bared fully, he struggled to break
my grip, tight on his reins,
to leap free into open space.

Was it the hour? The rich odors?
Was it the sea's deep saltiness?
The forest's breathing far away?

O had the meltemi wind held strong
a little longer, I would have gripped
the reins and flanks of mythic Pegasus!

Sikelianos's poetry offers a landscape that brings forth plausible images of the mythic country that still resided comfortably within his tradition, yet the landscape he describes, real enough in his day, will stir nostalgia only in those who have very distant memories. It is still possible, if rare, in turn-of-the-century Greece to run into a gypsy with an uninspired monotone voice, a warped tambourine, and at least one bear—fur tattered and dirty, its will to dance virtually dead from abuse and irrelevance—but the encounter is usually on a city street where charitable residents feel sorry for both the gypsy and his animal, rather than on one or another of the fast-laned highways that have taken over the old routes out of Athens. Kineta beach, just below the newly widened national highway, is now lined by hotels and restaurants that are crowding out the postwar campers who took over from the prewar goats. And any stallion climbing up steep Acrocorinth, however eligible for mystery, will have to bob his way slowly and dangerously against the traffic of cars of every make and vintage traveling the asphalt road to the top, where meandering tourists on the walls of the medieval citadel are likely to greet him with the wrong kind of wonder. Still, the poetry we've seen lives on with its truth about the way things are for those who are content to inhabit a land of the imagination where language and metaphor work to fix the past and the passing immutably.

Despite its quick access to the coast, modern Corinth is bound to strike the traveler who knows his ancient history as duller in most ways than its ancient pleasure-loving counterpart, which, according to local legend, roused the Apostle Paul to preach so ardently against the excesses of hedonism that he caused a small riot. But the minute you back out of the modern town's concrete-heavy streets into open country, you find a landscape rich in colors and still haunted by the liveliest of pasts. You can get a foretaste of that by walking as much as you can of the two-mile-long stretch of crenellated wall on the citadel, where the view in all directions tells you why it was the right place to put a temple to the goddess Aphrodite and her thousand sacred prostitutes. One might see that kind of homage to earthly love as the ancient bonus that went with a vigorous climb to take in the endless blue expanse of the Corinthian Gulf to the west, the Saronic Gulf to the east, and the true wonder of being there: the changing purple of the high mainland mountains to the northeast and the even deeper purple of the wooded mountain ridge along the Peloponnesian coast heading toward Patras.

It is here that you can also see why the Peloponnese (or more strictly, the Peloponnesus) was always thought of as an island in the old days, with just the narrow isthmus making it technically a peninsula, and that isthmus anyway cut through by the late-nineteenth-century canal which now brings a thin margin of water between it and the mainland. The name of the territory in Greek carries this identity: Pelops' island. And Pelops brings with him origins in violence that seem to brand the long history of the place. As a child he was slaughtered and then cooked by his father, Tantalus, who served him up to the gods to see if they could distinguish his flesh from that of an animal. Pelops was lucky: only Demeter inadvertently ate part of his shoulder, and when the rest of the gods brought him back to life, they were good enough to give him an ivory prosthesis. But that bit of paternal cruelty was the beginning of what ended up a curse on the house of Atreus, the son of Pelops, who, during a dispute with his brother Thyestes, served up Thyestes' cooked children to their father at a banquet of reconciliation, an act that caused the sun to turn backward and eventually led to further bloody deeds in the family: Agamemnon's sacrifice of his daughter Iphigenia, his wife Clytemnestra's adultery and murder of her husband, his son Orestes' murder of his mother and her lover.

But that history is farther south in the Peloponnese. The history of Corinth speaks less of bloodshed and more of wealth, extravagance, sensuality; and the country around it still offers a large portion of ripeness, an access to the goods of nature, space for hedonistic abandon, even the possibility of a return to Eden for those with a heart open to the beauty of this "living land," as one poet of Katsimbalis's *Ta Nea Grammata* generation, Odysseus Elytis, suggested back at mid-century in a bright, uninhibited display of surrealist images:

> *Drinking the sun of Corinth*
> *Reading the marble ruins*
> *Striding across vineyards and seas*
> *Sighting along the harpoon a votive fish that slips away*
> *I found the leaves that the sun's psalm memorizes*
> *The living land that passion joys in opening.*
>
> *I drink water, cut fruit,*
> *Thrust my hand into the wind's foliage*
> *The lemon trees water the pollen of summer*
> *The green birds tear my dreams*
> *I leave with a glance*
> *A wide glance in which the world is re-created*
> *Beautiful from the beginning by the measures of the heart!*

The Argolid, to the south of Corinth, is the region where the ancient dramatists most keenly felt the crucial influence of gods and demigods and where the demonic in mortals, especially in those given to revenge, seemed tragically out of control—until a goddess called Athena came in to prevent it from feeding on itself. She did so by setting up the first court of law to preside over homicidal excess, and though the court was established on the Areopagus Hill in Athens, we learn from Aeschylus that Mycenae, in the Argolid, was where the descendants of Atreus—specifically Agamemnon's son, Orestes—provided the occasion for the goddess's intervention to break the chain of murder breeding murder.

When Katsimbalis guided Miller into the Argolid, they came not by way of Corinth but by way of Nauplia (or Nafplion), Greece's capital from 1829 to 1834 after its War of Independence, and a town by the sea that many still find enchanting because of the remnants there of its long history of occupation—after the ancients and the Byzantines came the Franks, Venetians, and Turks—and its two surviving forts, essential pieces of the town's furniture. One of these is high enough to offer a perspective that opens out on a full spread of the Argive plain. The other, smaller, crowns an island that originally housed retired executioners afraid to go on living in Nauplia, but they were eventually removed to allow the fort to become a hotel for tourists with a taste for exotic accommodations. Yet in the late fall of 1939, Miller found Nauplia "dismal and deserted at night . . . a place which has lost caste," unlikable because provincial and because it offered unpalatable things such as "jails, churches, fortresses, palaces, libraries, museums, or public statues to the dead."

The latter presumably referred to the statue of Kolokotronis on horseback, which stands at the foot of the Palamidis rock bearing the fortress high above the town. Had Miller come to the Argolid by way of Corinth and Nemea, and had he asked his guide to give him at least a fleeting account of the history of modern Greece relevant to the region, he might have ended up pausing in front of that statue for a minute and taking off his hat, because Theodore Kolokotronis, grand old brigand turned war hero, was the kind of man sufficiently larger than life to rouse Miller's sense of the sublime. Early in the War of Independence, Kolokotronis masterminded a guerrilla ambush of the Turkish army when it was advancing through the narrow gorge of Dervenakia just south of the ancient site of Nemea, his small band of Christian militia forces called *armatoli* wiping out some fifteen thousand of the enemy and thereby causing the fall of Corinth to the Greek insurgents and the capitulation of the Turkish garrison in Nauplia. It was an action that some in the region have been heard to declare was under the influence of the great Herakles, the local demigod whose ancient labors included strangling the Nemean lion not far from where Kolokotronis strangled the enemy force.

On the other hand, news of that kind of massacre might have simply roused the pacifist in Henry Miller. His arrival in the Peloponnese by way of Nauplia led him to visit nearby Epidaurus first of all, a crucial stop during his voyage of discovery because it made him reflect on the "long and devious route by which I had at last come to this healing center of peace," and that in turn inspired his most ardent declaration against man's warring spirit and his hope for a return of man's lost innocence. He tells us that "the road to Epidaurus is like the road to creation," and sitting in "the strangely silent amphitheater" there, one of the grandest in antiquity, he is certain that Balboa standing upon the peak of Darien "could not have known a greater wonder than I at this moment." What the recollection of that moment brings forth in him is his strongest rhetoric against man's homicidal instinct, the demons that lead to wars and to slaying that has no end. "There will be no peace until murder is eliminated from the heart and mind," he declares. "Neither God nor the Devil is responsible and certainly not such puny monsters as Hitler, Mussolini, Stalin, et alia. Certainly not such bugaboos as Catholicism, Capitalism, Communism. Who put the demons there in our heart to torture us? A good question, and if the only way to find out is to go to Epidaurus, then I urge you one and all to drop everything and go there—at once." In this ancient center of healing one will encounter "the intangible residue of the miraculous surge of the human spirit" no matter into what vast hurricane "we may whip our evil passions," and it is here, in this area of peace and calm, that we will encounter "the pure distilled heritage of a past which is not altogether lost."

Miller was on to a truth. Anyone sitting in that great theater when it is empty and when the sun is well on its way down from the white heat or cold at the heart of midday will find the silence overwhelming and the light touched by enough mystery to bring forth the ghosts of the demigods and heroes who have strutted their hour of mimetic life on that stage and of the choruses encircling them who have chanted of their beauty, passion, and folly. With the dying sun a sense of absolute peace comes into the air, the silence penetrated only by those few who know the marvel of the theater's acoustics and choose to prove the point to someone sitting on the highest tier by quietly saying a word or two, maybe reciting a line of verse, from the center of the circular stage, this one as close as a stage comes to the ancient threshing floor that provided actors cleared ground for their first attempt to mimic and transform the human condition by rousing pity and fear.

In summertime, when one aspect of Epidaurus's distilled heritage comes to life during the annual productions of ancient Greek tragedy performed in modern demotic Greek, there is further occasion for mystery of a more public kind. When a production is being staged, the green meadows below the theater suddenly sprout row on row of chartered buses lined up to discharge theatergoers from Athens and elsewhere in clusters that soon merge into a great marching horde heading for the narrow passageways that lie at either edge of the stage where the curling rows of seats begin, and once they are inside the theater, their chatter fills the cooling air in a drone as steady as that of cicadas at high noon. When the actors suddenly appear out of the dusk walking slowly in procession toward the stage, coming along through one of the same narrow passageways, the audience is quickly hushed as though by otherworldly command, and in this new silence the actors find their places in the background or qui-

etly disappear, waiting out the long moment until the action begins. When it does, there is a sudden deep sigh of recognition
through the full length of the theater: Oedipus, eyeless by his
own hand, now comes onstage in rags, guided by his young
daughter Antigone. And then his voice at center stage, heavy with
the black history that he brings with him as his father's murderer
and his mother's lover:

> *My child, child of the blind old man—Antigone,*
> *where are we now? What land, what city of men?*

If that is the evening's play, those visitors who have the good
luck to know enough modern Greek or enough ancient Greek
drama to make their way through a performance of *Oedipus at
Colonus* in Epidaurus will find, as the dusk darkens over the
green country spread before them, just what land and city of men
the playwright has in mind when, later, he offers them a lyrical
moment that may put them, at least for that moment, in touch
with the gods. With luck, Epidaurus is transformed into Athens
and Colonus, and these in turn are a metaphor for that god-given
land, that abundant home on this earth, which all mortals know
in some measure, if too briefly and, more often than not, too
prodigally:

> *Here, stranger,*
> *here in the land where horses are a glory*
> *you have reached the noblest home on earth*
> *Colonus glistening, brilliant in the sun—*
> *where the nightingale sings on,*
> *her dying music rising clear,*
> *hovering always, never leaving,*
> *down the shadows deepening green*
> *she haunts the glades, the wine-dark ivy,*
> *dense and dark the sacred wood of god, untrodden*

rich with laurel and olives never touched by the sun
untouched by storms that blast from every quarter—
where the Reveler Dionysus strides the earth forever
where the wild nymphs are dancing round him
nymphs who nursed his life.

If, on the other hand, the evening's play happens to be Euripides' *Helen*, the high moment of illumination takes a more humanly domestic shape, reaffirming what Aristotle considered an essential element of dramatic literature: the recognition scene. Menelaus, King of Sparta, confused by two wives who look exactly alike—one the real Helen, carried to Egypt by the god Hermes, the other a phantom image of Helen sent to Troy by the goddess Hera—finally recognizes his real wife for what she is and opens his arms so that she can run to embrace him. That embrace, that moment of recognition accepted, again raises a sigh the length of the theater in Epidaurus, and though the action appears to be entirely on a human level—the level of marital love that Homer made so moving when Penelope finally recognizes her husband in the *Odyssey*—there is, as Helen herself puts it, "something godlike in recognition." And in this theater, the transcendence that attends a recognition scene of this kind can sometimes touch a modern Greek audience as it was meant to touch its ancient counterpart, further evidence in this place of the distilled heritage not yet lost.

When George Seferis took up Euripides' *Helen* for the source of a poem of that title written in the mid-1950s, what he chose to emphasize was not godlike recognition but the folly of both gods and mortals implicit in Euripides' plot. His speaker in the poem is a kind of modern Teucer, half brother of the famous warrior Ajax yet in his own right the best of the Greek archers at Troy, unjustly banished by his father as responsible for his brother's suicide and now an exile in Cyprus. The speaker ruminates over the implications of Euripides' version of Helen's story, in which

Teucer figured as a witness, having stopped off in Egypt on his way to Cyprus. In the guise of Teucer, the speaker tells us that he actually touched Helen, the real Helen, when he reached Egypt and that she spoke to him to verify that she had never boarded the blue-bowed ship for Troy but was indeed held hostage in Egypt during the whole of the Trojan War. If that was the truth, then who was the Helen at Troy?

> At Troy, nothing: just a phantom image.
> That's how the gods wanted it.
> And Paris, Paris lay with a shadow as though it were
>   a solid being;
> and for ten whole years we slaughtered ourselves for Helen.
>
> Great suffering had desolated Greece.
> So many bodies thrown
> into the jaws of the sea, the jaws of the earth
> so many souls
> fed to the millstones like grain.
> And the rivers swelling, blood in their silt,
> all for a linen undulation, a filmy cloud,
> a butterfly's flicker, a wisp of swan's down,
> an empty tunic—all for a Helen.

Since these thoughts, this fable, enter the mind of the part-ancient, part-modern speaker while he is "on sea-kissed Cyprus, / consecrated to remind me of my country," the setting raises implications for him which appear to be in sympathy with Henry Miller's view of the demon in men that drives them to perpetual slaughter, though in Seferis's poem it seems that the demon, and the unjust suffering it brings, are also the work of the deceiving gods who are given to the capricious use of a phantom Helen—or maybe even a real Helen—in some internecine conflict of their own. There is an implication that the gods may again be capriciously manipulating the Cyprus conflict involving Greece, Turkey, Britain, and the Greek and Turkish communities on the island that was once more heating up at the time the poem was written, but that sort of political inference is left to the reader:

> I moored alone with this fable,
> if it's true that it is a fable,
> if it's true that mortals will not again take up
> the old deceit of the gods;
>   if it's true
> that in future years some other Teucer,
> or some Ajax or Priam or Hecuba,
> or someone unknown and nameless who nevertheless saw
> a Scamander overflow with corpses,
> isn't fated to hear
> messengers coming to tell him
> that so much suffering, so much life,
> went into the abyss
> all for an empty tunic, all for a Helen.

From the healing influence of the theater at Epidaurus, its silence challenging the drums of war, Henry Miller, with Katsimbalis still guiding him, moved on one Sunday morning to the ancient sites of Tiryns and Mycenae in the Argolid. This was Agamemnon's country—another hushed world, he tells us, but different in feeling from peaceful Epidaurus; here no doubt gods and demigods had also once walked—and not only onstage—but mortals, though "artistic to the core," were at the same time "monstrous" in their passions. The aura here was "grim, lovely, seductive and repellent," the setting isolated, turned in on itself, full of secrets, and the ancient site of Mycenae a "great shining bulge of horror" on a high slope "whence man, having attained his zenith, slipped back and fell into the bottomless pit." Miller looks on the scene with "the eyes of a savage," walks between the huge slabs of stone and the great walls and wonders what dread darkness made these giants among men burrow into the ground to hide their treasures and "to murder incestuously in the deep bowels of the earth." Standing on the high slope, he gazes out at the great Argive plain where the mist is rising and thinks first of New York, "the grandest and emptiest city in the world" with its own underground murders, and then, crazily, of those American Indians he told us about at the start of his journey.

In his journal, he offers us a vision of smoke rising from imaginary wigwams in the misty plain, and he asks, "Where are the buffalo, the canoes . . . ?" But in the *Colossus*, he is pushed further back, to the very beginnings of history, where the Argive plain becomes the battleground of monsters, the rhinoceros man goring the "hippopotamic" man until the walls fall on them, flattening them "into the primeval ooze." Yet centuries later a mysterious race returns, godlike, now carving precious jewels and smelting ores, "blowing fresh vivid images of war and love on bright dagger blades." And soon the gods themselves return, "full statured, fearless," to create a new world of light that lasts until lesser men, "the initiates," hide them away in "the soft flanks of the hillocks and hummocks."

Miller apologizes, calling this the talk of a Brooklyn lad without a word of truth in it—"until the gods bring forth the evidence," presumably returning again at some point to replace the archaeologists. But it was the kind of talk that charmed George Seferis. In the interview he gave for the *Paris Review* series some thirty years after Miller's trip to the Argolid, Seferis spoke of his American friend as "the first man I admired for not having any classical preparation on going to Greece . . . There is such a freshness in him." He goes on to say that he gave Miller a text of Aeschylus in anticipation of his friend's visit to Mycenae, but "of course he doesn't see anything from Aeschylus; he sees, in the plain of Argos, *redskins* while he hears a jazz trumpeter. This is spontaneous behavior. And I admire it."

Miller's spontaneity apparently included a refusal to follow Katsimbalis down the slippery stairway leading to the well at the Mycenae site. Katsimbalis was ready to crawl down it on all fours—after all, he had "played the mole" on the Balkan front in the First World War and had been blown skyward, "his brain concussed, his rear blunderbussed," so what kind of challenge was a slippery staircase into the bowels of the earth?—but Miller would have none of it. No descent into the Mycenaean underworld for him, no search for what wisdom he might gain from those particular ghosts of the dead. What he wanted was "to see the sky, the big birds, the short grass, the waves of blinding light, the swamp mist rising over the plain," and, most of all, those imaginary wigwams. Yet a certain wisdom, another epiphany, does come to him when he reaches Agamemnon's tomb. First, on his way there, he runs into a shepherd, larger than life, his sheep all golden locks, moving leisurely "in the amplitude of forgotten time," in fact, "in Homeric times when the legend was being embroidered with copperish strands." This anachronistic vision evidently allows the present-day shepherd to talk to the dead and stroke their beards, clasping their fingers in the short grass, this power granted him because, unlike the poet who is "always a thousand years too late" and who speaks in the past tense about things that were, the shepherd lives in the present as an eternal earth-bound spirit, a "renunciator"—in short, Miller's spontaneously imagined contribution to the world of demons, the Nereids and Graeae and their modern counterparts (called *exotika*) that still inhabit remote regions of the country.

This discovery of an eternal earth-bound spirit puts the American visitor in the right mood to hover over Agamemnon's tomb and, as he puts it, to "take flight." In the journal he gave Seferis, he says Agamemnon's tomb was the building in Greece that most excited him, because—in comparison, for example, with the Parthenon—here there was mystery, and if you stood at a certain place in the tomb and spoke Agamemnon's name softly, he would answer you (a fact, the author tells us, to which Katsimbalis will testify). The journal proclaims grandly that Agamemnon is not a demigod, as the scholarly sources will tell you, but a full-blown god who lives on, even in death, as "a more powerful spirit than all the conquerors of the earth combined." But in the *Colossus*, though Agamemnon's spirit not only fills the beehive tomb but "spills out into the open, floods the fields, lifts the sky a little higher," his communication with the visitors is less certain, while the mystery he occasions is more profound. The shepherd, Miller tells us, walks and talks with Agamemnon by day and by night, but no civilized man can know and never did know "what took place in this sacred precinct." Miller finally decides that maybe somebody called by the name Agamemnon is buried in the giant stone beehive, but so what? "Am I to stop there, gaping like an idiot?" he asks. "I do not. I refuse to rest on that too-too-solid fact." So now, "as pure spirit," he moves on to a new hypothesis and a favorite theme: the gods who roamed in this place were like you and me in form and substance but free, "electrically free," and when they departed from this world they took with them the secret that will allow us one day to make ourselves free again in their image and to know what it means to have life eternal. That will come *"when we have ceased to murder."* The goddess Athena, lecturing Agamemnon's son, Orestes, before she established the first supreme court to deal with human murderers, could not have put it more succinctly—that is, had she believed in the possibility of life everlasting for mortals.

Miller tells his readers at the beginning of the second part of the *Colossus* that his grand tour of the Peloponnese was cut short at Mycenae because Katsimbalis had to return to Athens to take care of an unexpected piece of property that had come his way. We don't learn until we are nearing the end of the book that during his last days in Greece Miller made a return trip to the Peloponnese, including a second visit to Mycenae, this time with Larry and Nancy Durrell. They left Athens the day before Christmas, traveling not as usual in the automotrice train but in "a flimsy little English car which looks like an overgrown bug" borrowed from a Polish friend, and they entered the Peloponnese by way of Corinth. Miller finds the new town "anything but attractive," ancient Corinth from a distance "prehistoric," Acrocorinth "a sort of Aztec mesa" available to the bloodiest of sacrificial rites. Once inside the ruins, though, the author discovers luster and tenderness at every passing minute and ends up agreeing with Durrell that there is "something rich, sensuous and rosy about Corinth." His is not quite Elytis's vision, of a world where beauty is re-created from the beginning by the measures of the heart, since he discovers "death in full bloom" in the midst of voluptuousness, pillars that are fat, "almost Oriental," heavy and squat and rooted in the earth somehow "like the legs of an elephant stricken with amnesia," yet under the harmonious play of light between the dying sun and the rising moon the ruins "glow and vibrate with supernatural beauty." The travelers return to "the cold sweat" of modern Corinth and spend a cheerless Christmas Eve formulating quixotic messages on postcards to various world celebrities.

On reaching Mycenae, a different kind of cold sweat chills Miller's bones when he makes another attempt to descend the slippery staircase to the deep well there, this time aided by a flashlight and with Larry and Nancy in the lead. Halfway down, he again gives in to terror. It is not the ghosts of epic legend, metaphors of death, or the demons of local myth that get to him—at least not initially—but the very non-literary fear that the roof will cave in on him or that he will slip on the stairs and end up in a pit full of snakes, lizards, and bats. He persuades Durrell to abandon the descent, and, now in the lead, he comes out quickly into the world of light and metaphor again, "still going through the motion of kicking off the demons who were trying to drag me back into the horror-laden mire."

The theme of gods and demons haunting the Argolid is as

much Durrell's as Miller's, though it is hard to know if either influenced the other in bringing this preoccupation to the reader. Miller wrote the *Colossus* not long after leaving Greece in late December 1939, and about the same time Durrell wrote a poem, "To Argos," that seems to have come out of this winter trip with his American friend across an icy Argolid landscape, which Miller tells us was the Durrells' first visit to Mycenae. In any case, their approaches to the theme, though related, have the personal stamp of their distinct backgrounds and idiosyncrasies, Miller evoking the ghostly presence of monstrous antediluvian men and American redskins to join Agamemnon's legacy among gods and demigods, Durrell evoking the ghosts of English heroes, of Virgil, and of prehistoric menhir monoliths. Durrell's vision is less celebrative, more realistic, more melancholy. His poem projects an image of a land where the scholar, the traveler, or any sensitive modern visitor is bound to perceive that he is cut off from the local otherworldly presences and therefore end up feeling alone, in a land that is devoid of totems or remnants of a past that he can truly claim as his own. Only the resident shepherd may be situated to make that claim, because he at least knows "the natural history in a sacred place":

> *The roads lead southward, blue*
> *Along a circumference of snow,*
> *Identified now by the scholars*
> *As a home for the cyclops,*
> *For nymphs and ancient appearances.*
> *Only the shepherd in his cowl*
> *Who walks upon them really knows*
> *The natural history in a sacred place;*
> *Takes like a text of stone*
> *A familiar cloud-shape or fortress,*
> *Pointing at what is mutually seen,*
> *His dark eyes wearing the crowsfoot.*

Our idols have been betrayed
Not by the measurement of the dead ones
Who are lying under these mountains,
As under England our own fastidious
Heroes lie awake but do not judge.
Winter rubs at the ice like hair,
Dividing time; a single tree
Reflects here a mythical river.
Water limps on ice, or scribbles
On doors of sand its syllables,
All alone, in an empty land, alone.
This is what breaks the heart.

Durrell's travelers in an antique land may encounter Agamemnon in the voice of water falling in caves or the sound of the stonebreaker's hammer on walls, "memorials" in water and air like those that legend tells us were reserved for Virgil when his blood grew again in the scarlet pumpkin, but the poet tells us no such ghostly presences can be raised by "the cold sound of English idioms," nor do bones in beds of "companionable rivers dry" have mouths to smile with. The only smiling in the icy landscape of this poem is that of modern girls posing on a tomb from which they, unlike Miller and Katsimbalis, surely do not hear heroic voices out of the distant past. On this wintry road to Argos, the poem's speaker ends up with a tormenting epiphany: even the hyssop and vinegar of Christianity appear to have lost their meaning, and it is this recognition that perhaps most of all breaks the traveler's heart:

We say that the blood of Virgil
Grew again in the scarlet pompion,
Ever afterwards reserving the old poet
Memorials in his air, his water: so
In this land one encounters always

Agamemnon, Agamemnon; the voice
Of water falling on sand in caves,
The stonebreaker's hammer on walls,
A name held closer in the circles
Of bald granite than even these cyclamen,
Like children's ears attentive here,
Blown like glass from the floors of snow.

Truly, we the endowed who pass here
With the assurance of visitors in rugs
Can raise from the menhir no ghost
By the cold sound of English idioms.
Our true parenthood rests with the eagle,
We recognize him turning over his vaults.
Bones have no mouths to smile with
From the beds of companionable rivers dry.
The modern girls pose on a tomb smiling;
Night watches us on the western horn;
The hyssop and the vinegar have lost their meaning,
And this is what breaks the heart.

The overtones of some lines reminiscent of T. S. Eliot date the poem as an early effort in Durrell's poetic career, yet it offers an original and significant point of view, perhaps the most effective challenge in English poetry of the 1930s to the post-Byronic perspective on Greece that was promoted by nineteenth-century literary philhellenism. Durrell's road to Argos here is a century distant in time and sentiment both from Byron's road to Marathon and from that of most other English poets who followed Byron's well-traveled path in bringing Greece to the page decade after decade, even beyond the turn of the century. At the start, in his famous *Don Juan* "song," sometimes called "The Isles of Greece," the English lord assumed the mask of a peripatetic poet, a trimmer, who entertained his "enslaved" Greek listeners by dreaming that Greece might still be free, then, while taking on their fate, by bringing their valor into question through allusions to their nobler ancient history:

> Must we but weep o'er days more blest?
>   Must we but blush?—Our fathers bled.
> Earth! render back from out thy breast
>   A remnant of our Spartan dead!
> Of the three hundred grant but three,
> To make a new Thermopylae!
>
> What, silent still? and silent all?
>   Ah! no;—the voices of the dead
> Sound like a distant torrent's fall,
>   And answer, "Let one living head,
> But one arise,—we come, we come!"
> 'Tis but the living who are dumb.

In Durrell's poem the living are not so dumb—in fact, it seems they are the only substantial avenue to the ancient past—the living Greeks, that is, as distinct from "endowed" foreign visitors. The admonitory tone of the bard singing Byron's song, and his implicit disparagement of the modern Greek by comparison to his ancient ancestors that became a post-Byronic cliché, are replaced in Durrell by an implication that it is the modern Greek close to the land, the dark-eyed shepherd, who knows best how to read the remnant shapes of his inherited past, while the foreign traveler, now with no more than a borrowed access to local history and no faith of his own, will likely leave the Greek scene with a heartbreaking sense of what is beyond his reach. Poets and travelers in the post-Byronic tradition were given to evoking the landscape of modern Greece by way of bookish allusions to the country's ancient heritage and to political themes of freedom and slavery long out of date. That legacy of clichés wasn't Byron's fault, of course, even if it was his perspective that initiated it. Durrell—and Henry Miller, in his fashion—writing forty years into the twentieth century, were among the first to clear the Greek air of Byronic sentiment and imagery and to make room for a new perspective and a new mode of imagining the country based on what they could actually see and what might then be translated into a contemporary idiom, lyrical or otherwise. This way of writing about the country was to have a strong influence on the postwar generation of philhellenes, at least for a while.

The Durrells and Miller left the Argolid for Tripolis and Sparta in heavy rain, the delinquent car sputtering over narrow mountain roads where the danger was more from maniac bus drivers than from the sharp drop at the edge of countless hairpin turns. Miller found beauty in the lakes and rivers created by the downpour and in the powerful fragrance from the orange groves as they approached Sparta, but the town itself, though more animated and alluring than modern Corinth, had for him a "vulgar, pushing, somewhat aggressive air, as though it had been influenced by the return of Americanized Greeks." He saw in the Spartans traces of what he deplored in his own countrymen, yet it is here that he was somehow able to say "never in my life had I felt so American." It is also in Sparta that he felt "perversely gay" about the town because it revealed to him at last "the Englishman" in Durrell, who, normally "the most easy-going, amiable, jovial, forthright and outright fellow imaginable," here seemed to build a wall of ice around the group by quickly, if politely, getting rid of the several acquaintances who approached him, including a fellow Englishman. (When that surprised Miller, Durrell responded: "What would I do with an Englishman here? They're bad enough at home. Do you want to spoil our holiday?") Later Durrell became cantankerous and finally apologetic over a three-minute egg that was brought to him for his hotel breakfast first entirely uncooked and then, after traveling across town to the local baker and back, thoroughly hard-boiled, because the hotel had no stove of its own for boiling breakfast eggs for its foreign guests.

Clearly the holiday mood had collapsed somewhere south of Mycenae, caused in part by fatigue, by the eccentric behavior of the borrowed bug of a car, and by what Miller considered the natural look of Christmas: "sour, moth-eaten, bilious, crapulous, worm-eaten, mildewed, imbecilic, pusillanimous, and completely gaga." But the main cause of Durrell's "discomfiture" and Miller's sudden, at least partial, Americanization seems to have been the dissonant sounds from a German broadcasting station that bombarded them with "melancholy Christmas carols, lying reports of German victories, moth-eaten Viennese waltzes, broken-down Wagnerian arias, snatches of demented yodeling, blessings for Herr Hitler and his wretched gang of murderers, etc." The sound of approaching war sent Miller back to Athens and, a few days later, "back to jail"—that is, back to the United States under urgent pressure from the American Embassy, determined to help American nationals go safely home from this European war.

Miller left the Peloponnese feeling that it was full of "antithetical anomalies" and that it inevitably awakened "a suggestion of notness," these generalizations no doubt influenced by his departing image of Sparta as one of "bovine righteousness, a foul behemoth of virtue," the kind of place he thought Faulkner might settle in to write a huge book about its negative aspects, "its unthisness and its not-thatness." Faulkner would surely have found enough strong mythology and history in the place, enough evidence of gods and heroes and their good and evil still at work among the local mortals, to produce a rich spread of thisness and thatness. It is too bad that what Miller himself calls "Fate" did not allow him to stay long enough to find a more complicated Sparta, what the Greek writer Nikos Kazantzakis saw in those days as a source of both harshness and tenderness, home on the one hand of the god who dictates rigid commandments sent down from Mount Taygetus and on the other hand of Helen's "oft-kissed far-roving body." What you discover in Sparta, he tells us, is that "just as you begin to grow savage and to disdain the earth's sweetness, suddenly Helen's breath, like a flowering lemon tree, makes your mind reel." And what Kazantzakis's contemporary and friend Angelos Sikelianos discovered in the same place was the source for a sonnet, a bit of enticing local history from the time of Lycurgus, who, Plutarch reports, "freed men from the empty and womanish passion of jealous possession by making it honorable for them, while keeping the marriage relation free of all wanton irregularities, to share with other men in the begetting of children, laughing to scorn those who regard such common privileges as intolerable, and resort to war and murder rather than grant them." The sonnet, in the original a strictly rhymed dramatic monologue, is called, simply, "Sparta":

> "A long time now I've lain in wait for you;
> my eye singled you out from all the others
> as though you lived among them like a star;
> your grace and beauty gratify my heart.
>
> "Listen—let me grip your hand firmly:
> youth is tamed that way, like a stallion—
> for a single night, in my own bed,
> you will be partner to my wife!
>
> "Go. She is slim-waisted, a woman
> pledged to beauty as tall Helen was.
> Go, fill her with your generous seed.
>
> "Take her in your powerful embrace
> for one night only, and in Sparta's eyes,
> through a worthy son, exalt my dry old age."

The still-distant clamor of war that cut Miller's trip short cheated him of much in the Peloponnese that he would have found as worthy of celebration as the Greek writers of his day did, especially farther south, where the peninsula stretches three fingers toward Crete. The most western of these has its bright seaside castles at Koroni and Methoni and, up the coast, Nestor's palace with a bathtub still waiting to refresh Telemachus, and the eastern finger has medieval Monemvasia, walled in all around to protect its beauty and its self-governed independence. But what surely would have appealed to Miller most of all are villages on the middle finger south of Kalamata, the Mani, their stone towers and their will to fight strong enough to keep the enemy from bringing them to heel during four hundred years of Turkish occupation.

The Mani is the region—along with Crete—where the modern Greek could become most easily transformed into legend, where savagery could assume heroic dimensions, where men and women could appear to walk with some ease, if only briefly, in the company of gods. Their true strength was in their pride, sometimes too easily the excuse for turning against their own, deadly against whatever domestic or foreign enemy appeared in front of them. Katsimbalis thought the men of Mani the kind who, for the fun of it, could raise a bull by its horns, twirl it around in midair, and bring it back down to earth in a cloud of dust. But that is a tall tale he told not to Henry Miller but to the British writer Patrick Leigh Fermor, a later philhellene who knows the Mani like a native, settled there in a grand stone house he designed and helped to build with his own hands, and wrote a beautiful book called *Mani* about his postwar travels in the southern Peloponnese: full of learning worn lightly, full of lyricism, full of the way things really are where people live the hard life but manage to hold their faith in God and country. The village he settled in, which was once more or less inviolate, is now on the tourist route into the deep Mani, but it remains well preserved, open to the sea, untouched by the cheaper kinds of commerce except along the main road into and out of the village, where the flags of the tourist trade now fly in too many windows and doorways as though on perpetual holiday. There is another village high above that one, until fairly recently accessible only after a hard climb up something between a mule path and a goat path, a village that for some years was abandoned by the young and left to the care of a few old women, all dressed in black, usually sitting in a row on a natural bench of stone like the three Furies. If you were to arrive there hot to boiling from the climb, crazed by thirst and an image of cold beer, and were to ask the women in a moment of madness which way to the local café, what you could count on getting would be rock-hard Maniot irony: "Café? Where do you think you are, Chicago?"

But that was a decade or two after the Mani in Patrick Leigh Fermor's eloquent book, when the high villages were less deserted and visitors so rare that they were taken home for whatever even the humblest family might provide, and since then means have been found to pave almost any road leading anywhere a human being might go for solitude, so that trucks can now come in with more beer and bottled wine than the thirstiest tourists might need to satisfy their hottest daydreaming. And even Leigh Fermor's Mani is at least a decade later than that of an American philhellene named Kevin Andrews, whose *The Flight of Ikaros* portrays the southern Peloponnese with a like honesty and compassion, if a more muted lyricism, written as it was during a time when he persuaded the region to open its soul to him despite the stress of a civil war that had broken out in 1944, giving the local villagers no time at all to recover from the Second World War.

These were among the postwar writers who fell in love with Greece as passionately as Miller and Durrell and who were as available to the possibilities before them, perhaps with a touch less prejudice, but, like Durrell, without allowing their philhellenic sentiment and their knowledge of the gods and heroes of ancient Greece to distort their way of seeing both the good and the evil among the contemporary mortals they came to know so well. And they remained faithful enough to their initial passion to nurture it for life.

6

GARDEN OF EARTHLY DELIGHTS

*A*s in other Mediterranean countries with a Christian tradition, some in Greece keep their faith in God against all loose and even serious talk meant to undermine it; others take God for a metaphor; still others think Him dead or think He never existed. But whatever the level of their belief, some in Greece still talk as though they can speak of the ancient gods in exactly these same ways. And a few take their talk to the page. The best of the Greek poets in the first half of the twentieth century, in particular the mythmakers, were keenly aware of the dramatic and symbolic value of projecting their earthbound characters in territory that admitted the presence of ancient gods and heroes, and as we have seen in Sikelianos and Seferis, that projection was often not merely decorative but a plausible mode for representing the tragic and, at moments, otherworldly aspects of the human condition. These poets had the advantage of a landscape and a history in which mortals and immortals once appeared to have lived naturally side by side for generations; and if Christianity at one time did its best to bury the ancient gods and to make the heroes saintly-pure, these poets and others of their day were prepared to resurrect both gods and heroes for their own purposes in any form that they thought relevant to the contemporary struggle between good and evil.

Sikelianos sometimes succeeded in mixing his pagan gods with Christian presences or in transforming our everyday creatures into gods, while Seferis, more often interested in this world than in the other, succeeded in mixing Homer's heroes with their lesser counterparts, Christian and otherwise, in Seferis's contemporary landscape. Seferis's manipulation of a continuous parallel between contemporaneity and antiquity (to use Eliot's definition of the "mythical method") was governed by an impulse to demonstrate both the continuity and the discontinuity of the Greek past. In his published letter to Katsimbalis on the poem "*Thrush,*" he tells us regarding his use of Homeric mythology that he believes "men of inconstancy, of wandering and of wars," though they may differ in greatness and value, always travel among the same monsters and with the same longings; the poet therefore keeps "the symbols and names that the myth has brought down to us, suffice it that we know the typical characters have changed in keeping with the passing of time and the different conditions of our world—which are none other than those of everyone who seeks to express himself." Seferis's Odysseus, suffering from the "Waste Land feeling," struggles to guide his weak companions toward an Ithaka that seems to remain always just out of reach—at least in the years before and during the Second World War—and this Odysseus' hedonistic companions, unable to control their hungers despite warnings about hubris, either rouse the gods' deadly anger by feasting on the sun god's sacred oxen or remain indefinitely transformed into pigs in Circe's palace. In any case, we learn from *Mythistorema,* 4, that they are doomed to die forgotten. Both the average sensual man, the Elpenor figure of Seferis's prewar days, and his more sentient leader, the modern Odysseus figure, appear to have even less access to an earthly paradise than their Homeric counterparts did and little hope of an afterlife in memory—this presumably a consequence of the different conditions of our world, though the failure of the weak companions to survive is anticipated in Homer, whose hero finally reaches his Ithaka entirely alone.

Another poet of the famous Generation of the Thirties—though never part of the Katsimbalis circle—who found a significant new way to deal with the gods and heroes of the Greek past was Yannis Ritsos, a remarkable and prolific writer who ended up rivaling Elytis for the Nobel Prize. Ritsos began writing in his teens, published poems before 1930, and continued to write abundantly until his death in 1990, publishing more than a hundred volumes of verse and much else in fiction, prose, and dramatic forms. Unlike Elytis, Andreas Emberikos, and other older members of the same generation such as Katsimbalis and, to a lesser degree, Seferis, Ritsos did not have substantial resources to draw on from his parents, who were small landowners in the region of Laconia, in the Peloponnese. He was also sick with tuberculosis into his mid-forties, spending months in this or that sanatorium and supporting himself in between by occasional work as an actor and dancer. He was also not conservative or centrist politically, as were most in the group that published work in *Ta Nea Grammata,* but an unwavering member of the Communist Party from young manhood into old age, a commitment that led to his incarceration for four years under various postwar governments and again for a shorter period under the Colonels' dictatorship. Ritsos's political affiliation gave him over the years a broad following on the left, but it cost him entry into the cultural establishment that dominated Greece both before and after the war. Some of his early verse was blatantly propagandistic, some trivial, but some gave evidence of a strong emerging sensibility that in due course was to make him, along with Elytis, the heir to Seferis as one of Greece's two leading poets. Though the editors and most of the writers of the *Ta Nea Grammata* group could never bring themselves to recognize Ritsos's talent openly, he managed to get one up on them surreptitiously early in his career by publishing three poems in a 1936 issue of *Ta Nea Grammata* under the pseudonym Kostas Eleftheriou (a play on the word "freedom"), appearing beside Cavafy, Sikelianos, Seferis, Elytis, and Antoniou among the poets the journal offered its readers that year. But Ritsos apparently chose never to submit his work there again, and most of those others who had been published with him in 1936 chose to ignore his work under his real name and his subsequent eminence. Seferis, never remotely a connoisseur of Ritsos's poetry, did say in conversation late in his life that he considered it outrageous that the Colonels had sent him into exile.

Ritsos's mode for bringing Homeric mythology alive was in keeping with a broader commitment in his work to dramatize his sympathy for the dispossessed common man and woman, especially those who become subject to tyranny. His impulse is to defend the humanity of mortals who are defeated by the sometimes unreasonable or uncaring or simply omnipotent will of immortal gods who appear on the scene and who have the power to determine man's fate. And he also defends mortals suffering unequal treatment as the lesser companions of heroes, who at least sometimes earn the gods' special favor. In several poems his perspective seems to challenge Seferis's less-forgiving image of the weak companions who frustrate their leader's long, tormented effort to guide them to their island home. In "Eurylochus," for example, the companion to Odysseus who brings his captain news that Circe has turned some of his sailors into swine speaks in defense of those who did not have their leader's advantages, notably the herb the god Hermes gave him to counteract Circe's magic:

Had we too the good will of the gods, and had they given us
that herb with the black root and the milky flowers
that wards off the evil eye
or a woman's wand—who would not have drawn his sword,
    really,
who would have sat down here with the ships,
alone and angry, and carved swallows on the keel
or trimmed his nails with his penknife? Who would not have
    gone
into the baths, to be soaped by the maidservants, rubbed down
    with oil,
guided to the silk sheets of their mistress
and her silken breasts? And then the other one calls you:
cowards, fools, and above all, "the pigs."

When Ritsos takes up the crucial Oxen of the Sun episode in Homer, his impulse again is toward forgiveness—the poem's title—for the condemned mortals. The poem considers the logic of the situation: what else could these poor sailors do, hungry as they were, with not enough on board to eat and the sea ungenerous, with their captain—the man of many stratagems—having a nap and therefore not around to warn them in time; and besides, what they did was fated. The poem ends with a final touch of victory for the mortal "transgressors," very much in the modern Greek tradition: at least they went out with a full belly:

What were they supposed to do? They were only human. All
    that was saved
from the ship's hold—and that barely—was the wine and flour;
    they were patient quite a while,
caught some fish with hooks—small fry—hardly enough to fill
    up on. In the end
they put the knife to the broad-browed oxen of the Sun. So what
if the meat on the spits bellowed like real cattle and so what if

their skinned hides walked? Eurylochos and the others had the
joy of them hot.
The man of many stratagems was having his beauty sleep on
the grass. He didn't get to them in time.
The warnings were no use at all.
The further developments, what happened after Thrinacia, we
know well enough. Besides,
both those things and these were fated—unavoidable, as they
say.
For once in their lives they went out with a full belly—who can
blame them?

Ritsos's master in this mode is C. P. Cavafy, who wrote earlier in the century. Cavafy's defense of the human condition included a celebration of earthly pleasures so encompassing, so uninhibited for its time, and so compelling that the gods he brings into his poems return to earth not to parade their godliness but to show their avid and undying taste for mortal delectation. In the poem called "One of Their Gods," we encounter one of Them, hair black and perfumed, "like a young man" but with "the joy of being immortal in his eyes," who has come down from the August Celestial Mansions into the streets of Selefkia for unnamed if suspicious pleasures in "the quarter that lives / only at night, with orgies and debauchery, / with every kind of intoxication and desire." The message is clear: how compelling those mortal pleasures must be if the immortal gods come down to our level to seek them out. And in "Ionic," a beautiful lyric set in the early post-Christian era, what allows the Christian speaker to reaffirm the continuing presence of the ancient gods is the quality of the earthly paradise his people have desecrated: Ionia, sensuous like other Mediterranean lands, this one so loved by the gods that it haunts their memory still and sometimes works to bring one or another of them back for a fleeting view of what has been taken from them:

That we've broken their statues,
that we've driven them out of their temples,
doesn't mean at all that the gods are dead.
O land of Ionia, they're still in love with you,
their souls still keep your memory.
When an August dawn wakes over you,
your atmosphere is potent with their life,
and sometimes a young ethereal figure,
indistinct, in rapid flight,
wings across your hills.

Cavafy lived in the cosmopolitan though often narrow-minded and intolerant society of late-nineteenth- and early-twentieth-century Alexandria, the "small corner" of the world that he some-times found unbearably restricting, but he worked his way out of that confinement by creating another Alexandrian world, an imaginary ancient city with counterparts in other Mediterranean cities, where it was possible century after century for initiates in Cavafian hedonism to live an elegant life devoted to art, theater, the Greek language, and the love of beautiful bodies. Sin as Christianity came to know it was irrelevant to this mode of life; in fact, Cavafy's early Christians were often far more ardent in their devotion to the satisfactions of the flesh than puritan pagans such as Julian the Apostate who were out to reform Christians and deny them what the poet called the "range of their daily plea-sures, . . . / delectably sensual, in absolute good taste." It had taken the poet himself more than a few years to learn to accom-modate remorse, fickle though his sense of guilt was, and to transform the memories of his own early sensuality into some of the most enduring erotic poetry of his day, whether the setting was his re-created world of ancient diaspora Hellenism or his contemporary Alexandria. It was still early enough in the twenti-eth century to require a certain courage for him to take the route he took, but once the transformation began, all traces of remorse vanished, replaced finally by "understanding," the title he gave a poem he wrote at the age of fifty-two:

> *My younger days, my sensual life—*
> *how clearly I see their meaning now.*
> *What needless, futile regret . . .*
>
> *But I didn't see the meaning of it then.*
>
> *In the loose living of my early years*
> *the impulses of my poetry were shaped,*
> *the boundaries of my art were plotted.*
>
> *That's why the regretting was so fickle.*
> *And my resolutions to hold back, to change,*
> *lasted two weeks at the most.*

Cavafy's mode of accommodation cannot be everybody's, yet it is in keeping with what has now been deemed a characteristic Mediterranean sensibility, and his celebration of an imagined Alexandrian way of life, though appearing to some as idiosyncratic, is not entirely out of key with an attitude pervasive in Greece that holds pleasure to be as sacred at times as the sacred itself. It is sometimes difficult for the Anglo-Saxon traveler to understand how a country that appears to be steeped in the Byzantine tradition of Orthodox Christianity, so visible in the churches of the smallest village and the monasteries that crown the remotest mountainside, can be so given to the earthly pleasures, to food and wine and the games of love that seem to dominate any hour that allows people escape from the hard tasks of everyday living. One answer is that people give the Church its due in the rituals of baptism, marriage, and burial, and the Church, heavy on liturgy, easy on confession and righteous moralizing, allows more room for private sin than most religions. Also, through its plentiful feast days, the Church joins openly in the celebration of God's bounty on earth, especially so at Easter, when the countryside is resplendent with the roasting fires of skewered lamb and white-decked tables piled with other traditional delicacies. As Seferis has suggested, the spring celebrations of Christ's Resurrection, the platforms decked with flowers and carried through the streets in holy procession, bring back latent images of the resurrected Adonis of spring in pagan times, as does the feeding orgy that follows on Lenten fasting. And for those mortals who find it difficult to feel remorse for their indulgence in the fleshly pleasures, the Church provides a reserve of penance through the lifelong devotion to prayer and self-denial of those who live in monasteries and nunneries.

There is a scene in Patrick Leigh Fermor's superb book on the Mani that would appear to capture the essence of Greek hedonism as one could know it in the decades before and immediately after the Second World War, when the influence of foreign television and commerce had not yet altered the imagery and substance of pleasure in the provinces. Leigh Fermor tells his readers that it was a 1950s feast day in the "glaring white town" of Kalamata, north of his village, perhaps the festival of St. John the Baptist that marks the summer solstice; the heat was explosive, the town waterfront "crowded with celebrating citizens in liquefaction." Leigh Fermor, his wife, Joan, and their friend the writer Xan Fielding sat down to eat their taverna dinner at a table set out at the water's edge on the flagstones that "flung back the heat like a casserole with the lid off." Suddenly they decided to pick up their iron table, neatly laid out, and set it down a few yards out to sea, followed by their three chairs, then by the three of them sitting down with the cool water up to their waists. They weren't the first or the last to offer that kind of challenge to the heat at a Greek shore, but they were unusual in that they were fully dressed. Yet the really significant action occurred when the waiter came out, gazed in surprise at the space they'd left empty on the flagstone quay, then, "observing us with a quickly-masked flicker of pleasure," stepped without further hesitation into the sea and "advanced with a butler's gravity" to put down their meal before them: three broiled fish, "piping hot, and with their golden brown scales sparkling."

That waiter's tolerant flicker of pleasure tells all, even more than that others on the quay sent their seaborne fellow diners can after measuring can of retsina, and a dozen boats gathered around to help them consume the complimentary wine, and a mandolin arrived with the moon and the Dog Star to accompany *rebetica* songs in praise of hashish. Anyone sitting by or in the Mediterranean who has slowly taken apart and savored a broiled porgy or snapper or sea bass (even Leigh Fermor's *kefali*), the fish fresh from the sea and bathed amply in an olive-oil-and-lemon sauce, will recognize why no Greek citizen devoted to pleasure would think of disturbing, except in a celebratory way, any table holding such a succulent, earthy gift from the gods.

As we have seen from the gourmet commitment of Katsimbalis's Athenian circle, the provinces weren't alone in their devotion to the ecstasies of food and drink at mid-century, but even today, in the remoter areas, they still provide easy means with local products and often an essential backdrop: land in touch with the sea, or mountains delineating the sky. In the remoter provinces you encounter the kind of landscape closest to that which Seferis identified as essentially Greek, not grand or stately, as one might say of landscapes outside Greece, but "a whole world: lines that come and go; bodies and features, the tragic silence of a 'face' "—a perception he finds difficult to put into words but summarizes as "a kind of process of humanization" that comes with the Greek light. It is a process that extends to legendary figures in the landscape, that brings the grand old men of literary history down to earth and allows the poet to see

Aeschylus not as the Titan or Cyclops that some imagine him but as "a man of feeling" who expresses himself "close beside us, accepting or reacting to the natural elements just as we all do."

Henry Miller made his own discovery of a process of humanization during the late stages of his Greek journey when he visited several ancient sites outside the borders of contemporary urban confinement and architectural poverty—two in Crete for a start—that seemed to have the mysterious attraction of sacred places that were in fact devoted to joyful worldliness. Between his trips to Mycenae, he took a boat to Crete, now traveling on his own, and after a night in the "shabby" town of Herakleion, its main street "almost a ringer for a movie still in a third-rate Western picture," he fulfilled a long-standing dream by taking a bus and then walking a mile to the palace of Minos at Knossos. We learn that he felt "drawn to the spot," and once there, standing among the restored columns "painted in raw, bold colors," he experienced the kind of illumination that most visitors experience at that site—not including pedantic archaeologists who insist that all ruins remain ruins. Miller tells us how grateful he was to Sir Arthur Evans for the restoration that allowed this uncritical visitor to descend the grand staircase, to sit on the throne chair that had served the Hague Peace tribunal in replica for so many years. For Miller, Knossos represented the splendor and opulence of a powerful if peaceful people, yet there was something "down to earth" about the place. The religious aura seemed to be graciously diminished, allowing for a clearly evident "spirit of play." He concluded that the prevailing note was one of joy, because you felt that here "man lived to live, that he was not plagued by thoughts of a life beyond, that he was not smothered and restricted by undue reverence for the ancestral spirits, that he was religious in the only way which is becoming to man, by extracting the utmost of life from every passing minute." In short, he found Knossos "worldly in the best sense of the word."

One aspect of that worldliness was the Minoan women, who

Miller thought played "an equal role with men in the affairs of this people." He doesn't cite a source for that opinion, but it suggests an attitude to the female sex that at least in this context is not entirely consistent with the unmitigated male chauvinism that some feminist critics find throughout his work. On the whole, his view of Greek women is flattering to them if you accept the terms he uses in establishing their particular qualities, which is not always easy, and if you accept his generalizations about them in comparison to women of other nationalities, which is even less easy. Seferis's sister Ioanna (called Jeanne in his book), "most gracious and lovely," appears to have impressed him above all others. He thought her "of royal descent, perhaps of the Egyptian line—in any case, distinctly trans-Pontine." And he found other women in Ioanna's company offering attributes that made "even the most beautiful American or English woman seem positively ugly," most of all the fact that a Greek woman is "first and foremost a woman" who "sheds a distinct fragrance; . . . warms and thrills you." The negative comparison is surprising—let alone hyperbolic—especially in view of what a Greek companion of the Durrells' 1941 exodus to Crete once spoke of in conversation as the thrilling beauty of Durrell's English wife, Nancy (Larry Durrell had persuaded him to join the couple in a final nude swim off the southern Peloponnese, just as Miller had done on the island of Corfu).

How intimately Miller got to know Greek women during his visit remains an open question. The *Colossus* is, on the whole, uncharacteristically spare of sexual action and innuendo. We get a clue as to why this was so from an entry in the *Diary Notebooks* of George Theotokas, a distinguished Greek novelist of the Generation of the Thirties and long-standing friend of George Seferis. Theotokas had a warm evening with Miller in early December 1939 talking of "a thousand and two things" and "becoming friends" to the point where Miller asked him for possible contacts with women. That Theotokas readily granted him in hopes that his American visitor would "be pleased." He goes on to say that it was clear his new friend had missed out on this "game" since coming to Greece. He thought Miller hadn't been able to find his bearings in the confusion of Greek eroticism. The hotel staff had sent him to well-known local brothels, but he'd retreated, panic-stricken, as soon as he'd crossed their thresholds. It was something awful, Miller reported; you couldn't do a thing in surroundings like that. At other times young women had smiled at him in the street and he had approached them, but he couldn't communicate with them because they spoke neither English nor French. The end result was that Miller had "ended up living like a monk." Theotokas adds: "A ridiculous situation for a writer whose books were banned in England and America because of their sexual content."

Monastic or not, Miller indicates that there were at least two women besides Seferis's sister Ioanna who appear to have thrilled him more than any others he came across during the days he recorded in the *Colossus*. The first of these was a ten-year-old girl he encountered one day at the foot of the Acropolis whose features seemed to him as noble, grave, and austere as those of the Erechtheum's caryatids, and who occasioned in him the kind of adoration that evoked *Death in Venice* and that thereby made him fear he might commit he knew not what folly were Fate to put her in his path again. The other was a decidedly ugly "peasant woman" on Corfu who had six toes, in fact thought to be a monster by everyone else but capable of rousing in Miller the rhetoric of sexual heat as no other character in the *Colossus*. He watched her at the village well as she stood in mud in her bare feet washing clothes, and he thought of Renoir, who would have found her beautiful, ignoring her six toes: "he would have followed the rippling flesh, the full globes of her teats, the easy, swaying stance, the superabundant strength of her arms, legs, torso; he would have been ravished by the full, generous slit of her mouth, by the dark and burning glance of the eye, by the massive contours of the head and the gleaming black waves which fell in cascades down her sturdy, columnar neck." And this would have led him to capture "the animal lust, the ardor unquenchable, the fire in the guts, the tenacity of the tigress, the hunger, the rapacity, the all devouring appetite of the oversexed female who is not wanted because she has an extra toe."

Whatever Renoir might have made of this woman who was "not wanted," Miller makes more of her during a high-flying exercise in fantasy than a woman should possibly be asked to suffer outside hyped-up fiction. He sees in her a "starved dream of love" that has her embracing a void "beyond the imagination of the most love-lorn woman," and her "powers of seduction" are therefore driven back "into the coffin of sex where, in the darkness of her loins, passion and desire burned to a dark smoke." Since she has no hope of seducing men (presumably not counting the Miller persona), her lust turns to forbidden things: animals of the field, inanimate objects, objects meant for veneration, mythological deities. Finally, her smile becomes that of "the insatiable one to whom a thousand burning kisses are only the incentive to renewed assaults." All, presumably, because of an extra toe.

But the problem doesn't rest there. Miller's lurid fantasy of the woman's insatiable lust for forbidden things remains in his memory not simply as a recollection of what he imagines to be her private obsession but in "some strange and inexplicable fashion" the symbol of "that hunger for unbounded love which I sensed in a lesser degree in all Greek women." Strange and inexplicable indeed. Even stranger still, that symbol becomes "almost the symbol of Greece itself, this unappeasable lust for beauty, passion, love." Alas, poor Greece, to be so unappeasably described. But the reader should remember that Miller is writing this only a few months after his trip to Crete (though in the chronology of the *Colossus* it comes on the eve of his setting out), and in the context of the Cretan landscape that introduced the subject his exaggerated and occasionally grotesque image of the sexuality of Greek women is at least in keeping with some of the local mythology. It was at Knossos, after all, that the god Poseidon caused Pasiphae, wife of Minos, to love Minos's handsome bull so passionately that she managed to persuade the artist and inventor Daedalus to create a wooden cow that she could enter for the bull to mount and thereby satisfy her lust, the product of which was the monstrous half man and half bull known as the Minotaur. To be generous, let's say that Crete may have been responsible for releasing a Daedalian spirit of invention in the author of *The Colossus of Maroussi*.

When Miller takes up the subject of Greek women in the journal he left with Seferis, his talk not only is more down to earth but actually becomes polemical on behalf of women's rights. He tells us that the more he sees of the country, the more he believes that women "were always predominant, always the unseen power." That is a shrewd insight, as anybody who has been close to the power structure in a village family, or even a city family, of prewar Greece could testify. Miller then goes on to call for the total emancipation of women, for the abolition of the dowry system and the "trading in virginity." He declares that the Greek woman "should become the celestial bee of the hive." And he berates Greek men for moping in the sun while their women do all the work: "May they die of the pox, all of them!" Conjuring up the image from Corfu that haunts him so grotesquely, he tells the reader of his journal that the woman he would most choose to honor is the one walking in the mud in bare feet "with a pack on her back and an ache in her womb"—the woman he would "train to walk upright, to grow five toes and not six." He concludes that in all his travels he has never seen women more beautiful than Greek women or more miserably treated.

It is clear that there is less juice, less color, less hot fantasy in the characterization of Greek women that Miller offers in his journal than in the book that emerges later, but there is also more significant reality—and, perhaps, a sounder insight into Miller's actual attitude toward women at this point in his life, whatever the sometimes curious generalizations he offers us in the *Colossus*. In any case, some of the more muted aspects of his portrait of Greek women were shared by his friend and traveling companion Lawrence Durrell, as we gather from a short article that Durrell wrote for *Réalités* some twenty years later. The article, on "Women of the Mediterranean," focuses on Greek women especially, and it repeats some of the same definitions that we've seen in Miller: the Mediterranean woman is a woman first of all, and in contrast to her northern neighbors, "she can do just as great deeds without once sacrificing the female side of her character." Though she may seem "enslaved," she is nevertheless "the queen bee of the family hive." The "violent coherence" of her character is composed of "fierce extremes," one of which is the "poetry and vehemence of her feelings," the "sacredness of emotion," and "the uncritical enjoyment of feeling for its own sake," parallel in some measure to Miller's "hunger for unbounded love." The difference is that Durrell balances this attribute with what he perceives to be another attribute equally extreme: "a certain innocence, a purity of mind." And he summarizes the Mediterranean woman's violent coherence in a telling sentence: "She can let her sensuality overturn a whole world if it is given free rein, but on the other hand she can become an anchorite because no other men (except the one she loves) seem worth loving."

In his article, Durrell himself points to the problem with both his and Miller's generalizations: they are too black-and-white. Though his portrait is more complex than Miller's (and what is quoted here is too sketchy to do it justice), Durrell admits that "it lacks much fine detail." He concludes that, in the end, the Mediterranean woman "defeats words, as all true goddesses must." Still, words are what Durrell has done his best to offer us, and whether he calls her goddess, demigoddess, or mere mortal, the fact is that the contemporary Greek woman, like any woman, has an essential individuality that can be described in terms that lie at every conceivable point between Durrell's fierce extremes of uncritical enjoyment of feeling and purity of mind. Also, several aspects of his composite portrait are rather out of date, and they were so at the beginning of the 1960s, when he wrote the article. By that time, what Miller called "trading in virginity" was fairly dead, and purity of that puritan kind was no longer very relevant, certainly not in the Greek cities and even in most villages, where the saying had it that few women over eighteen had not, of their own volition, "been taken for a walk" beyond innocence. By the 1960s the liberation of women from the injustices of an out-moded tradition was well on its way, not so much by government decree—that was to come later—as by women themselves (and many of their men) choosing to ignore absurd social pressures and family manipulation. The dowry system was under threat everywhere; sexual freedom was close to being equally shared be-tween the sexes; abortions, though illegal, were easily available and much availed of in the cities; and not far hence, divorce was to cease being solely a Church prerogative and to move into the civil courts.

But Greek women—anyway, some Greek women—still im-press foreigners who get to know them well as prone to certain refreshing characteristics. For one, they appear to be less inhib-ited than most Anglo-Saxon women about expressing their emo-tions, sexual and otherwise, wherever their passion and their purity may actually lie between Durrell's extremes. For another, they tend to speak their minds. And though some are unusually gentle in manner, what is fiercest about almost all of them is their pride: personal, familial, national. They are proud enough not to be shy about demonstrating their love both for their lovers and for themselves, or for their children, or for their country, and they will defend what they love with a vehemence that is hardly innocent. Challenged about their lack of political objectivity, they will say simply, "I'm a Greek, after all." Most of them, anyway. There are foreigners who think that in our day Greek women are easy prey to the kind of abuse shown on local television, or melancholy prey to cuckoldry at noontime, but those foreigners surely know too few Greek women in the flesh or know them not well enough. Abuse of women is now no more prevalent in Greece than anywhere else in Europe, and these days noontime or any other time is a woman's time if she so chooses. Yet Durrell is right in the end: whatever words one uses, the portrait still comes out too black-and-white. Greek women in our day are probably not very different from women anywhere in the West, with maybe a stronger historical sense to nourish their pride— though that, too, is no doubt an oversimplification.

Miller's Cretan visit took him from Knossos southwest to the equally ancient site of Phaestos near the southern coast of the island, across "quick bad lands," rolling fields "with a serene steady smile" that reminded him of Virginia, up and down a mountain where nature was in "a state of dementia," beside a lake of "waving champagne," and finally to the infinite "magic carpet" of the plain of Messara. We see that this stretch of his trip evoked emotion recollected in rather strained metaphors, but the essential imagery soon became that which had been shaping his Greek journey all along. He had been building a mythical country from his first encounter with Athens in weeks gone by. And in Phaestos—with a history of construction going back to neolithic times but without the benefit of Sir Arthur Evans's reconstruction—Miller's country, and his exultation in making it, reached a kind of culmination.

It was high noon when Miller arrived at the site, the rain had stopped, the clouds had opened to reveal the violet light that made everything Greek seem "holy, natural, and, familiar," and he suddenly had the impulse to take off his clothes and leap naked into the vault of the blue and float there like an angel because he was now in "the perpetual dawn of man's awakening." He tells us that this was among the few times he was fully aware of being on the brink of a great experience, which caused him to be grateful not only for the sound life he has been given but for what he had known of the gutter, of hunger, and of humiliation, since it had all culminated in "this moment of bliss."

The first illumination came to him as he climbed up to the ruins, an intuition that he thinks will make the historian smile: Phaestos "became the abode of queens." His second moment of truth arrived after he was greeted by the caretaker, Alexandros, as having been sent by God. Pacing back and forth to survey the grandeur of the setting, Miller now felt slightly demented, "like the great monarchs of the past who have devoted their lives to the enhancement of art and culture." No longer in need of enrichment, he felt he had reached an apogee that made him want to give indiscriminately of all he possessed. In this mood, he sends out a benediction to all things great and small, old and young, to the neglected savages in the forgotten parts of the earth, to both wild and domesticated animals, birds of the air, creeping things, to trees, plants, and flowers, rocks, lakes, and mountains, because "this is the first day of my life," and that being so, he blesses the world, "every inch of it, every living atom." When he finally descends the broad steps of the leveled palace, totally indifferent to such details as lintels, urns, pottery, children's toys, and votive cells, he has a vision of the plain below that seems to reshape all the otherworldly images of his journey into a grand reaffirmation of our world as it might be:

> From this sublime, serene height [the plain] has all the appearance of the Garden of Eden. At the very gates of Paradise the descendants of Zeus halted here on their way to eternity to cast a last look earthward and saw with the eyes of innocents that the earth is indeed what they had always dreamed it to be: a place of beauty and joy and peace. In his heart man is angelic; in his heart man is united with the whole world. Phaestos contains all the elements of the heart; it is feminine through and through. Everything that

man has achieved would be lost were it not for this final stage of contrition which is here incarnated in the abode of the heavenly queens.

We have seen that Miller told his readers some twenty years after his Greek journey that falling in love with Greece is the easiest thing in the world because it is like falling in love with one's own divine image reflected in a thousand dazzling facets, and he might have added that it is especially easy if one has the imagination and the will to make the country itself into a divine image that can reflect those many dazzling facets, as Miller and Durrell both succeeded in doing in their separate ways. The *Colossus* makes it clear that one of the most dazzling facets of Miller's image emerged from his visit to Phaestos. His creation there is especially compelling because, along with Zeus' descendants, it brings the reader back from the gates of heavenly paradise to the Edenic possibilities of this world, to the beauty, joy, and peace that have been Miller's aspiration since he left Paris and to the humanity, the elements of the heart in man and woman alike, that his Greek journey has helped him rediscover.

That he had left France far behind at this point in favor of another country, both real and imaginary, is verified in the *Colossus* by his dialogue with a "dried up prune" of a French woman he meets on the eve of his departure for Phaestos—what he calls, in retrospect, "the last Paradise on earth" in the "barbarious passacaglia" of a monologue that the following dialogue initiates. The woman tells him how much she hates Crete—too dry, dusty, hot, bare—and how much she misses the high-walled gardens and orchards of Normandy. Miller replies that he doesn't miss any of that, neither her pretty little orchards nor her well-cultivated fields, because what he likes is the dusty road outside with its "sorely-laden donkey . . . plodding along dejectedly." The woman shrilly retorts: "But it's not civilized," to which Miller answers: "Je m'en fous de la civilisation européenne!"

This earns him, just within his hearing, the parting label of typical American barbarian who doesn't know what life is, and that earns the French woman in turn a postmortem from Miller: "Je n'aime pas la Normandie. J'aime le soleil, la nudité, la lumière . . ." He follows this with a wild eight-page "barbarious" monologue addressed to "Madame" and celebrating Agamemnon's son Louis of the golden torque on his journey from Monemvasia in the Peloponnese to Memphis, Tennessee, in order to join the Count and the Duke on the Fourth of July, Dipsy-Doodle Day, in a missionary jam that will blow the woman so low "she will quiver like a snake," will "Blow dust in the eye. Blow hot and dry, blow brown and bare! Blow down them orchards, blow down them walls Boogie Woogie's here again." We can hear George Seferis in the wings—ardent jazz enthusiast who talked to Miller about Louis Armstrong, Fats Waller, Count Basie, and Pee Wee Russell in the same breath with Erskine Caldwell and William Faulkner—cheering on his barbarian friend's passacaglia about this torque-bearing son of Agamemnon, surely no less plausible and charming from Seferis's point of view than those redskins and their tents on the Argive plain.

The importance of Miller's visit to Phaestos is confirmed by his account of it in his journal, which, though more literal and less rhetorically evocative, still offers a description that is not very different in substance from the image of the last paradise on earth that he creates in the *Colossus*. In the journal he tells us that Phaestos is the closest we'll ever get on this earth to "the Shangri-la of the cinema." As he looks out toward Mount Ida, he finds the autumn colors ravishing, and for the first time in his life he sees "a symphony of umbers." Toward the sea, he discovers red earth that is "the primordial clay out of which man was formed in God's image," and though man has fallen from a state of grace, here nature is seen to remain eternally holy. Miller concludes, as he later did in the *Colossus*, that the place is feminine through and through and that the female line of the Minoan dynasty is what has given the landscape "its character, its charm, its subtlety—and its inexhaustible variety." In the end, the site strikes him as so marvelous and his well-being there is so complete that he suddenly feels guilty about enjoying it all alone. This is a theme that he picks up in the *Colossus* to explain, having received "this stupendous gift" of Phaestos by himself, why he leaves a princely gratuity with the caretaker, Alexandros, after sitting down with him to a meal of olives, ham, and cheese, and a bottle of "heady, molten wine" called *mavrodaphne* (in fact sweeter even than the sound of its name). The authenticity that the journal brings to what Miller has felt and learned during this visit shines through with a somewhat less dazzling light when, describing the same meal, the author calls the olives "lousy—without taste, unless it be the taste of mud."

Miller's Cretan tour was the high point of his new liberation and new self-definition, but it was not the end of his journey, nor did it totally mute the ominous drumbeat of war. He returned to Herakleion for a few days and, according to the journal, found himself wondering if maybe he hadn't been wrong about America, this because of the lavish gratitude for the generosity of the United States that he heard from his Cretan hosts and others, in particular from a Greek gentleman named Eliadi, who was serving as British vice consul in Herakleion and who put his services entirely at Miller's disposal "especially because you are an American." Miller decides that, despite the many things he has said against his compatriots at times, they are after all kind and "give without motive other than natural human sympathy." Clearly his Cretan experience has mellowed him regarding his home country, though by the time he writes the *Colossus*, the "magnificent homage" of the character based on Eliadi, including praise for America's unswerving loyalty to the ideals of freedom, manages to overwhelm the author for only a moment and becomes the excuse for his launching into what he himself calls "an equally florid, sweeping testimonial" of his love and admiration for Greece and its people.

The Cretan visit ends with quick stopovers at the towns of Chania and Rethymnon. Miller then heads back to Athens by ship, and he is barely at sea before thoughts of the war intrude, first when the steward asks him why he was knocking about in Greek waters with the war imminent, then when the radio in the saloon brings the latest news, "always just enough progress and invention to fill your mind with fresh horrors." He goes up on deck for a walk, then returns to write a few lines in the book he has promised Seferis. He tells us that he had completely forgotten about the war, but now it won't go away. And he ends up suggesting—this while writing in America some months later—that the reality of it should in fact *not* go away. Having heard on board this ship about the horrors of the Smyrna catastrophe of September 1922, in which, following the Greek army's withdrawal in retreat, "thousands of innocent men, women and children were driven into the water like cattle, shot at, mutilated, burned alive, their hands chopped off when they tried to climb aboard a foreign vessel," Miller is reminded of how a French cinema audience watching a newsreel about the destruction of Shanghai was divided between outrage at the injustice of the event and outrage at being shown such a nasty slice of reality when they had paid to see a drama of love. "Such is America today," he concludes. And he adds—the Paris pacifist apparently taking a new turn: "as long as human beings can sit and watch with hands folded while their fellow-men are tortured and butchered, so long will civilization be a hollow mockery, a wordy phantom suspended like a mirage above a swelling sea of murdered carcasses."

When Miller arrived in Athens he found both welcome and unwelcome news: money waiting for him at American Express and a letter from the American Consulate asking him to come in and have his passport validated or invalidated. After a conversation with a young woman at the consulate who grilled him about where he lived, who his relatives were, and who he worked for, he answered that he had no home, no relatives, no boss, and was a free man who could write anywhere he chose, even in America, though he chose not to—after all this candor, his passport was invalidated. That meant he had to clear out and go home to America. He decided it was Fate; at least he was free to leave when others had to stay, and with the war spreading, it occurred to him that he would soon have no choice, even with a valid passport.

But after a meeting with amiable Lincoln MacVeagh, the American Minister to Greece and an ardent philhellene, Miller found that he still had some time for further travel in his new country, and Katsimbalis was fully prepared to organize last-minute excursions, real and imaginary, the former by arranging for Miller to go to Thebes and Delphi before a quick visit to Eleusis and his final trip to Mycenae with the Durrells. The imaginary travel was by way of endless monologues over endless lunches and dinners that took Miller down the Nile, up to Constantinople, on to Monte Carlo and Paris, then, among other places, back to Mount Athos and Salonika, where the Colossus claimed that he had gone "crazy with boredom," no doubt because, like most Athenians, he knew the city and its sensual pleasures too little.

The real excursions served to confirm what had already captured Miller's spirit. At Thebes, accompanied now by Ghika, he suddenly burst into tears when his eye caught "the full devastating beauty of the great plain." He found himself "in the dead center of that soft silence which absorbs even the breathing of the gods," and in his effort to distinguish this seemingly empty if fertile plain from other "irrigated Paradises" known to man, he came up with some of his best poetry in prose: "In the belly of this emptiness there throbbed a rich pulse of blood which was drained off in black furrowed veins. Through the thick pores of the earth the dreams of men long dead still bubbled and burst, their diaphanous filament carried skyward by flocks of startled birds."

As Miller takes us through a winter landscape that includes the "Alpine" village of Levadia and a breathless ride to high Arachova as though through "a tropical Iceland," he suddenly brings us down to earth again by reporting that Ghika got out of the car to vomit. Such is one reality, winter or summer, of the narrow winding roads up and down the mountains of prewar (and even postwar) Greece. But the author doesn't keep us on that mundane level for more than a moment. He moves to the edge of a deep canyon to see "the shadow of a great eagle wheeling over the void," and beyond that, the outer precincts of Delphi, where the earth presents a sublime and dramatic spectacle: "a bubbling cauldron into which a fearless band of men descend to spread a magic carpet . . . composed of the most ingenious patterns and the most variegated hues," a task that they have been at for several thousand years. And still beyond that, in "a state of dazed, drunken, battered stupefaction," the travelers come upon Delphi.

What they find there first of all is Katsimbalis, who had preceded them by bus, and a bit later, the ancient theater where the Colossus strides to the center of the bowl, and holding his arms aloft, delivers the closing line of the last oracle as it was delivered to Julian the Apostate in the mid-fourth century. Miller calls this an impressive moment, but he doesn't give us the closing line. The whole of the oracle reads, in Philip Sherrard's translation:

> Tell the king the well-wrought hall has fallen to the ground.
> No longer has Phoebus a hut nor a prophetic laurel,
> Nor a spring that speaks. Quenched is the speaking water also.

Katsimbalis's few words, lifting the curtain from what seemed a world that had perished, gives Miller "a long glimpse down the broad avenue of man's folly," and he recalls other oracular utterances from his Paris days in which the current war had been represented as just one item in a long catalogue of impending disasters, news that was then received skeptically. His meditation leads him to prophesy: "a thousand years hence men will wonder at our blindness, our torpor, our supine acquiescence in an order that was doomed."

But what appears to be an even more compelling theme for him, in keeping with his mood since Phaestos, emerges from his contemplation in the Delphi Museum of the statue of Antinous, last of the gods. He sees this as a bold but simple Greek idealization in stone of "the eternal duality of man," presumably the duality of body and soul. Christianity, he tells us, by emphasizing man's soulful qualities, disembodied him, while the Greeks "gave body to everything," thereby incarnating man's spirit and eternalizing it. He concludes that in Greece one is ever filled with a sense of eternality that is expressed "in the here and now," a sense that is shattered when one returns to the West, whether in Europe or in America, where "we move in clock time amidst the debris of vanished worlds, inventing the instruments of our own destruction."

George Seferis, also much taken by Delphi and its aura, wrote about it two decades later with something of the same prophetic vision, though in a more frugal style. Seferis had obviously read the *Colossus* by then (though the preliminary impressions in the journal Miller gave him end before Miller goes to Delphi), but whether or not he shared his understanding of the place during Miller's time in Greece, we cannot say. In any case, when Seferis speaks of the coming and going of the oracle and quotes in full its final message to the Emperor Julian, the reference to the wheel coming full circle again seems to allude to potential disasters of the postwar atomic age: "again we find ourselves facing the fury of natural powers that we have released and we don't know whether we will be able to control them." What we do know, he tells us, is that life on this earth is relative and that "tomorrow or after some millions of years it will come to an end"; so, on speaking of eternity, we have in mind not something that can be measured in years but what the Pythia at Delphi saw when seized in ecstasy, namely, "all space and all time, past and future, as one." Seferis's conclusion carries a message that Miller would surely have honored. Remembering E. M. Forster, the poet suggests that "we must call things eternal in order to struggle and to rejoice in life till our last moment." To this degree Seferis participates in Miller's conviction that the eternal paradise must be seen as the possible Eden of our life on earth.

Miller's persistent concern during the late stages of his Greek journey with the virtues of living in the here and now finds its most overt—if most prosaic—expression in his response to one of the final excursions that Katsimbalis arranges for him, this one to an Armenian soothsayer who earns his credence by telling him things about his past that no one in Greece could possibly have known. But what excites Miller most is the soothsayer's insistence that Henry Miller will never die. He tries to explain that metaphorically—reaching eternity through his work or his deeds—but no. The soothsayer, with the Colossus as interpreter, says he means it literally, because he finds in his American visitor a baffling and impressive fact: "all the signs of divinity" in a man who, at the same time, has his feet "chained to the earth." The soothsayer goes on to say that the American leads a charmed life and always will, with only one possible enemy: himself.

Miller feels so profoundly "chastened" by this interview that his liberation rises to yet another level: he decides that the artist's devotion to his art is "the highest and the last phase of egotism in man," and this leads him to the exalted aspiration to live unselfishly, to give abundantly, in the end to pass from art to life so that he can exemplify whatever he has mastered through art by his living. To live creatively, he asserts, means to live more and more "*into* the world," and the mastery of any art, of any expression, should lead "to the final expression—the mastery of life." A year after his visit, as he writes these words, the conviction still holds. He tells the reader that since he has returned to America, one fulfillment has followed another like clockwork, and his only desire that has not been fully satisfied by that time is the desire to give more and more. By "living openly," he now expects to become "a medium, a transmitter." And he concludes with a metaphor that appears to convey his ultimate understanding of the soothsayer's prediction: "living thus, as a river, one experiences life to the full, flows along with the current of life, and dies in order to live again as an ocean."

But Miller's Greek journey doesn't end with this visit or this belated perception. We have already seen what new illuminations came to him on his return to Mycenae with the Durrells. And there is also a quick visit to Eleusis after dark, with Ghika guiding him rapidly through the ruins by lighting one match after another—an unforgettably "weird spectacle," he tells us. Yet what seem most unforgettable, because of the passion he brings to his recollection, are his parting images of Athens and of "the little band of friends" he made there. From Eleusis, Athens "sparkles like a chandelier"; it "swims in an electric effluvium." And in the heart of the city, on any slight eminence such as the bluff at the end of Anagnostopoulou Street where the Durrells lived, he finds that you can stand and feel "the very real connection which man has with the other worlds of light." He reports that "in some mysterious way, this soft, peaceful city never wholly lets the sun out of its grasp." Yet the nights have their particular light as well, and walking back to his hotel home from Seferis's home on Kydathenaion Street, Miller would sometimes cross the Zapion garden that had so enchanted him during his first night in the city and stroll under dazzling starlight, repeating to himself: "You are in another part of the world, you are in Greece, in Greece, do you understand?" And it is here, in the Zapion garden, that his last nights, filled with wonderful memories, "were like a beautiful Gethsemane."

The light-caressed landscape has figures equal to it. Miller tells us that it was in Athens, and in Greece more generally, that for the first time he met men who were what men ought to be: open, frank, natural, spontaneous, warm-hearted. In France he had known "another order of human being," types he admired and respected but never felt close to. Greece proved to be the center of the universe, "the ideal meeting place of man with man in the presence of God," the place that made him free and whole. And in offering silent homage and thanksgiving to his Greek friends, he declares: "I love those men, each and every one, for having revealed to me the true proportions of the human being." He also loves the soil in which they grew, the tree from which they sprang, the light in which they flourished, "the goodness, the integrity, the charity which they emanated," and he does so because they brought him face-to-face with himself and cleansed him of "hatred and jealousy and envy." He ends his hymn of praise to Katsimbalis, to Seferis, to Ghika and the others, with an encomium to the country they revealed to him: poor though it may be and seemingly unimportant, it is still "the mother of nations, the fountain-head of wisdom and inspiration."

Yet after Miller says goodbye to Larry and Nancy Durrell in Tripolis, his horse-drawn carriage vanishing into "a teeming mist which was made up of rain and tears," he realizes that the war will change everything he leaves behind—not only the map of the world but "the destiny of everyone I care about." He remembers the consequences of the First World War, and he predicts that what he sees as the chaos and confusion that the current war is engendering will never be remedied "in our lifetime." If he is sentimental, in his way, about what he is soon to lose as he leaves Greece, in retrospect he does not seem so at all about what lies ahead. "There will be no resuming where we left off," he concludes. "The world we knew is dead and gone. The next time we meet, any of us, it will be on the ashes of all that we once cherished." This dark prediction may explain why Miller, for all his passionate response to the "man-sized world" of Greece and for all his intense affection for the little band of friends he met there—especially the human phenomenon (in Seferis's phrase) whom he made into a world-renowned colossus—why Miller never returned for a single hour or day to the country he fell in love with, then re-created in his liberated image, then left forever.

Had he returned he might have found that even out of the ashes of an earthly paradise, new life can sometimes rise in time. Twenty-five years later, the bluff at the end of Anagnostopoulou Street where the Durrells once lived usually offered you a vision of more cement than even a carefree heart might want to study under misty daylight or cluttered starlight, yet on some days the wind cleared the air so thoroughly that you could see Salamis and Aegina near enough to think you might swim there, and at night the stars would sometimes come down close enough to dazzle earthbound mortals as they always had. In the forest just above that street and the others curling around Lycabettus, you could follow the old paths that lovers still climbed to hide their intimacy among the trees just as their more courageous or impassioned parents had. And now there was a new road leading to the bald dome of the hill and a parking lot for those who had the freedom and the imagination to mix their loving with a view that could sometimes take them to another world. Years after Miller left that hillside behind, it was still—and still is—a garden of both open and secret pleasures, which the American poet and philhellene James Merrill, who lived nearby for decades, captures brilliantly in his poem "Days of 1964," the title echoing a number of titles of poems by C. P. Cavafy that celebrate earthly love in the Alexandrian mode half a century earlier. The days that Merrill locates in the opening stanza present an image of Lycabettus in mild November:

Houses, an embassy, the hospital,
Our neighborhood sun-cured if trembling still
In pools of the night's rain . . .
Across the street that led to the center of town
A steep hill kept one company part way
Or could be climbed in twenty minutes
For some literally breathtaking views,
Framed by umbrella pines, of city and sea.
Underfoot, cyclamen, autumn crocus grew
Spangled as with fine sweat among the relics
Of good times had by all. If not Olympus,
An out-of-earshot, year-round hillside revel.

The poem's speaker climbs the hill regularly and brings home wild flowers of the season. One fall day, lying beside his lover, he tells of having headed downtown that noon along the hillside and having run into their cleaning lady, Kyria Kleo, a woman "fat, past fifty," like "a Palmyra matron / Copied in lard and horsehair," who sighs the day long with pain from her hurting legs or with love for so much of what is around her—including him, his lover, the bird, the cat—that the speaker thinks "she *was* love." But on this day, when he sees her trudging into the pines of Lycabettus hill—actually or only in his mind's eye?—her face is suddenly painted "Clown-white, white of the moon by daylight, / Lidded with pearl, mouth a poinsettia leaf" that says *Eat me, pay me,* in short, what he takes to be "the erotic mask / worn the world over by illusion / To weddings of itself and simple need." Startled mute, the two can only stare at each other, and he now wonders: Was love an illusion? A bit later, after crossing an outdoor market "through a dream-press" of hagglers who are leery of being taken, plucked like a "flower of that November mildness," he heads back home, offering his listener an image of "self" (myself? yourself?) now "lost up soft clay paths," or maybe "found" there, "where the bud throbs awake / the better to be nipped" and where "self" ends up on its knees in mud. Here the speaker stops his revery "cold," for both his own and his lover's sake, and, calmer now, buys fruit to bring back from his noontime excursion into this garden of erotic dreaming and questioning. He asks forgiveness of both Kyria Kleo (if his poem is ever translated into Greek) and of his lover:

> I had gone so long without loving,
> I hardly knew what I was thinking.
> Where I hid my face, your touch, quick, merciful,
> Blindfolded me. A god breathed from my lips.
> If that was illusion, I wanted it to last long;
> To dwell, for its daily pittance, with us there,
> Cleaning and watering, sighing with love or pain.
> I hoped it would climb when it needed to the heights
> Even of degradation, as I for one
> Seemed, those days, to be always climbing
> Into a world of wild
> Flowers, feasting, tears—or was I falling, legs
> Buckling, heights, depths,
> Into a pool of each night's rain?
> But you were everywhere beside me, masked,
> As who was not, in laughter, pain, and love.

Such, in the Athens of 1964, is the god come down into the garden of earthly love that grew out of the ashes of the Second World War and that Henry Miller never came back to see.

7

SAILING OUT OF PARADISE

In late December 1939 Henry Miller boarded an American Export Lines ship in Piraeus bound for New York. The evening before his departure, he said goodbye to George Katsimbalis and George Seferis at a farewell dinner he arranged. He tells us in the *Colossus* that at that time, Larry and Nancy Durrell were either still marooned in Tripolis or sitting in the Epidaurus amphitheater. Captain Antoniou was at sea, taking his ship to Salonika. Theodore Stephanides was back in Corfu, getting his X-ray laboratory in order. Of Miller's closest Greek friends, only Ghika was free to see him off the next day. The painter was impressed by the ship's "luxurious appearance," which apparently matched his anticipation of what an American ship would look like, but Miller was not so impressed. The minute he got on board, he felt "in another world"; it made him think he was back in New York, with a familiar atmosphere that was "clean, vacuous, anonymous" and that he detested. He says, without evident irony, that he would have preferred a Greek boat. And we learn from the preface to a book he began to write after he finished the *Colossus* (this one published some four years later as *The Air-Conditioned Nightmare*) that, when the ship stopped in Boston on its way to New York, he came back on board from this first return encounter with his home country "praying that by some miracle the captain would decide to alter his course and return to Piraeus."

But the fact is, Miller never did get back to Piraeus after it became possible. He never again saw Seferis, Antoniou, or Stephanides, and it was not until fifteen years later, at his home in Big Sur, California, that he met Katsimbalis again briefly, and not until twenty years later, on a trip back to Europe which ended short of Greece, that he and his third wife, Eve, visited Durrell and his third wife, Claude, in Sommières, France. One gets the impression from *The Air-Conditioned Nightmare*, despite its revelations of ardent distaste for much that the author came across after his homecoming and during the eighteen-month journey around the United States that Miller recorded in it, that the writing of *The Colossus of Maroussi*, soon after his departure from Piraeus, and the fading recollections of his recent adventures in Greece while he was on his American tour, served to wean him gradually from his uncompromising passion for Greece and from the image of Eden engendered there. For a start, we learn in the preface that for Miller the whole earth was by now a paradise, "the only one we will ever know," and that we don't have to "make it a Paradise" because it already is one. All we have to do is make ourselves fit to inhabit it. This means that even in America you can find a paradise if only you can recognize it and make yourself fit to live there; if you have murder in your heart you won't know it when it's shown to you. Without murder in his heart and presumably cleansed of hatred and bitterness, it still took Miller some years to recognize a paradise in America, but he was already working his way toward it in the months after he left Greece, and when he finally found it, in Big Sur, he never quite let it go.

Among the various allusions in *The Air-Conditioned Nightmare* to Miller's time abroad are a few that focus specifically on his experience in Greece: the Armenian section of Athens is rich in flora, fauna, and spirit compared to the "unorganized lunatic asylum" that is Chicago's South Side; the graceful yet sturdy masonry columns of "The Shadows" in New Iberia, Louisiana, remind him of the "roseate, insidious opulence" of Corinth, "fragrant with the heavy bloom of Summer"; and along with Phaestos, Mycenae, and Epidaurus, the author finds that the Grand Canyon is among the few places on this earth that have not only come up to his expectation but surpassed it. (The place is "mad, completely mad, and at the same time so grandiose, so sublime, so illusory, that when you come upon it for the first time you break down and weep with joy.") Yet when Miller writes of the enduring monuments that man has created out of his faith and love that might be mentioned in the same breath with nature's creation of the Grand Canyon, he cites the cathedrals of Europe and the temples of Asia and Egypt. Gone from the front of his memory are the theater at Epidaurus, Agamemnon's tomb, and the palace at Knossos, among the pagan monuments of Greece that he thought vital to the education and liberation of his spirit in the fall of 1939.

Now, as he walks through St. Louis considering its horror and misery, his passionate recollection of another country that he loves perhaps beyond reason and that is now desperately threatened by the war turns out to be not of Greece but of France, in particular of the last place he visited before going to Greece, the town of Sarlat. Remembrance of it brings on an emotion that would strike a reader of the *Colossus* as implausible were he to read it close upon Miller's "barbarious passacaglia" addressed to the despised French "Madame" in Crete who eulogized the orchards and walls of Normandy. But the war has turned disastrous for France in the meanwhile, and Miller's words in *The Air-Conditioned Nightmare*, written soon after the agony of its fall, are obviously genuine: "Glorious gentle France! God, with what love and reverence I think of you now . . . If the great flame of the spirit be extinguished the little flames are unquenchable; they will burst through the earth in millions of tiny tongues. Another France will be born. France lives. *Vive la France!*"

But neither of the books Miller wrote during the war tells the whole story. We learn from his letters that his understandable nostalgia and sympathy for the country where he had lived for a decade and which was now suffering under Nazi occupation went hand in hand with a certain nostalgia and concern for the other country he had fallen in love with, intensely if more briefly, which had its own terrible experience of war during the period Miller was touring his home country and writing his books. Greece's intrepid challenge to the Italian aggression that began in the fall of 1940 succeeded in pushing the enemy far back into Albania and in keeping it there, but then the German army invaded Greece in April 1941, bringing utter famine and devastation, much of the latter in reprisals for the Greeks' resistance to the occupying forces. There is evidence especially from Miller's occasional (and still largely unpublished) correspondence with George Seferis during this period that he not only was homesick for Greece at moments but, as the war progressed, became increasingly worried about the fate of the friends he had left behind. In January 1940 he was stirred to send Seferis a card saying that he is where he is "but not of it," and that he has come across a chapter on Sikelianos in an American book by Claude Bragdon. A month later he writes that he has found Sherwood Anderson rather disappointing on first meeting, but Louis Armstrong—a passion for whose music he shared with Seferis—is playing at the Cotton Club and advertised as TERRIFIC on Broadway (Miller adds that he can't afford the price of admission). He goes on to say that he still does not feel at home in America, but he may soon begin to write again because his having written letters to Seferis, Durrell, and Katsimbalis is a good sign, and he is certain that the scale of public entertainment in his home city of New York—thousands of blocks of nightlife—would be a source of pleasure for Seferis if it didn't drive him crazy. Miller concludes that while the war is in the newspapers, it is billions of miles away to most Americans, so that the faces he looks at seem callous and unreachable. Still another month later, a postcard reports that Sherwood Anderson is now a good pal and that Miller, presumably remembering his effort to promote what he considered the best of American literature among his Greek friends (Walt Whitman first of all), has now arranged to send Seferis, Antoniou, and Katsimbalis signed copies of Anderson's work.

In late May 1940 Seferis receives a letter together with a section of the *Colossus* manuscript describing the Epidaurus visit. We see in the letter that the war is now much on Miller's mind, and his attitude about it is changing somewhat, as it did during the writing of certain late passages in the *Colossus*. He hopes that what he is sending in the mails will make it through before Italy declares war and blockades the Mediterranean, though he is sure France and England will wipe her off the map in short order. He also believes that the United States is getting ready to go in and will soon be sending over planes by the thousands, along with men and munitions—and that once she is in, the war will become a war of annihilation, with Germany and Italy totally destroyed. Americans will not be gentlemanly, like the European Allies, he declares, but—as the man in the street would have it—gangsters and murderers, which is what they become when their blood is up. He still thinks that the war was unnecessary and that it would be better if it were to stop, but since the fire has now started, only great loss of blood will quench it. He ends up hoping that Greece can stay out of it, and he adds, along with his fondest greetings, a promise he will never keep: as soon as the war ends, he will take the boat for Piraeus. A month later, now well into the composition of Part II of the *Colossus* manuscript, he reaffirms the same hopes, first that Greece will be spared and then that he will be seeing his Greek friends again not too long hence.

Before the correspondence is finally fractured by the war, it takes a new turn in August 1940 and for several months thereafter, as we learn that Seferis has now managed to get through to his American friend. In late April, Seferis had sent Miller a note in French commenting on Poros and their trip there as a way of reminding him where the island was located, but this did not reach Miller until more than three months later, when he answered by postcard (from "Sparta, Va.") that he was curious to get what he calls "the fragment of your letter from Poros" written, evidently, while Miller himself was writing about the island. He asks: "Or haven't you yet received the first 100 pages of the MS?" He asks the same question in late August, when he forwards the "Boogie Woogie Passacaglia" section of the *Colossus*. Seferis mails an answer on October 10, but again it takes some months for his letter to arrive. In the meanwhile, as Miller is about to set out on his tour of America, in mid-October he writes Seferis from New York to say that he is forwarding the two parts of the manuscript that complete the *Colossus* (one enclosed, one to follow) and asks him to pass on both of them to Katsimbalis because he is no longer sure that the subject of his book is at his Athens address. He is clearly eager for a response to his manuscript (he instructs his Greek friends to write to him via his agents, Russell and Volkening, or the Gotham Book Store "as usual"), and he reports that a fragment about Katsimbalis talking, with two or three illustrations by Ghika, will appear in *Town and Country*. He ends up offering Seferis his literary agent in case he has anything translated that he would like to submit in America, and he signs off by saying that it looks as though everybody will be in the war soon: Greece, the United States, Turkey, Russia, the whole world.

About Greece, Miller was right: two weeks after the letter was mailed, General Metaxas, who had been mobilizing Greece for months, said his unequivocal (and now legendary) "No" to an

Italian ultimatum, reportedly delivered in the middle of the night, and the Greek army soon forced the invading Italians back across the Albanian border. We don't know when the letter Seferis sent earlier in October was actually delivered, but his mood at the time he wrote it was not what it was to become all too quickly. He reports that he has received both the "Passacaglia" and the first hundred pages of the *Colossus*; regarding the former, he compares his reading of that wild section of the manuscript with what he felt when he first heard Louis Armstrong in London. He also reports, "Larry is now in Kalamata, and very pleased with the place," but their friend Max Nimiec, the Polish aristocrat who had lent his sputtering car to Durrell and Miller for their trip to Sparta, "died a week ago of heart failure while dancing in the Argentina bar . . . a foreign land." Less than a month later, Miller's prophesy in the *Colossus* that "the world we knew" will end up dead and gone seems on its way to fulfillment.

On November 7, a little over a week after the Italian invasion, Seferis sent Miller a solemn telegram: "FIGHTING AGAINST BRUTAL INVADER FOR OUR SOULS FOR EVERYTHING YOU LOVED HERE STOP SUPPORT YOUR FRIENDS STOP EXPECT YOULL DO YOUR BEST FOR OUR CAUSE STOP GEORGE SEFERIADES." The telegram was sent by way of the Ministry of Press and Tourism to 137 East Fifty-fourth Street, New York City. It never reached his American friend. A reply telegram in French a day later notified Seferis that his message to Henry Miller was not delivered to the addressee, who had left New York without a forwarding address. The correspondence lapsed for a full year. During that time the Italian invaders had been repulsed through the winter, Hitler had come to Mussolini's rescue in the spring and had occupied the whole of Greece after a final fierce battle with Greek and Allied forces in Crete, and the country was under an increasingly harsh occupation by the Axis enemies.

Miller next wrote to Seferis from Nevada in October 1941, on his way back to New York, by which time Seferis was with the

Greek government-in-exile in South Africa, having left his country in advance of the German army by way of Crete and having spent some months in various Foreign Ministry assignments in Egypt. He had apparently written his American friend from Johannesburg two months earlier, and it took that long for the letter to arrive; Miller reported that he had heard nothing from Greece. From Larry Durrell, then in Cairo but now he knows not where, he has heard that Katsimbalis is a prisoner of war and Theodore Stephanides has been killed (news that proves to be wrong). Miller adds that he has had no word from Antoniou but hopes the captain has been spared. People who have all the comforts are not crazy about going to war, he reports, and in his travels across America he has gotten the impression that they are indifferent to the fate of Europe; it is too remote for them. Anyway, it appears that Russia is now holding its own, but, he asks, for how long?

It must have become clear to Miller by then that "the little band of friends" he had made in Greece was now shattered, and though we see from this letter that he longs for news of those with whom he has lost touch and feels for those who are suffering from the dislocations brought on by the German invasion of Greece in April 1941, the image of paradise that he created in their company is now between the covers of a book being published as he writes, and his attention has begun to turn elsewhere. He tells Seferis that he had a good stay of four months in Hollywood, where he met a number of famous movie stars, John Barrymore included, and that he liked California more than any other state because of its climate and scenery and because you can live cheaply—an "easy Paradisiac life there," he suggests, "almost too easy." He reports that he could write movie scripts for $100 to $2,000 per week, but the work would be terrible and the life ghastly, so he refused to be tempted by the offers he received from three different companies. Still, California, he concludes, has "everything—everything a man needs." Miller has surely begun to see the brightly paved road ahead that will eventually lead him back to his American version of Eden for the rest of his life.

During the war years, Miller will send Seferis one more letter from New York in early 1942, a postcard six months later, a Christmas card from Los Angeles in 1943, and a postcard from Monterey ("the first capital of California") in 1944. By 1945 he has settled in Big Sur. For his part, Seferis sends a second letter—from Pretoria, South Africa, on Christmas Day in 1941—to say that he had the feeling he was throwing a bottle into the sea, as Captain "Tonio" Antoniou used to say of his poems, which brought to mind Larry Durrell's recent mode of sending a letter to him, that is, by first publishing it in a Cairo magazine—and Seferis then quotes the letter in part.

I think of you, my friend, in the unfamiliar continent of Africa; a subtropical man out of his element, defeated by a world where the black compromise is king . . . We are on the edge of winter; and yet thinking of that day when the somnambulists tried to break through the border into Greece, I find myself thinking not of a winter but of a spring . . . But what have you and I to do with history? We are dwellers in the Eye, dedicated to the service of the blue . . . I think you understand, and I think Maro [whom Seferis identifies for Miller as his wife] understands. Meanwhile this is simply a message in a bottle to tell you that we will meet again in the blue islands one day;—perhaps islands kinder and lovelier than ever.

Seferis goes on to describe an encounter with Durrell in Crete and his effort to find some food to share with the Durrells and their hungry child during the chaos of those days, when so many people were trying to leave Greece. Katsimbalis in his uniform tells "another story": to Seferis it seems that, in comparison to his new stature, he was a mere dwarf when he was a civilian, every-thing in his new military getup has been made to measure—boots, belts, even his sword—because "he was too big for anything ready-made." And Theodore Stephanides, also in uniform, now seems to be still dreaming and just as lost "as he always was under the sun." But the dark note is there throughout: everyone in Greece is suffering terribly because there is no food. When Seferis received Miller's last letter (presumably that of October 1941 from Nevada), he was "going to ask you how you were feeling in those dark days" because he considered his friend a "man with justice in the heart." But now he can no longer ask that question because "the silence which raped so many of us, during *our* war, seems to take me back again."

Miller's response to this message "in a bottle" in late January 1942, some weeks after the United States entered the war, seems a touch apologetic: the situation in Greece must be frightful, but the United States is trying to send shiploads of food in, and various "expeditionary" forces are on their way to various places—a beginning, Miller says, "but a very late one too." He has no doubt about the ultimate defeat of the Axis powers, and there will be a new alignment in which China, Russia, and India will play a big part, but the British Empire is sure to crumble. About his friends: he wishes he knew how to reach Katsimbalis, he is pleased to learn that Stephanides is still alive, and he has twice written Larry in Cairo, where he must be having an exciting time of it. In New York, by contrast, life is stupid, dull, plentiful, secure. It is business as usual, he reports, so that you wouldn't dream that America was at war, the only pinch being sugar rationing. He tells Seferis that the *Colossus* has found a British publisher, but the book on America which he has just finished is a failure, his first: no inspiration, no joy in it. He still hopes to get to Mexico but, he says, a bit wistfully, that rather than be where he is he would prefer a thousand times to be where Seferis is, in Africa, a great continent, and he urges the poet to go to Timbuctoo. The letter ends: "Don't worry. We will all be together again. If not here, then in the next world!"

As though that thought becomes a plaything for the gods, Seferis's long reply, dated March 1942, apparently never reaches his American friend (the only text of the letter that has surfaced is in the poet's archive: a faint carbon copy in Seferis's hand). Surely it would have pleased Miller to know that Seferis has not only learned some of what he wanted to about America from a book Miller sent him, identified in the letter as "Powell's book on Jeffers," but, jealous of Jeffers's mode of life, plans to settle in a fisherman's house by the sea "if I ever go back to Greece." It would have pleased Miller even more to receive Seferis's compliment about "your ways of giving: a plain and whole gesture," the remark referring in this context to the marginally annotated copy of Powell's book he had just received, yet no doubt alluding also to the gift of the single copy of Miller's notebook called "First Impressions of Greece." But the largest compliment concerns the *Colossus*, which Seferis finally acknowledges receiving: "It has been a rainbow against the sky. You are a spring of life, Miller."

Further along in the letter, in answer to the advice: "Go to Timbuctoo," Seferis quotes Miller to himself about his book on America: "no joy, no inspiration." There is a war on: "we are in the game and eaten by the game—no matter how"; and besides, in Africa he has so far found to his liking only the sea, the sea wind, and the flowers in Cape Town. He concludes his long letter with stirring news of Kyrios Ypsilon (as Miller chose, in the *Colossus*, to call Seferis's brother-in-law, Constantine Tsatsos, the Athens professor of philosophy then exiled on Spetses). Kyrios Ypsilon, in Seferis's account, under orders by the puppet government in Athens not to interrupt university classes on October 28, 1941, the anniversary of the Italian invasion, chose that occasion to give a lecture to his students which reminded them that though the body of Greece was now enslaved, the spirit of the country, its freedom, would never die. Moved by his words, the students then went out and gathered flowers to spread over the marble statue of the poet Solomos, author of the "Hymn to Liberty," the country's national anthem. The Gestapo came for Kyrios Ypsilon that evening, but he had disappeared. An announcement of his dismissal from the university was published in the Athens press the next day, but by then his real name had become "a password among Greek students."

The gods play on, the war god especially. No news reaches Seferis from the New World until some months later, when a postcard from Miller points to a short circuit in both their communication and elsewhere: Miller reports that he is asking his publisher to send Seferis three more copies of the *Colossus*, presumably because he thinks the three he sent originally never arrived, and he adds that he hopes when Seferis goes to Cairo he will run into Larry Durrell, from whom he never hears a word. Then there are the two quick cards from California (one announcing a letter to follow that doesn't follow), and finally, a post–VE Day letter from Big Sur to an address supplied by Durrell: "Salut! Mille fois salut! Et Pax Vobiscum! What an age since we heard from one another!" and the perennial request: "Tell me where to write Katsimbalis, please," which introduces what seems an incredible question were it not coming at the end of an incredibly disruptive war: "Has he seen the 'Colossus' yet?" The letter ends: "Tell me how you are and what you lack. Perhaps I can help in some way. We know very little here of the true conditions in the outside world." The rest, in keeping with Miller's discovery of peace in Big Sur, is silence—anyway for some three postwar years.

The correspondence between Miller and Durrell after Miller left Greece just before New Year's Day in 1940 is even more uncoordinated and incomplete than that between Miller and Seferis, and in this case it is Durrell's writing from Greece that provides most of what survives from 1940–41, partly because Miller was able to save what letters reached him during this period and Durrell apparently was not. That there were letters from Miller to Durrell—and at least one life-saving check—we know from Durrell's several acknowledgments. In any case, Durrell was a voluble correspondent, despite the personal and professional disruptions during the war, as though keeping in touch with Miller was equivalent to keeping up with his muse at a time when writing letters—some of them both expansive and eloquent—had apparently become his most productive creative activity.

In the winter of 1940 Durrell provides tantalizing bits of local news: Nancy has flown off in an Imperial Airways plane from Phaleron to have their child in England; the Acropolis is covered in snow during days when branches of almond blossoms are being sold in the streets; the carnival is on but the clowns and harlequins are rather squalidly dressed and without masks, these forbidden because the government suspects that seditious words will be uttered behind them; and Durrell is off for a week's holiday in the islands with Captain Antoniou. In the spring the focus is on Katsimbalis. He is described lighting up after his thirtieth drink with a "small blue bud of flame inside his waistcoat" to begin a Wagnerian cycle of stories, and after much bad philosophy and boasting, ending up "fucking in my bed like a Trojan horse." We learn that the Colossus is unquenchably not his normal self for a week or so after getting news of Miller, because that makes him, "like a mock-turtle out of nowhere," turn into a mock colossus, some of his stories not funny at all or even humane, so that his audience "winces for him and wonders why." But that doesn't stop him: he "goes on roaring and washing the air with his long flat dead-looking hands, trying to carve out this mythical personality for himself from the rubble of language." Now that he has heard that Miller is writing a book about him he is "more unreal than ever." Yet by the summer Durrell offers an account of Katsimbalis in action that is reminiscent of the wonderfully flamboyant old Katsimbalis at his best: the Colossus in his cups standing on the edge of the Acropolis hill in the late evening, squared like a bird about to fly into space and flapping his coat-tails as he rouses all the cocks of Attica one after the other with his blood-curdling clarion call of cock-a-doodle-doo. Durrell's evocation of this episode seems so essential to the reality of one memorable aspect of the man that Miller simply quotes the letter as an appendix to his book "to round off the portrait of Katsimbalis."

On the other side of the coin, along with the Colossus beginning at times to take his mythical role so seriously as to bore people, we find signs in Durrell's letters that he has come to see that the little band of friends and the charmed life they created together is falling apart under the pressures of separation and the anxieties of impending war. In March he reports that he is now officially an exile because in England his age group has been "called" and he can't go home for fear of being "called out." Later in the month, he asks Miller not to do any more for him regarding an American edition of *The Black Book*, because things have changed so much, with new and more powerful enemies on the horizon and "the system closing in"; he feels he has to use every ounce of anonymity to keep from being thrown out of the British Council, where he now works. He tells Miller that he can write what he wants about him in print—which the censors will allow to pass as "an utterance, a pronouncement"—but any quotes about him in manuscript form could do him harm. In late June we learn that Theodore Stephanides has passed through with a commission in the army and is heading for Cyprus via Turkey because these days only fishing boats go by way of the other route, from Beirut to Cyprus. It now looks like war with a vengeance, he says, but "without the offensive spirit, we are lost." And he reports that he and Seferis and Katsimbalis still meet, "but it's like the meeting of ancients; we exchange silences rather and pipe smoke: and the weather is impervious to it all, smiling blue and green."

There were still darker days ahead. Durrell moved from Athens to Kalamata, in the Peloponnese, during the fall of 1940 in order to run a school there under the British Council, and now he began to feel himself in exile from his friends as well as from England. His letters to both Miller and Seferis report that he is writing nothing and that he has little to report because the action is all elsewhere. In October he sends Seferis an apology for not having been in touch but says he has been "so busy and so miserable" that he really had nothing to tell him "except never to come to Kalamata"—his experience of the place obviously less fervent than Patrick Leigh Fermor's was to be a decade or so later. And there is growing nostalgia for what Durrell has left behind in Athens: "God bless you and George [Katsimbalis] and the cheery drunkards of Syntagma; Max [Nimiec]'s death was a hole in the ranks of the gay which we will not fill easily. I suppose someone else has the car now." The war seems to be elsewhere than Kalamata but is nevertheless much on his mind now that some of his Greek friends have joined up. He writes Seferis again to say that his heart goes out to the great Colossus "riding off to the wars like Galahad," a "living piece of mythology" whom Durrell plans to honor with a memorial one of these days, but he envies Seferis the excitement and parades he has in Athens; he himself has nothing at all other than the good news of the campaign against the Italians and air alarms. When word of his Athenian friends gets through to him, he touches it up with some romantic highlighting, maybe as compensation. In November he tells Miller that Katsimbalis has "ridden off gigantically with the artillery"— though exactly where remains vague—while Tonio Antoniou is reported to be somewhere "away with the fleet." About the same time he tells Seferis that he'd love to see Katsimbalis on his horse "riding over the Albanian hills" and Tonio "scouring the sea for the Italian fleet," images that will come down to earth as the war progresses. The rusticated Durrell calls these "great moments," but in Kalamata he feels that by contrast he is in a tomb. He wonders if perhaps British naval intelligence could use him, even if he can't resist a bit of irony about his fellow countrymen: for both his correspondents he quotes a "wonderful" letter in *News of the Week* that begins "Englishmen! You are the ancient Greeks of modern times."

But there is no irony in Durrell's celebration of the "wonderful" spirit of the Greeks: in a letter to Seferis he tells him they have every right to "enjoy their shattering victories in Albania," and in his view the dictator Metaxas has deservedly been given the affectionate nickname Barba Yanni (Uncle John) by his triumphant troops, after the famous folk figure of the popular song "Barba Yanni with His Jugs." Durrell concludes this letter to Seferis with a grand—if now rather desperate—vision of possibility on the model of what he and his friends had managed to create in more serene moments: "With him [Barba Yanni Metaxas] and Tonio and you and Katsimbalis and Karageozi [the "hero" in Greek shadow theater, in which cutout figures act out folk versions of legend and history behind a backlit screen] we do not need to worry. Between us we will make a new myth of Greece, and a new style of heart for Europe: and a souvlaki of the Eyetalians."

The euphoria of this vision was short-lived. By March 1941 Durrell tells both his correspondents that he has no feeling left— for either the dead or the living, about either living or dying— and for Miller he adds the news that it is now impossible for him to write anything "except bad poems." He goes up to Athens and finds big changes: "all blacked out and grim, with planes patrolling over the statues." In April, following quickly on the German invasion that began on the fifth of the month, Durrell and his family are suddenly evacuated from Pylos, in the Peloponnese, to Crete. Before departing he scribbles a note to Seferis at the Press Ministry on the back of a hotel registration form: "They came in the middle of the night and told us to be ready by 5. No time to do anything—not even to say goodbye. I am very miserable at the thought of leaving. But will you please take over my trunks when they come . . . There is some very fine crockery and cutlery which would help you to set up house with your wife. The clothes you could keep for me until après la guerre if there is any après . . ." Seferis was hardly in a position to respond as he, too, was shortly evacuated to Crete with other members of the Greek government. After Durrell's brief meeting there with Seferis, he, Nancy, and their daughter, Penelope, set sail out of the land of blue and green for the desert sands of Egypt and those hot cities that in due course would help him create a new myth and a new country elsewhere.

The harsh reality that the war brought into the lives of the little band of friends in Athens obviously affected each in particular ways, but the clearest difference was between the experience, and attendant perception, of those who stayed behind and those who sailed away; there was a further difference in the latter group between the expatriates who had settled in Greece for a time, such as Durrell, and the members of the Greek government going into exile, such as Seferis. One of Durrell's expatriate companions on the sudden voyage to Egypt was the British novelist Olivia Manning, who eventually became a member of a literary group in Cairo that included, along with Durrell and Seferis, Bernard Spencer, Keith Douglas, and Robert Liddell, among others, and that published, for a while, a journal called *Personal Landscape*. Some of its contributions were subsequently reissued in the collection *Personal Landscape*, subtitled "An Anthology of Exile." Manning's contribution to the collection is a poem that perhaps best captures the mood of the departing expatriates during their final days in Greece, when it became clear that they were about to lose their second home and faced new expatriation in yet another country while they waited to return to Greece. She writes that on the bright spring day when the lorries full of soldiers went north from Athens to confront the German army, everyone watching had a flower and a flag, and the Greeks carried "the bearded sailors, like classic heroes, aloft on their shoulders," calling out "We're off to Berlin" in answer to the onlookers wishing them good luck. The soldiers who began to return from the front just a week later had nothing to say:

> They stared with blank eyes over the lorry sides, the bandages
>   muddy on their heads.
> We watched with compassion and bewilderment.
> It seemed a long way to bring the wounded. We were not
>   told how close the Germans followed.
> When the lorries stopped and the men slid down like old men,
>   blind, without response for us,
> We felt then a thing unknown to our generation, the sorrow
>   and the terror of defeat.

The poet now becomes aware of her own particular kind of defeat as an expatriate about to lose everything that sustained her expatriation, including the friends returning to their Athenian homes:

> As we lay in the harbor amidst sunken ships,
> Our decks crowded, the guns uptilted on the quayside,
> The creeping sun for the last time lit for us
> The Acropolis and its tokens of ancient wars.
> Others were driven out before this; we had held ourselves an
>   unbiddable people.
> When the brilliance of the Peloponnese went down in darkness,
>   when the night came between us,
> Our friends returned to Athens, excited a little, more afraid.
>   We faced the sea
> Knowing until the day of our return, we would be exiles from
>   a country not our own.

The poem, entitled "Written in the Third Year of the War," concludes with a hard lesson that the war may or may not teach

those who had chosen self-exile out of longing and who now
have little prospect of a return to what once was:

> *The future may lead elsewhere now. It will not matter.*
> *Have we not learnt enough?*
> *Separation become for ever had brought us low, and victory*
> *   will have an emptiness.*
> *There's not much spared us. Born into war and ignorant of*
> *   peace, our arrogance*
> *Grew from longing. In the end we may know a thing withheld*
> *   us from our birth.*

Athens, seen from the perspective of Greek nationals forced to
leave their country in the last days before it was occupied by the
German army, is characterized by a somewhat different imagery
and a somewhat different tone. An account that had particular
relevance to the Greek friends of Miller and Durrell came from
Katsimbalis's old First World War army companion and Gerald
Durrell's mentor, Theodore Stephanides, biologist and radiologist
in civilian life. When war arrived again, he became a lieutenant
attached to the Royal Army Medical Corps as regimental medical
officer. His 1946 book, *Climax in Crete*, based on his memory of
events in which he took part, was recommended by Durrell in a
foreword that praised the book's freedom from "literary inflation
of any kind" and its "clearness, accuracy, and unselfconscious-
ness." The praise is in one sense appropriate for a document
which the author tells us was written immediately after his evacuation to Egypt and without benefit of notes, but it seems rather
faint in view of the drama in the narrative whenever the good
doctor comes under fire, which is often, and in view of the room
he allows for entertaining anecdotes, humorous and sometimes
penetrating comments, and poetry of various kinds that he encountered on his hard trek across Crete. All this is offered in

Stephanides' low-key style, which is less open to eloquence—and inflation—than at times Durrell's own is.

During the retreat from the German advance in mid-April 1941, Stephanides, then back from service in the Near East, ended up in the Daphni Camp outside Athens, and he tells us that he took a few hours of leave to go into the city for lunch with his friend Lieutenant George Katsimbalis. Everything in the city that day seemed quiet and normal except for the occasional air-raid alarms; the people he ran across were cheerful and optimistic despite the recent suicide of the Prime Minister, Alexander Koryzis, in despair over the quick German advance, everybody apparently confident that the Germans would be held on the Lamia–Thermopylae line, well north of Athens. Lieutenant Katsimbalis told him that while the situation was grave, he, too, was of the opinion that the Lamia line could be defended, and Stephanides was reassured by this news because his friend was serving in the Greek G.H.Q., where he would presumably have access to inside information. When Stephanides came into town again two days later for a second lunch with Lieutenant Katsimbalis, Athens still looked calm, and though Katsimbalis was a bit more perturbed because he had word that the Lamia line "was cracking," he hoped it was "only an alarmist rumor." As they finished their meal the telephone rang in the next room. Katsimbalis got up to answer it and then called out that somebody at the other end of the line was telling Lieutenant Stephanides to return at once to his new billeting in the Old Phaleron district of Athens. The phone went dead, and by the time Stephanides reached Old Phaleron, the villa he'd been assigned to was deserted, his unit was gone, and so was his medical kit.

Though it took Stephanides some time to believe it, a wholesale evacuation had now begun. He found himself assigned to a Cyprus regiment, and, in short order, after picking up a new medical kit, on his way to Piraeus to board one of the several steamers waiting in the harbor. The first group to be evacuated that day included personnel of the British Legation and some of the staff of the Greek Press Bureau "who might be treated rather roughly by the Germans if they remained behind." Among these he spotted "Mr. Seferiades . . . whom I knew," but he apparently couldn't approach his friend, let alone send him the kind of parting note Durrell managed to send Seferis.

Under cover of darkness, Stephanides boarded the old Greek collier SS *Julia*, and, not far down the coast the first morning—sea very calm, sky clear—the ship was attacked by seven Stuka dive bombers. The author tells us that they made "a most terrific screaming sound as they dived," but somehow not one of their bombs hit home, and when they came back to machine-gun the deck, the bullets causing "a tremendous clatter, like a violent hailstorm on a galvanized-iron roof, as they skipped and ricocheted all over the place," there were still no serious casualties that Dr. Stephanides felt he couldn't cope with on his own. The ship then dropped anchor at Ghika's island of Hydra, where the rock cliffs provided a shield. Stephanides continued to attend to the wounded, now with the help of an Australian corporal.

That was to be his fate for the next five weeks, with his untrained medical orderly occasionally changing rank and nationality once he reached Crete. He was the lone medical officer in his unit, working day in day out as best he could with inadequate equipment to clean, stitch, and bind wounds or provide what paltry medicine he could from this or that kit or stock of supplies left behind by the departed, including food tablets (Dextrosan? he wondered) gathered up from the enemy dead. The voyage south took him through further Stuka attacks—bomb after bomb somehow missing a direct hit on his now-limping ship—and after he reached Crete, he was moved back and forth from one camp to another in the Chania and Suda Bay region, only some few kilometers east of inadequately defended Maleme airport, which proved to be the Achilles' heel of the failed Allied defense of the island.

During his first weeks on Crete, after increasingly intense strafing attacks by the Luftwaffe, one relief from treating the wounded came with a bit of casual botany, sometimes to gather herbs for medicinal purposes, sometimes to court good fortune: "On May the 14th I found a four-leaved clover, the first one I had seen since 1907. I pressed it for luck in a little notebook my daughter had made me and kept it there with my snapshots from home. I also found a four-leaved yellow wood-sorrel (*Oxalis*); this was the only four-leaved specimen I had ever observed." There were also relaxed moments over "bully beef" and strong tea to build morale by exchanging stories about the mythical Near Eastern sage Nasr' Eddin Hodja. ("Hodja claimed that he could have created a far better world than God. 'For instance,' said he, 'I would make the sun shine warmly in the winter when people are half-frozen, and I would send snowstorms during the summer when they would be really appreciated.' ") Even in wartime Crete there were wedding festivities one could join from a distance, listening to the lyrae and watching the wedding party dance the *pentozali* in a circle "to make the war seem misty and remote." And for the translator still living within the doctor and botanist, there was the chance to render the rhymed couplets of the Cretan *distich* "in which the whole idea must be succinctly expressed":

The youth who never has aspired to ride the clouds unfurled,
Of what use is life to him, of what use the world?

Yon tiny cottage is accursed and shamed in every stone,
For there a lovely maiden sleeps—and she doth sleep alone.

I weep in secret, for the world now points at me in scorn,
I have been wounded once again—and by the selfsame thorn.

But there was no sure and lasting escape from the war. The evening of May 19, Stephanides watched the sun sink "into a sea of blood against which the black branches of olive trees were strikingly silhouetted." He tells us that, had he known what was coming, he might have read an omen in this "grim outlining of the symbol of peace against that crimson ocean," and though its angry glow faded as the calm stars came out one by one, these, too, appeared to be symbols of a peace that was "as distant and as unattainable as the heavens themselves." Early the next morning hundreds of German planes began crisscrossing the sky to bomb and strafe without break, followed by low-flying silvery machines that proved to be gliders, and then by bombers dropping wave after wave of parachutists to fill the skies with little white umbrellas that soon vanished behind the trees.

The resistance to this airborne invasion was fierce in the days that followed, both by regular troops—Greeks, British, Cypriots, New Zealanders, Australians—and by the local Cretans, using any weapons they could grasp, from clubs to pitchforks. One old Cretan with a bullet in his leg called Metaxas an "old baboon" for having made Cretans like himself give up their weapons out of fear of revolt against his dictatorship, and Stephanides, in apparent disagreement with Durrell's view that Metaxas was justly celebrated as Barba Yanni, adds that he himself emphatically doubts if the dictator was ever popular anywhere in Greece. But within less than ten days, the retreat to the south of the island had begun, with Lieutenant Stephanides and his faithful Greek orderly, Kokkinos, first leading a small band of wounded into the mountains, then carrying a Scotsman named Ironsides on a stretcher and in a hand chair for some kilometers until an overcrowded lorry picked him up, and finally making their way gradually on their own over the White Mountains in a three-day trek to the southern port village of Sphakia.

Stephanides' account of that trek is harrowing even from his modest, understated perspective: the strafing by Luftwaffe planes was constant, the water sparse when not bug-filled and muddy, the rations minimal even for somebody who no longer had any appetite, his tattered boots replaced by a new pair so large he had to fill them with cardboard to bring them down to his size and finally so wounding that his orderly had to hold him up on one side with an arm and a shoulder while he supported himself on the other side with a shepherd's crook. He also supported himself by muttering, every time a fresh German plane passed overhead, "I won't give up, damn you; I won't give up." During the final descent to Sphakia, he fell in with a group of wounded who were under strict orders to travel in the open with a Red Cross flag in the lead. To his surprise, the German planes not only honored the flag again and again but sometimes dipped their wings in salutation as they flew overhead. Stephanides found that hard to understand. After considering possible explanations—the pilots didn't want to waste ammunition on such a miserable target, they were just saving their bombs to blow up the rescue ships about to head out toward Egypt—he decided that maybe there were still some Germans in whom "all the humane feelings had not been entirely obliterated." A bit later, when several pseudo-casualties tried to join his group of wounded and were threatened with lynching by the others, he concluded that after all "war does *not* bring out the nobler side of one's character" and that with perhaps a few exceptions "primitive instincts . . . gain the upper hand." The good doctor would hardly be the one to say so, but from this low-key account of the attention he gave to others who he felt were suffering more than he was, the reader is likely to place him among those exceptions.

During the night of May 31, Lieutenant Stephanides and his orderly, Kokkinos, boarded a barge that carried them off the Sphakia beach to the cruiser HMAS *Perth* waiting offshore. After a meal in the wardroom, Stephanides took off his boots and spent the night in a bunk handed over to him by a fellow officer. The next morning, sometime after the cruiser managed to survive a direct hit by a bomb, he got up to discover that he couldn't get his boots back on. He walked to the wardroom that day in his swollen stockinged feet, and not until frequent cold baths and more sleep had reduced the swelling did he manage to get his feet back into his oversized boots in time for the 2:00 a.m. disembarkation at Alexandria, Egypt. He tells us that he took leave from his "staunch and willing comrade" Kokkinos with "a hearty hand-clasp" and that he was pleased to see Kokkinos subsequently mentioned in dispatches "for his good work in Libya and Crete."

The next day word went around in Alexandria—presumably "a rather rude joke"—that every man who had taken part in the Cretan evacuation would be presented with a medal inscribed with the words EX CRETA. We learn from an appendix to *Climax in Crete* headed "Anticlimax" that what in fact Lieutenant Stephanides received some three months later was the following:

Information has recently been received from D.M.S. Branch, G.H.Q.M.E., that you embarked from Egypt on 7/3/41 for Greece and disembarked on 1/6/41 ex Crete. As Colonial Allowance is inadmissable for this period, an overissue of £5 1s. 0d. has occurred representing 3s. 6d. per day issued over the whole of this period.

Will you please either remit the amount to the Command Cashier or forward written authority for the deduction of the sum from your allowances by suitable monthly installments? In the latter event will you please inform me the amount that you wish to be deducted each month.
[Signed] Lieut. [illegible] for Officer in charge of Officers Accounts, M.E.F. Jerusalem, 3/9/41 W.R.S.C.

So much for medals, dispatches, and other commendations for this particular medical officer. He deserved at least "a hearty hand-clasp" from somebody for serving others more than himself during one of the bitterest defensive battles of the Second World War.

We know from Stephanides' account that for Seferiades of the Press Bureau the voyage to Crete and beyond began on the "small steamer" SS *Elsie* a few hours ahead of Stephanides' exodus on the SS *Julia*, both ships sailing away shortly after another steamer outside the harbor was attacked by several German aircraft and, in the good doctor's words, "blew up with a tall column of black smoke." Seferis's journal of these days confirms his friend's image of "exultant arrogance" on the faces of German prisoners of war who were forced to join the exodus from Piraeus on the SS *Elsie*, passing in front of the Greek and British officials to board the ship "with no sign of the defeated" in their bearing. But at the same time the poet tells us that he believes the presence of German prisoners on board his ship is what made for a calm crossing to Suda Bay, evidently nothing like Stephanides' harried crossing under dive-bombing Stukas. We also know from Seferis's Christmas 1941 letter to Henry Miller that when he and his wife, Maro, reached Crete he ran into Durrell ("Larry, I love him. He has wonderful moments. I remember him in Crete . . ."), who had arrived from Kalamata with Nancy and their daughter, Penelope (nicknamed Bouboulina), "in a sort of boat like the one you [Miller] used to go to Spetses." The united friends went off in search of a taverna because they were all very hungry, and Seferis tells Miller that everything was full up in the town, the taverna "stuffed with a queer crowd of soldiers and homeless civilians sweeping the dishes like grasshoppers in a vineyard." After "a tremendous struggle," they managed to get some cold rice, then left without paying because the waiters were "drowned in the compactness of this mad crowd." They parted in a blacked-out street under an "extraordinary sky," and one or two days later, Durrell left with his family for Egypt.

Seferis did not mention this meeting in his journal, and the report to Miller, for all its details about the scarcity of food and the crowding, has a tone quite different from the deep melancholy, disillusionment, and sense of inadequacy that color the journal entries he made during the three weeks he spent in Crete before sailing for Port Said, Egypt. From these entries we learn of intense maneuvering among certain members of the Greek government after the death of Metaxas and particularly after the suicide of Prime Minister Koryzis; once the remnant government reached Crete, there was much in-fighting and undercutting by the ambitious or the cowardly. The Cretan air was heavy with rumors that the Greek people had been betrayed by their leaders, both politicians and the military. Seferis was surprised by the lack of military preparedness. "The government has done nothing," he writes from Crete. "That is in its nature. But the English?" Three days later we learn that still nothing in the government is functioning. And in the days that follow he reports that "really, we have dried up from bitterness, from uncertainty, from shortage of breath . . . The English are still dizzy from the blow they got in Greece. They chew their words; they don't know if they're going to stay here or go." He feels surrounded by "a dry fever," everyone thinking of himself. The quality that had sustained the front in Albania is missing here: the group sense of impetus, of high spirits, of sacrifice—"the common flame." What began there the October before has been spoiled, humbled. Rather desperately he adds that it can't have spoiled totally; surely "the time will come when it will blossom again."

Seferis finds his position in Crete, never clearly defined, increasingly irrelevant, and an "atmosphere of escape" everywhere. A pity, he says, that there aren't more "living" people around like the many thousands who went to the front in Albania. He had expected things to be different here from what they were in Athens, but alas, they are not. News comes that Antoniou's ship, the *Kios*, has been sunk, but nobody can tell him whether Tonio survived or not. He finds great bitterness in that. And Athens radio reports that the Germans have told citizens of the city to walk the streets at a fast pace. "Poor Katsimbalis," he writes, "you who stopped at every street corner to converse endlessly." Yet Crete moves him, makes him feel that were this land his, he'd never leave it, whatever happened. "One minute a springtime downpour, another minute the great mountains still snow-covered here and there, the tranquil sea, the lively air—these things that are much more mine than all the wars of the world."

During his third week on the island, he writes that he can't understand why the government came to Crete if it didn't plan to stay. He finds it horrible for people to be faced with the pervasive atmosphere of escape: "We ask a multitude to make heroic decisions and at the same time we rip morale to shreds by our stance." Later he records what a British officer in Athens had said when asked whether the British would stay in Greece or head for Egypt: "Crete isn't really all that important to us" was the casual answer, the "us" presumably meaning the British army. Seferis is now tempted by the idea of staying in Crete as long as the island holds out—that would be the best that could happen to him—but he wonders if that may not be unwholesome romanticism. Then, on May 14, he gets word that he is to be evacuated with the rest of the Greek government. Around him everyone is digging foxholes in the ground, as though digging their graves. At that moment he truly feels "the shame of flight." Later in the day he is ordered to be in Suda by 6:30 a.m., ready for embarkation.

The ship that George and Maro Seferis boarded for the voyage to Port Said was a Dutch ocean liner. "What a nice trip we could have taken on a ship like this," Maro remarked, but Seferis records laconically that *this* is the real trip: you don't know where it will take you or if you will arrive. When they reach Egypt, he finds low land, the lowest he has ever seen, no mountains, the sea yellow, the sea of Proteus, full of jellyfish but also deep blue. The scene evokes two celebrants of the Aegean: "Where is Tonio?" the poet cries. "And Elytis?" Seferis and his wife take the train to Cairo, where the British greet them as evacuees and put them in a "horrible pension" called Imperial House. At the Greek Embassy, the people he meets, totally unconcerned, believe themselves to be in an idyllic situation; for them the war might as well be on Mars.

The couple soon move on to Alexandria—at least there they encounter traces of Cavafy and a few Greeks who can talk literature—but within a week Seferis reports that he is sorry he left Greece, sometimes bitterly sorry: that is where his friends are, and his people. Crete remains a "great wound." Maro tells him that "all of us are to blame, you, me, the Government, the British," and he agrees. At dinner the next day an English officer just in from Herakleion reports that the Cretans are fighting back desperately with any weapon they can find, including sabers. "You go ahead and leave," they tell the British. "We have the mountains." With the full British evacuation of Crete on June 1, Greece's government-in-exile, which has been hovering in Egypt, is reduced to only a few members. Seferis is designated to accompany a new Greek ambassador to South Africa, first to Johannesburg and then to Pretoria, where the embassy will be located. "I am indifferent," he says. "I'll go wherever they send me." Meanwhile he lectures to high-school children in Alexandria about the poetry of Antoniou and Elytis—a release because it is *only* to children that he now chooses to talk poetry—then on to Cairo, where "the head has no soul" and nobody can do anything "in this paste of petty self-interest." Whatever is done is done "crookedly and upside-down."

On the SS *New Amsterdam*, heading for South Africa, the poet decides that Egypt at least gave him Alexandria, and at least he can take solace in "the bit of writing" that his journal entries provide him. But his dislocation and isolation continue. He remarks that he doesn't travel now—he is "transported": first to Durban, then to Johannesburg, then to Pretoria. His associates are no help. Prime Minister Emmanuel Tsouderos is like the ghost of Hamlet's father. Seferis writes that when he left Greece he did so in order to go on serving "the struggle" as best he could, but his associates quickly "neutralized" him, and he has no friend among them or anyone else in whom to put his faith. Now, in mid-July, he is working alone in the Pretoria embassy under the ambassador. He decides, since he can't carry on the struggle among his friends, luck may have provided him the best deal after all. He buys a book of Edward Lear's limericks and has the feeling that the book is like a much loved pet returning home. By late September he senses himself more than alone: *he* is now the *stranger*, with nothing to do in Pretoria, and his country doesn't wait for him any longer: "in the pain and the night of its slavery, it struggles to save its soul"; though Greece's struggle is his, too, he is shut off from it, stranger that he is, and his bitterness is like a poison in his guts, in his veins.

Seferis's decision to leave his friends behind in occupied Greece and to serve his country by going into exile with the remnants of his government had obviously cost him dearly, but in South Africa he couldn't escape the fact that it had been his decision, and though he continued to suffer a deep sense of futility and isolation through the fall and winter of 1941–42, he gradually found ways to accommodate the agony of his situation by writing. First there was a long commentary on Cavafy, then poems that were made to carry the burden of his pain and to transform the imagery of his exile into something richer than he could manage in his journal. One of these poems, bearing the Cavafian title "Days of June '41" and the postscript "Crete—Alexandria—South Africa, May–Sept. '41," evokes piercing images of war-ravaged Crete following his exodus:

> *the beautiful island bleeding,*
> *wounded; the calm island—the strong, innocent island*
> *And the bodies like broken branches,*
> *like roots uprooted.*

Another poem, written in October 1941, raises the question "who is he who commands and murders behind our backs?" The answer, "don't ask, just wait," is followed by a cry of hoped-for retribution: ". . . the blood, the blood / will rise some morning like St. George the rider / to nail the dragon to earth with his lance."

The poem that speaks most eloquently of the poet's sense of dislocation and of his passionate concern for his suffering compatriots across the sea is "Stratis Thalassinos Among the Agapanthi," the speaker being Seferis's Odyssean persona. His last name means "sailor" or "mariner," and he finds himself surrounded by African lilies with the Greek name agapanthi ("love flowers"), but these are unfortunately not the flowers that carry the message he needs to find his way home. What he needs and longs for are the asphodels, violets, or hyacinths of his native country, flowers that might help him talk to the shades in Hades who alone can guide him, as they guided Odysseus, toward the day of his return. And the companions who remain with him merely frustrate him, cutting the silver strings so that "the pouch of the wind empties" again and again. In despair, the exiled persona asks, "How can I grasp this religion?" The answer is a creed that declares all his anguish but little of his hope:

> The first thing God made is love
> then comes blood
> and the thirst for blood
> roused by
> the body's sperm as by salt.
> The first thing God made is the long journey;
> that house there is waiting
> with its blue smoke
> with its aged dog
> waiting for the homecoming so that it can die.
> But the dead must guide me;

it is the agapanthi that keep them from speaking,
like the depths of the sea or the water in a glass.
And the companions stay on in the palaces of Circe:
my dear Elpenor! My poor, foolish Elpenor!
Or don't you see them?
—"Oh help us!"—
On the blackened ridge of Psara.

The companions here presumably include ancient relatives of the modern associates who "neutralized" Seferis during his journey out of Greece. These exist in the condition of those ill-fated members of Odysseus' crew who were changed into pigs by the goddess Circe, among them Elpenor, the youngest and least valiant of them, who broke his neck in a drunken fall from the roof of Circe's palace and whom Odysseus left unburied. The call for help that Elpenor utters as the first of the shades Odysseus encounters during his visit to Hades to consult the soothsayer Tiresias about his homeward journey is a plea that he be given a proper burial—in a mound by the shore with his oar planted to mark the grave for passing sailors. The call for help in Seferis's poem appears to extend beyond this Homeric source to encompass a desperate plea from the contemporary Greeks left behind in Seferis's homeland and now struggling for the soul of their country under a hostile foreign occupation, as their nineteenth-century ancestors did on the island of Psara, which was razed and its people massacred by the enemy in 1824 during the Greek War of Independence, which liberated the country from Turkish occupation under the Ottoman Empire. That tragic moment in Greek history, commemorated by Dionysios Solomos in what is perhaps the most famous short poem in modern Greek literature, returns hauntingly to the speaker's consciousness by way of the line that opens Solomos's poem and that Seferis borrows to conclude his:

On the blackened ridge of Psara
Glory walking alone
Recalls the gallant young men:
On her head she wears a crown
Made of what little grass
Remained on that desolate earth.

Seferis wrote "Stratis Thalassinos Among the Agapanthi" on January 14, 1942, in Transvaal. By that time Henry Miller was "cooling [his] heels" in New York City, Lawrence Durrell was a press officer attached to the British Ministry of Information in Cairo, Theodore Stephanides was a medical officer somewhere in the Near East, Tonio Antoniou was without his ship and probably landlocked, Ghika was a professor at the Polytechnic University in Athens under the harsh and confining occupation regime, and the Colossus of Maroussi was walking the streets of Athens under the nose of Axis soldiers, perhaps still at his own pace but no longer in uniform and mostly alone. For each of these companions, the vision of an earthly paradise in Greece that they had fashioned together was now a casualty of the war, its many-faceted image an increasingly distant memory.

8

EDEN BURNING

If Glory walked alone in the foothills of Lycabettus any day during the fall and winter of 1941–42, she saw both horrors and gallantry equal to anything she encountered on the blackened ridge of Psara during the War of Independence, but in the beginning horrors dominated the landscape. Seferis knew that all too well. And his American friend, back in New York in January 1942 from his trip to Hollywood, had heard enough by then to surmise that "it must be frightful in Greece now." The historical record tells us that the massive requisitioning that the Germans initiated with the occupation of Athens in April 1941, the hoarding that followed, the weak harvest that summer, soaring inflation day in day out, a breakdown in transport, arrogant squabbling among the Axis occupiers, the quisling government's flaccid and corrupt bureaucracy—all of this in a country that in the best of seasons was not self-sufficient in wheat and other essential footstuffs—led to a severe famine in Athens and Piraeus and other urban areas where there was limited access to the countryside. By December the shortage of food in the capital, especially in its shantytown suburbs, was so severe among those without special resources in goods or gold or luck that three hundred people were dying each day of starvation or disease brought on by malnutrition, some reports said; as many as forty thousand died between October 1941 and October 1942.

Those who died at home might be buried in unmarked shallow graves or dumped in cemeteries at night by their weakened relatives and their ration cards used to help the living, but those who collapsed in the streets lay for hours where they fell, their emaciated bodies eventually hauled away by municipal carts barely able to cope with the weight of their anonymous cargo. Inflation grew rapidly; the official price of bread rose from 70 drachmas in June 1941 to 2,350 a year later, soap from 65 drachmas to 3,100; and the black-market rate was whatever bargaining might make it. During the worst days, before the British lifted their blockade of Piraeus in June 1942 and the International Red Cross took over supervision of relief shipments, only those Athenians with marketable furniture and valuables, gold sovereigns, or some access to sources beyond the city could regularly provide their families with enough food to keep them from malnutrition, and many both in Athens and in its suburbs had to survive on sparse rations of sawdust bread, wild herbs, gathered weeds, and garbage leavings.

We have seen how Solomos commemorated so simply and movingly the price paid by those who gave their lives on the blackened ridge of Psara during the Greek War of Independence. The devastation of Athens during the famine, the yearning in its citizens to transcend the horror around them and to know the hope of ultimate justice, found their most moving expression in a late 1941 poem, "Agraphon," by Angelos Sikelianos, a poet whose usual organ tones heralding a personal vision were muted by the tragic experience of those days in a sublime narrative voice offering the following parable:

Once at sunset Jesus and his disciples
were on their way outside the walls of Zion
when suddenly they came to where the town
for years had dumped its garbage: burnt mattresses
from sickbeds, broken pots, rags, filth.

And there, crowning the highest pile, bloated,
its legs pointing at the sky, lay a dog's carcass;
and as the crows that covered it flew off
when they heard the approaching footsteps, such a stench
rose up from it that all the disciples, hands
cupped over their nostrils, drew back as one man.

But Jesus calmly walked on by Himself
toward the pile, stood there, and then gazed
so closely at the carcass that one disciple,
not able to stop himself, called out from a distance,
"Rabbi, don't you smell that terrible stench?
How can you go on standing there?"

Jesus, His eyes fixed on the carcass,
answered: "If your breath is pure, you'll smell
the same stench inside the town behind us.
But now my soul marvels at something else,
marvels at what comes out of this corruption.
Look how the dog's teeth glitter in the sun:
like hailstones, like a lily, beyond decay,
a great pledge, mirror of the Eternal One, but also
the Just One's harsh lightning-flash and hope."

So He spoke; and whether or not the disciples
understood His words, they followed Him
as He moved on, silent.

The poet, walking outside his once-Edenic city, his own ravaged Zion, now joins those who follow Jesus and offers up a prayer that he, too, might find a like token of inner transcendence and hope that will allow him to rise above the stinking corruption around him:

> And now I,
> certainly the last of them, ponder your words, O Lord,
> and, filled with one thought, I stand before You:
> grant me, as now I walk outside my Zion,
> and the world from end to end is all ruins, garbage,
> all unburied corpses choking the sacred
> springs of breath, inside and outside the city·
> grant me, Lord, as I walk through this terrible stench,
> one single moment of Your holy calm,
> so that I, dispassionate, may also pause
> among this carrion and with my own eyes
> somewhere see a token, white as hailstones,
> as the lily—something glittering suddenly
> deep inside me, above the putrefaction,
> beyond the world's decay, like the dog's teeth
> at which you gazed that sunset, Lord, in wonder:
> a great pledge, mirror of the Eternal One, but also
> the Just One's harsh lightning-flash and hope.

One of those who found ways to rise above the desolation of the great famine and feed the spirit while the body hungered was Ioanna Tsatsos, Seferis's sister, celebrated by Henry Miller after his prewar encounters with her. A journal that Ioanna kept from September 1941 to October 1944 and published some twenty-five years later records how she lived through these days in her house on Kydathenaion Street in the Plaka district of Athens, under the Acropolis, in the company of her two daughters and her famous husband Constantine Tsatsos, Miller's Kyrios Ypsilon. Her account of the winter of 1941–42 is generally unrhetorical and filled with the kind of detail about day-to-day things done and known and thought that best illuminates the mood of the times. The darker aspect of her experience comes over at moments in a sort of staccato shorthand: "5 November 1941. Ghastly atmosphere. Everywhere a dead end. I don't want to speak to anybody about us. I'm ashamed of the slavery, as I'm ashamed of the ugliness . . . 25 November 1941. It's night. Cold, snow, hunger . . ." The entry that day also records a "wonderful" dream of long tables spread with "the most beautiful, sweet food," where Greek children eat greedily, with relish, faces smeared to the ears. And then a bad awakening: "I woke feeling I was coming out of paradise and sinking, wide-awake, into a familiar nightmare. My room is freezing. I'm hungry. I never get up from the table full."

And there are bad-dream-like imaginings. Returning home on New Year's Eve, 1941, the night bitter cold, the darkness dense, Ioanna hears "something like weeping, like a complaint," and she imagines skeletal hands stretching out, begging for something she can't possibly give. She concludes that even the most trivial hope can't penetrate this night. "The Germans triumph everywhere. And this hunger, like a mass extermination of the race, kills all of us." A month later, there is still no relief: "7 February 1942. We've never been so cold. Freezing inside and out. When [her daughter] Dora shuts herself up of an evening in the living room and tries to practice on the piano, her fingers are too numb. The cold in the streets and the cold in the house the same . . ." Even after the climate turns summery, there is still the aura of a country once rich in pleasures of the mind and spirit now desolated by what has been done to it: "5 June 1942. What happened today is unbearable. The prewar hours of intellectual joy are over. We will never find them again as they were then. A bullet cut off the life of Michali Akyla. Don't these Huns understand who they have in front of them and who they kill? They kill the spirit, they kill this rare sensibility that is a thousand lives together."

But knowledge of good things lost and of death for the spirit at the hands of triumphant barbarians is not the whole of Ioanna's story. She finds ways to transcend the desolation by helping others in more need or more danger than she. She writes of an English soldier who has stayed behind in Athens because he is in love with a Greek woman and is willing to hide out and take any risk he has to in order to go on seeing his loved one. Ioanna helps him by packing some food and escorting him to a safe house, in this case with the added satisfaction, as she feels every time she helps an Englishman, of thereby somehow answering the violence of the occupier: "because, whether by deception or by rebellion, we feel the answer to violence as a law of necessity." (From a later entry we learn that the Englishman marries the woman he loves and apparently survives the occupation.) Then there is the case of Robert Levesque, French translator of Sikelianos, Seferis, and Elytis, "a man of profound spirit and a good friend," who tried to leave Greece when the Germans invaded but who was shipwrecked on his way out and then returned to Athens without money, clothes, or livelihood. "How is he to live, refined and cultured in a time when only black marketeers can make a living?" Ioanna asks. She answers her own question by organizing a course in literature in her home and charging "something" for those who attend. The first of Levesque's lessons, on André Gide, draws eighty to the house in Kydathenaion Street—a great success, Ioanna reports, that takes the participants back to "the familiar intellectual atmosphere" where the "nuances of the authentic aesthetic thinking" on the part of Levesque enters inside the audience "to calm the demon of hate and action that had possessed us from the beginning of our enslavement."

This was still early on during the famine. As it grew, Ioanna records that at one point she had to sell her daughters' bicycles for a gold pound in order to buy vegetables. She hopes for some olive oil as well and maybe an egg, but ends up with five pounds of beans and five pounds of yellow peas. At the same time, she joins other women to distribute milk to the children of the Plaka district, and in December she organizes a system whereby each family that can agrees to provide a plate of food for one destitute child every noon. By mid-February 1942 she can report that her "Life to the Child" program has helped to ensure that, despite the cold and hunger, "the children of the Plaka are healthy." But the occupation authorities decree that those who hide English soldiers will be shot, and the enemy has occasional open confrontation with Greek citizens. The expanding activity by resistance groups inside and outside Athens soon brings on a demoralizing series of arrests and reprisals, including regular executions, by the occupying forces as they encounter more and more clandestine resistance. On March 25, 1942, in celebration of Greek Independence Day, there is an open demonstration by young men and women, some with feet swollen by malnutrition, and by invalid veterans, who come out into the streets in what Odysseus Elytis dramatized many years later as "The Great Sally," in one of the prose sections entitled "Readings" of his best-known poem, *The Axion Esti*:

> . . . they came out early in full view of the sun, with fearlessness spread from top to bottom like a flag, the young men with swollen feet, those they called bums. And many men followed, many women, the wounded with their bandages and crutches. And suddenly you'd see their faces so lined that you'd think many days had gone by in those few hours. And the Others, hearing about such daring impudence, were greatly disturbed. And after sizing up their own possessions three times over, they decided to move out into the streets and squares with the only thing they had: a yard of fire under their steel, with the black muzzles and the sun's teeth—there where no sprig or blossom ever shed a tear. And they hit at random, their eyes shut out of desper-

ation. And Spring overran them more and more. As though there were no other road in the whole world for Spring to take except this one, and as though they themselves had taken it silently, gazing far ahead, beyond the edge of despair, at the Serenity they were destined to become—these young men with swollen feet, those they called bums, and the men and the women, and the wounded with their bandages and crutches.

And many days went by in those few hours. And the beasts cut down a multitude and rounded up others. And the following day they lined up thirty against the wall.

Through the office of Archbishop Damaskinos, Ioanna Tsatsos organized a group of mostly women who supplied aid and comfort to the victims of these reprisals in the months and years ahead. And at her home on Kydathenaion Street her husband's friends gathered regularly to discuss postwar political prospects, the group including at one time the young Constantine Karamanlis, destined to be a major statesman after the war, and Prime Minister during the years when Ioanna's husband, Constantine, was President. These gatherings, and the traffic of those passing through for help and comfort, eventually put the house under suspicion, but somehow Ioanna and Constantine made it through month after month of increasingly intense resistance activity matched by increasingly severe reprisals, until the professor managed to escape to Turkey and Egypt. He did so despite having to leave Athens with his real identity card rather than the fake card he was supposed to carry but couldn't find at the last minute. Ioanna reports that this real identity card finally protected her husband: when German soldiers searching the bus he was traveling in found a can of German meat in his knapsack and accused him of stealing it from their army, he was forced to get off the bus and produce the only identity card he had. "Herr Professor," said the soldier examining the card, and he handed it back to him, saluted, and apologized. A university professor stealing meat? Excuse me. Out of the question.

During Ioanna's day-to-day account of these harrowing years there are only two substantial references to her brother George Seferis. In July 1943 a friend planning a trip to Egypt asks her if she wants him to convey any message to George, who had returned to Cairo to serve as Press Officer with the Greek government. She doesn't answer him, but she asks herself, "Will I see him again?" and wonders what he is going through in Egypt, a man so in need of free space for himself. Surely he must find some time for pure creation to refresh himself, while she at that moment feels that she is in Dante's hell, pursued by madness. "How I would like to see him," she writes. "He always strengthened my spirit." When the friend returns almost four months later, he reports that George was tormented by nostalgia but even more by worry about his country, which allowed him no rest. "When the two of us sat down together," he tells Ioanna, "his agonies came before us and then came back again." Ioanna thinks to herself: "All of us pay for this war, wherever God assigned us."

The third sibling, the younger brother of George and Ioanna, appears to have been the family member who ended up paying the largest cost for the war, and his fate proved to be cause for much agony for both his sister and his brother. Angelos was living on the second floor of the house on Kydathenaion Street at the start of the occupation. In July 1942, his wife, Roxani, had some sort of nervous breakdown and left him, taking their son with her. Angelos then had surgery for an ulcer, under exacting circumstances, and in mid-September disappeared from his home. It turned out that he was incarcerated by the Germans, and, after some days in the Averoff prison and more time in a ghastly prison in Lamia, he was released in November, the victim, apparently, of mistaken identity. He survived the occupation but not its debilitating influence. After the war he settled in Monterey, California, where for a period he taught Greek to officer candidates in the U.S. Army Language School there, and at one point he visited Henry Miller in Big Sur. In January 1950 he died alone with a copy of Plato in his lap. Miller wrote Seferis that he had been expecting another visit from Angelos when he got word of his death "after your brother had already been buried." This was a shock to him, and he added perceptively: "It must indeed be terrible for you to learn that he died so far away and lies buried in a foreign land." Seferis, then serving in Ankara, sent his sister a telegram that suggests what the news had cost him: "A few hours ago I received the terrible news that we have lost Angelos . . . My pain is very great, here alone . . . I am in no condition to write to you at length . . . Be brave." And the entry in his journal that day consists of a single word: "Angelos."

Ioanna tells us that George tried to conceal his lingering grief over the death of his brother "by doing interesting things with his life," including a trip in late June of 1950 to Ephesus and from there to Smyrna and his childhood home at Skala, nearby. In his journal he portrays the "little house" he searched out after an absence of some thirty-five years as a ruin with broken windows, rotting shutters, leprous walls, and a rusted iron door through which children scuttled like huge rats. However "interesting" this visit, the poet's grieving for his brother did not go away easily, nor his persistent sense of isolation in a foreign wilderness, nor his nostalgia for a paradise that has vanished. These still color passages in his poetry, as in the following lines from "Memory II: Ephesus," which appear to have been inspired by his tour of the ancient site and its theater that summer (the poem was first published five years later). The third-person figure here invokes the ghost of the so-called melancholy philosopher, Heraclitus of Ephesus:

> . . . I remember still:
> he was traveling to Ionian shores, to empty shells of theaters
> where only the lizard slithers over the dry stones,

and I asked him: "Will they be full again some day?"
And he answered: "Maybe at the hour of death."
And he ran across the orchestra howling
"Let me hear my brother!"
And the silence surrounding us was harsh,
leaving no trace at all on the glass of the blue.

An episode that surely stirred another aspect of George Seferis's brooding nostalgia—this when he was in Egypt during the occupation—occurred in Athens on February 28, 1943, at the funeral of Kostis Palamas, the eighty-four-year-old poet and man of letters who had long since been recognized as the unofficial poet laureate of Greece. ("We had forgotten that he was mortal," commented Ioanna Tsatsos.) The funeral became the occasion for a public release of national feeling, as many local literati and ordinary Athenians packed the small church for the service and then joined the huge entourage that crammed the pathways of the First Cemetery in Athens, passing unconcerned in front of German observers planted here and there. The church service ended with Angelos Sikelianos placing his hand on the coffin and reciting his commemorative poem to Palamas in grand, sonorous tones, a ringing call for bugles to sound and bells to peal in honor of the great poet's passing, while Greece herself stood there beside the coffin. (This poem soon became one of the standard texts memorized by Greek schoolchildren.) Sikelianos, the dead poet's heir to the mantle of national poet, was in the front row of pallbearers carrying the coffin through the cemetery to the burial plot, and George Katsimbalis was among those at the head of the procession of mourners. After the coffin had been lowered to its resting place, the Colossus stepped up to be the first to throw a handful of earth into the grave, and then, turning to face the vast horde of mourners, he began to sing out in a booming voice the verses by Dionysios Solomos that had become the Greek national anthem, an anthem that the German authorities had banned. The crowd eventually joined in. And when they finally turned to leave, the attendant German observers moved off without a word, either ignorant of what had gone on or indifferent to it.

In mid-February exactly three years later, Lawrence Durrell sent Henry Miller a report on Katsimbalis's version of this story as told to him during a visit Durrell made to Athens while he was back in Greece (on the island of Rhodes). According to Katsimbalis's account, he shouted insults at the German Embassy representative laying a wreath on the tomb, then broke into the national anthem, which, he pointed out, was banned under pain of death. Katsimbalis told his English friend that he was like a man in a nightmare, ten thousand people and nobody would sing along, while his voice was breaking on the top notes, his eyes bulging, and then silence at the end of the first verse as he stood there trembling, his wife trying to shut him up, Ioanna Tsatsos pulling at his arm. But on he went into the second verse, still singing alone, the Germans looking around angrily, he feeling "like a drowning man in the midst of that huge crowd," until suddenly he was joined by a fat Corfiot friend whose rich voice finished the second verse with him as a duet. And then, Katsimbalis reported, "as if you had thrown a switch," the roar of the crowd took up the hymn and sang along, the "tears running down our faces." Katsimbalis now felt in danger of being shot and, terrified for some time, went into hiding, here and there— the source of further entertaining stories, Durrell adds.

Poetry in the cause of national honor was not to have another day like that in Athens until some thirty years later, when, in 1971, the funeral of George Seferis became the occasion for a mass gathering of the young and not so young, some of whom knew his work in one form or another, most of whom had come out to show their respect for the courageous public stand that Seferis had taken two years previously against the dictatorship of the Colonels. After his 1963 Nobel Prize, Seferis had struggled *not* to assume the role of national poet or to act as spokesman for his country, but the tradition of Solomos, Palamas, and Sikelianos was too strong for him in a land where, at least in time of crisis, poetry still mattered enough to raise up heroes even against their will.

Seferis had always been wary of the moments when politics forced its way into the life of his imagination during his daytime hours or into the landscape of his dreams at night, and he recorded the occasions when it did so during his diplomatic career with distress. But politics is one thing and a sense of history is another. His friend Katsimbalis had that sense, and it was always an impulse behind Seferis's work. When in 1968 the poet felt that the rhythm of current history under the dictatorship was moving Greece toward the abyss, he decided after some soul-searching that he had to speak out as his country's conscience—no other leading writer or intellectual yet had—and that is what he did in March 1969, his statement first broadcast abroad:

It has been almost two years now that a regime has been imposed on us which is totally inimical to the ideals for which our world—and our people so resplendently—fought during the last world war. It is a state of enforced torpor in which all those intellectual values that we succeeded in keeping alive, with agony and labor, are about to sink into swampy stagnant waters . . . Everyone has been taught and knows by now that in the case of dictatorial regimes the beginning may seem easy, but tragedy awaits, inevitably, in the end. The drama of this ending torments us, consciously and unconsciously—as in the immemorial choruses of Aeschylus. The longer the anomaly remains, the more the evil grows.

Those in power who heard the poet and understood his message at first ignored him, then accused him in the government press of betraying the Greek people, then revoked his diplomatic passport. But most of those without power honored him with affection and respect, and these were openly demonstrated at the time of his death outside the small church where the funeral was held by singing en masse a poem of his that had been set to music by Mikis Theodorakis and then by following his casket to the grave, swarming up the lanes and over headstones to get as close as they could. One young man who climbed up a headstone was accused of being a donkey by a mourning friend of the poet. "But I love Seferis. Why do you call me a donkey?" The friend: "Because you put your ass in my face."

Writers who belong to a tradition where creativity and political history do not mix quite so naturally as they sometimes do in Greece might find it a surprising aspect of the occupation years that at a time when it might have seemed Athens provided barren soil for the creative spirit, poetry not only continued to survive but prospered, though mostly in private and underground. The large gathering on Kydathenaion Street to hear Robert Levesque was typical except in size, for smaller groups often met to hear poets read their poems to friends, try out work in progress, or simply talk shop as they used to in the open-air cafés. These were times, it seems, when a new vitality managed to enter the life of the mind, as though hunger and despair could best be challenged by a rise in imaginative energy. And some poets, especially those working in a contemporary Greek version of surrealism—Andreas Emberikos, Nikos Engonopoulos, Odysseus Elytis, Nikos Gatsos—occasionally found new ways to root their free-wheeling imagination in the marsh of current history.

Nikos Gatsos, the youngest of these along with his friend Elytis, proved to be the brightest voice that emerged in the occupation period. His was a curious career. In 1943 he published his first work, a six-part poem called *Amorgos* that he wrote during the terrible winter of 1941–42; then he published a few more poems in the same mode several years later; then he turned for the rest of his life to producing translations and song lyrics, the latter among the most popular of their kind set by Manos Hadjidakis, Theodorakis, and other postwar composers. But *Amorgos* was a remarkable debut, in both its language and its sensibility.

Gatsos's despair over what he called "the forces of evil at the forefront of history" was the essential source of the poem's mood, and his timely mix of personal and national emotion became the impetus for a more universal melancholy regarding man's bitter fate through the ages. Yet his dark vision was modified at times by what he saw as a heroic tradition in Greece and elsewhere, and by the forceful effort of some—poets included—to express their more humane impulses in the face of barbarity. The two aspects of the poem's perspective are manifest in a constant tension between the horrible and the lyrical, the violent and the tender, the crude and the beautiful, with the demonic often prevailing over the angelic. Its startling juxtapositions are presumably meant to rouse the reader out of sleep-induced lethargy—as his favorite ancient teacher, the "tearful" philosopher Heraclitus, had recommended—and to give access to the hope for "one ordered universe common to all," even in the presence of despair. But what most serves to stir the reader's heart, and made Gatsos the most influential poet of his generation, is his highly original fusion of traditional and colloquial diction and imagery. What follows is perhaps the most impassioned, if still surreal, representation in poetry of the imposed bitterness of the Italo-German occupation—especially during the winter of famine when it was written, a tragic moment in Greek history:

> *In the griever's courtyard no sun rises*
> *Only worms appear to mock the stars*
> *Only horses sprout upon the ant hills*
> *And bats eat birds and piss out sperm.*

In the griever's courtyard night never sets
Only the foliage vomits forth a river of tears
When the devil passes by to mount the dogs
And the crows swim in a well of blood.

In the griever's courtyard the eye has gone dry
The brain has frozen and the heart turned to stone
Frog-flesh hangs from the spider's teeth
Hungry locusts scream at the vampire's feet.

In the griever's courtyard black grass grows
Only one night in May did a breeze pass through
A step light as a tremor on the meadow
A kiss of the foam-trimmed sea.

And should you thirst for water, we will wring a cloud
And should you hunger for bread, we will slaughter a nightingale
Only wait a moment for the wild rue to open
For the black sky to flash, the mullein to flower.

But it was a breeze that vanished, a lark that disappeared
It was the face of May, the moon's whiteness
A step light as a tremor on the meadow
A kiss of the foam-trimmed sea.

What hope emerges from Gatsos's searing portrait of an Eden turned unnatural by the intrusion of barbarity comes over best in lines that move out of the surrealist mode into a more direct language and precise rhythm, yet resonate with overtones from the folk tradition and its biblical roots:

Enough if a sharp sickle and plow are found in a joyful hand
Enough if there flower only
A little wheat for festivals, a little wine for remembrance, a
    little water for the dust.

Gatsos acknowledged that the method of *Amorgos* owed a debt to French surrealism, what he called "the somewhat arbitrary movement of the imagination, the complete freedom in the synthesis of images, the dreamlike association of emotions," and there are moments when this mode of synthesis and association produces striking results. The sixth part of his long poem opens with lines that suggest a love lyric ("How very much I loved you only I know / I who once touched you with the eyes of the Pleiades . . ."), but that end up addressed to a metaphoric landscape: "Great dark sea with so many pebbles round your neck, so many colored jewels in your hair." These opening lines reappear at the poem's conclusion, a kind of coda following on a surrealist tour which at one point has taken us into the high mountains of unconquerable Mani and down its slopes with a cruising windmill that has mended its rotten sails "with a needle of dolphin bone." In this coda we see that the lines concern an idyllic landscape that blends the speaker's memories of his loved one and of his sea-girt country, as he once knew them. Now, in a far from idyllic time, all he can offer both as a gift of hope is his "embroidery" of a poem:

> For years and years, O my tormented heart, have I struggled
>   with ink and hammer,
> With gold and fire, to fashion an embroidery for you,
> The hyacinth of an orange tree,
> A flowering quince tree to comfort you—
> I who once touched you with the eyes of the Pleiades,
> Embraced you with the moon's mane, and we danced on the
>   meadows of summer
> On the harvest's stubble, and together ate cut clover,
> Great dark loneliness with so many pebbles round your neck, so
>   many colored jewels in your hair.

The other important writer who came to full maturity as a poet during the occupation was Yannis Ritsos, whose career was of course very different from Gatsos's: incredibly prolific, highly popular with the left, almost totally ignored by the established writers of the *Ta Nea Grammata* group. Ritsos, ill with tuberculosis before the war, spent the occupation years mostly in bed, living in the Thymarakia section of Athens with friends who fed him what little he ate, his self-imposed therapy reportedly an effort to breathe as little as possible and to remain speechless and motionless except when writing, which he continued to do as relentlessly as he was able.

Given the general dearth of publication during the occupation years and the inevitable gaps in Ritsos's own oeuvre at that time, it is hard to plot the specific effect those years had on his work, but a certain stylistic catharsis and a sensibility that penetrates deeper than politics are evident in a volume he wrote shortly after the war's end, *Parentheses, 1946–1947*. These are short, condensed, often subtle poems in free verse, the opposite face of his longer, more diffuse, more overtly political poems of the period such as the famous *Romiosyni*, written about the same time. The poems in the *Parentheses* volume appear to be a distillation of the poet's response to the occupation and the early phase of the civil war, but their form reveals an attempt at directness, an imposed simplicity, an effort to turn subjective impressions into narrative and rhetorical flourishing into dramatic representation by way of figures, acts, and objects. This suggests that Ritsos had been through a period of apprenticeship in Cavafy's workshop. The volume's opening poem, one of the very few written in the first person, establishes the volume's mode when the speaker tells us: "I hide behind simple things so you'll find me; / if you don't find me, you'll find the things, / you'll touch what my hand has touched," and that is the impulse we feel in poem after poem, where things, voices, and gestures are allowed to speak for themselves in portraying the harsh reality of the times:

WOMEN

Women are very distant. Their sheets smell of "good night."
They set the bread down on the table so that we don't feel
    they're absent.
Then we recognize that it was our fault. We get up out of
    the chair and say:
"You worked awfully hard today," or "Forget it, I'll light the
    lamp."

When we strike the match, she turns slowly and moves
    off
with inexplicable concentration toward the kitchen. Her
    back
is a bitterly sad hill loaded with many dead—
the family's dead, her dead, your own death.

You hear her footsteps creak on the old floorboards,
hear the dishes cry in the rack, and then you hear
the train that's taking the soldiers to the front.

The landscape of these poems conveys a bitterness that is as strong as in Gatsos, but the imagery remains closer to the earth and what is actually seen on the earth, metaphoric but more real than surreal. And again at the heart of the rendering are gestures and objects, sometimes offered to provide a sense of cosmic indifference:

AFTERNOON

The afternoon is all fallen plaster, black stones, dry thorns.
The afternoon has a difficult color made up of old footsteps
    halted in mid-stride,
of old jars buried in the courtyard, covered by fatigue and
    straw.

Two killed, five killed, twelve—so very many.
Each hour has its killing. Behind the windows
stand those who are missing, the jug full of water they don't
    drink.

And that star that fell at the edge of evening
is like the severed ear that doesn't hear the crickets,
doesn't hear our excuses—doesn't condescend
to hear our songs—alone, alone,
alone, cut off totally, indifferent to condemnation or vindication.

The subtlest poem in the volume, "Miniature," tells the very short story of a meeting over tea between a woman of undesignated age and a young officer. We are not told whether they are lovers or mother and son or neither, but we encounter them as they are about to take part in a moment of mystery. The surface action couldn't be simpler: the woman stands up at the tea table and with sad hands cuts slices of lemon that are compared to the wheels of a fairy-tale carriage, while the officer, deep in an armchair, lights a cigarette without looking at her, his hand trembling. At that moment the clock suddenly "holds its heartbeat." We are told that "something" has been momentarily postponed but not exactly what. Could it be the imminent separation between the two, or at least a recognition of its inevitability? We are left knowing only that what might have happened has now become what can never happen and that the lemon-wheel carriage was transformed into a carriage that came and went bearing death. Is it the death of the moment's possibilities and its suggested link to the fairy-tale world of childhood, or is it a more ominous foreshadowing of the officer's anticipated death in action? Again, we are left to answer for ourselves. But when the carriage with its little wheels of lemon reappears as the story draws to its end, the only remnant of the past, it brings with it a profound sense of loss, the sadness of knowing that things as they once were have now gone their way and that the best that lies ahead is a gentle passage into oblivion:

The woman stood up in front of the table. Her sad hands
begin to cut thin slices of lemon for tea
like yellow wheels for a very small carriage
made for a child's fairy tale. The young officer sitting opposite
is buried in the old armchair. He doesn't look at her.
He lights up a cigarette. His hand holding the match trembles,
throwing light on his tender chin and the teacup's handle. The clock
holds its heartbeat for a moment. Something has been postponed.
The moment has gone. It's too late now. Let's drink our tea.
Is it possible, then, for death to come in that kind of carriage?
To pass by and go away? And only this carriage to remain,
with its little yellow wheels of lemon
parked for so many years on a side street with unlit lamps,
and then a small song, a little mist, and then nothing?

When Ritsos's "Afternoon" speaks of "Two killed, five killed, twelve—so very many. / Each hour has its killing," the lines encapsulate both a reality and an attitude toward it that were pervasive in desolated Greece during the late years of the occupation, when the Germans' policy of reprisal became increasingly vicious, no longer tempered as it sometimes had been by their Italian allies, who themselves became victims of severe Nazi retribution after their surrender in September 1943. Early in the occupation precise quotas for reprisals had been established: fifty to one hundred hostages were to be shot for any attack on, or death of, a German soldier; and though it was sometimes impossible to carry out this directive because not enough hostages could be arrested on the spot, it was quite effective in Athens. The best historian of the occupation period in Greece, Mark Mazower, tells us that if there was one place "where the use of terror was refined and exploited to the full, it was in the SS-run camp at

Haidari," a few kilometers outside the city on a rocky hillside along the road to Eleusis, just beyond the Byzantine church at Daphni. This was both a transit camp for Italians, Jews, and others to be sent out of Greece and a warehouse for hostages awaiting execution; its name became synonymous with death. There were no beds, the corridors served as latrines, water was brought in by truck when there was enough gasoline for transport of that kind. It was from here that, as late as May 1944, two hundred hostages were taken to the firing range in Kaisariani to be shot, and Ioanna Tsatsos's diary reports that even later, one month before the German withdrawal, a woman friend of hers who had helped to organize resistance was executed at Haidari along with seventy others.

In the provinces, the German army had other ways of intimidating and terrorizing the occupied population. A few weeks before the Italians capitulated, guidelines were issued for a German First Mountain Division operation in the Epirus region that called for killing any armed man encountered, while villages where shots had been fired or where armed men had been seen were to be razed and the male population shot, and elsewhere all men between sixteen and sixty years old capable of bearing arms were to be rounded up and sent to the town of Yannina. In practice, the Wehrmacht perpetrated still worse things. On August 16, 1943, the morning following the Feast of the Virgin, soldiers from the 98th Regiment were ordered to enter the peaceful village of Komeno, south of Yannina, in an exemplary "surprise operation." This was done, presumably, in response to a report by a two-man Wehrmacht reconnaissance team that had run into some *andarte* (resistance) guerrillas who had visited there some days previously. Three hundred and seventeen villagers, including seventy-four children under ten years of age and twenty entire families, were killed that day. And as the defeat of the German army became simply a matter of time, the reprisals became more and more capricious, brutal, and extensive. By July

1944 the Greek government-in-exile reported that 879 villages in Greece had been totally destroyed and 460 destroyed in part.

At least two of the villages destroyed during the summer before the German army withdrew have raised enduring memorials to the victims of Wehrmacht atrocity, one in the village of Distomo, not far from Athens, the other in the village of Hortiati, on the mountainside behind Salonika. In June 1944 a German patrol outside of Distomo came under fire by a guerrilla unit, and after the guerrillas withdrew, the patrol turned around and entered the village to shoot anything they could search out that moved, then burned the village to the ground. Some three hundred villagers of both sexes and all ages died that day. Ioanna Tsatsos's diary entry comments: "It was as if, in order for [the perpetrators] themselves to survive, it became necessary that there be only desolation around them." And at Hortiati in September 1944, the death of one German soldier in an ambush by a guerrilla unit below the village resulted in the massacre of 146 villagers, mostly the young and the aged under the care of women, all of whom had stayed behind when the Wehrmacht trucks approached the village and the men escaped up the mountainside. Sixty of the victims were crowded at gunpoint into the village bakery, which was then sealed and lighted, as though the heart of a bonfire. Burning villagers to death, here and elsewhere, was said to be for the purpose of saving ammunition for the Germans' retreat from Greece. Though the village of Hortiati was deserted after the bakery was fired, the saber-wielding Sergeant Fritz Schubert in charge of the reprisal ordered all houses stripped and then torched.

Lieutenant Kurt Waldheim, the Wehrmacht intelligence officer whose assignment it was to gather information for anti-partisan operations in the Salonika area—as had been his assignment earlier in southern Greece—was apparently not a witness to the Hortiati massacre on September 2. He returned from his honeymoon in Austria the following day to take up his duties again at intelligence headquarters in the village of Arsakli, some six kilometers away, where the bloodbath in Hortiati had caused an enormous commotion and much indignation in the German army group stationed there, as one of his fellow officers in the room next to his subsequently reported. Asked many years later about the incident by the historian Hagen Fleischer, Waldheim, now President of Austria, replied that he was not familiar with "the event." For his part, Sergeant Schubert had the audacity to return to Greece after the war, was arrested, and was finally executed for his role in the massacre and for other crimes under a death sentence issued by a Greek military court. Schubert is now hardly a footnote to the history of the occupation and Waldheim a participant in that history with convenient amnesia regarding his past in Greece, but in both Distomo and Hortiati there are monuments large enough to attract the curiosity of passing tourists, even if most have no clear idea how a memorial dated for a single day in the summer of 1944 can list so many names of people with such a variety of ages, from one to ninety-eight.

Six weeks after the Hortiati massacre, the German army withdrew from Athens and soon was on its way out of Greece. On October 12 Ioanna Tsatsos's diary announced: "Greece is ours again." People that day went crazy: embracing, kissing, weeping, waiting for the English to arrive. The German flag on the Acropolis, she reports, came down as though swallowed by the Holy Rock, and in its place rose the flag with "the beloved color of our sky." An English friend of hers named Macaskey who had just arrived in town in civilian clothes was told by Archbishop Damaskinos to put his uniform back on, and he and the archbishop moved through the streets in an open car to the cheers of gathering celebrants, some of whom tried to raise the car to their shoulders. The archbishop returned to the cathedral the next day to hold his first service there, and Ioanna Tsatsos's diary ends with her kneeling, surrounded by "noise and liberation," to join with broken voice in praise of the Holy Virgin. (Some months later Damaskinos became Regent of Greece and George Seferis director of his political bureau, the regency established in anticipation of the plebiscite in September 1946 that returned King George II to the Greek throne.)

The euphoria of those moments in October 1944 was short-lived. The undeclared civil war, which entered what has been called its "second round" toward the end of the year, had been foreshadowed by months of violence between the left and the right in parts of occupied Athens (as in large areas of the countryside), with EAM-ELAS guerrillas of the left often in open confrontation with collaborationist Security Battalion forces or the gendarmerie of the quisling government of Ioannis Rallis; the Wehrmacht, for its part, used masked informers to round up and kill anyone identified as a leftist by their rightist or opportunist henchmen. Then, on December 2, 1944, during a protest demonstration in Syntagma Square by thousands of EAM followers, several city policemen panicked and fired into the crowd, killing some ten demonstrators and wounding another fifty. A British armored brigade cleared the square, but the uprising against the police that followed resulted in further bloodshed, and soon the British forces came in with a vengeance, including RAF Spitfires that strafed the suburbs. Prime Minister Churchill, having concluded a secret agreement with Stalin that placed postwar Greece within the British sphere of influence, was mistakenly convinced that the expected attempt by the Greek left to seize power had begun in earnest and that the city now under British protection ought to be treated as—in his words—a captured city with a local rebellion in progress. By early January the "rebellion" was put down; but not long thereafter, with the failure of the Varkiza agreement (which had promised ELAS amnesty for what were designated "political crimes" if it disarmed and which called for a plebiscite on the monarchy before general elections, a term of the agreement that was reversed in practice), guerrillas on the left took to the mountains again to begin the "third round" of the civil war, which lasted until a revitalized Greek army and massive

American military assistance brought the war to an end in the fall of 1949.

In early October 1944 George Seferis, waiting near Salerno, Italy, to return with the government-in-exile, appears to have anticipated the inevitable progress of bloodletting in his devastated homeland despite its imminent liberation. He tells us in his journal account of the days just before his return that he continually had before his eyes a Greek landscape "with images of the horror that I believe lies in wait for us." Now that his eyes were about to survey the literal landscape of his country across the sea, he realized that the ways in which his "spirit" saw it during the war years created a reality different from what was actually "*over there*" and he'd just as soon not yet have to drink from the cup of this actuality. A poem he wrote at this time, "Last Stop," is a meditation on the expense of the war, and it is one of the finest poems to emerge from that catastrophic period, even if his initial estimate of the war's human cost does not tally up the occupation horrors illuminated by his sister's diary so much as the moral corruption among public servants who confronted the war from its peripheries:

> . . . *We come from the sands of the desert, from the seas of Proteus,*
> *souls shriveled by public sins,*
> *each holding office like a bird in its cage.*
> *The rainy autumn in this gorge*
> *festers the wound of each of us*
> *or what you might term otherwise: nemesis, fate,*
> *or, more simply, bad habits, fraud and deceit,*
> *or even the selfish urge to reap reward from the blood of others.*

And then a more general image of the corrosive effect of war on the human spirit:

Man frays easily in wars;
man is soft, a sheaf of grass,
lips and fingers that hunger for a white breast
eyes that half-close in the radiance of day
and feet that would run, no matter how tired,
at the slightest call of profit.
Man is soft and thirsty like grass,
insatiable like grass, his nerves roots that spread;
when the harvest comes
he would rather have the scythes whistle in some other field;
when the harvest comes
some call out to exorcize the demon
some become entangled in their riches, others deliver speeches.
But what good are exorcisms, riches, speeches
when the living are not there?
Is not man perhaps something else?
Is he not that which transmits life?
A time to plant, a time to harvest.

The poem moves on to a vision of what the war's devastation and killing have cost the poet's once-green homeland, not least "a virgin forest of murdered friends." It is a vision the poet must express in "fables and parables" because the wordless horror is too alive to be talked of openly, it keeps on growing, and, as Aeschylus's chorus teaches us in *Agamemnon*, it is also inescapable: the wound of remembered pain drips in both daylight and darkness—though it seems, ominously, that now it is in darkness alone that an image of wounded heroes comes forth:

But the country they're chopping up and burning like a pine
*   tree—you see it*
either in the dark train, without water, the windows broken,
*   night after night*
or in the burning ship that according to the statistics is bound to
*   sink—*

this is rooted in the mind and doesn't change
this has planted images like those trees
that cast their branches in virgin forests
so that they rivet themselves in the earth and sprout again;
they cast their branches that sprout again, striding mile
    after mile;
our mind's a virgin forest of murdered friends.
And if I talk to you in fables and parables
it's because it's more gentle for you that way; and horror
really can't be talked about because it's alive,
because it's mute and goes on growing:
memory-wounding pain
drips by day drips in sleep.

To speak of heroes to speak of heroes: Michael
who left the hospital with his wounds still open,
perhaps he was speaking of heroes—the night
he dragged his foot through the darkened city—
when he howled, groping over our pain: "We advance in
    the dark,
we move forward in the dark . . ."
Heroes move forward in the dark.

Few are the moonlit nights that I care for.

Cava dei Tirreni, 5 October '44

The poem had opened "in our final port," with the moon outstripping the clouds to make the houses on the slope opposite glow as though enameled—a tableau recorded in Seferis's journal—and on that moonlit night the constellations, the "abecedary of the stars," had stood out so that they could be read more clearly for their "new meanings and new hopes" under what Virgil called the friendly silences of the moon. But by the last line of the poem, where the poet reaffirms that the moonlit nights he cares for are in fact few, we are left to wonder if the memory-wounding pain that "drips by day drips in sleep" can ever really end, and in our wonder there can be little prospect of hope. As it turned out, Seferis sailed back to a homeland that remained at peace for scarcely a month. Greece had indeed been chopped up and burned like a pine tree. Before long he began to witness the so-called December events from his home on Kydathenaion Street: armed British soldiers with their burgundy berets below his window, and on a corner farther along, a dead ELAS fighter standing upright beside his weapon holding a khaki handker-chief against his forehead. The poet's journal succinctly records the actuality he feared in the last days of his exile: "My premoni-tions and the nightmares of these past two and a half years turn out to be real."

Perhaps Seferis's immediate consolation in these still-dark days was finding that his family and most of his closest friends had not been murdered during the occupation. Brother Angelos, sister Ioanna, and brother-in-law Constantine Tsatsos were there to greet him, and soon he was reunited with Katsimbalis, Stepha-nides, Antoniou, Ghika, and, eventually, Larry Durrell. The only missing member of "the little band of friends" was the author of that phrase, but Seferis had Henry Miller very much on his mind and had honored his friend's loyalty in a journal entry during the final trip home: "A desire for the first time after years to write Henry Miller who didn't forget me. May he excuse my not re-sponding to his messages."

Miller's premonitions recorded in the *Colossus* had proven to be as accurate as Seferis's. He had rightly predicted that when the little band would come together again, it would be "on the ashes of all that we had once cherished," and there would be "no re-suming where we left off." He himself chose not to test this pre-diction in person, and anyway it allowed him to turn his talent elsewhere after having invented a beautiful otherworldly country that he must have known could not survive too much literal suffering. His turning elsewhere cleared the way for other writers, from both inside and outside Greece, to herald new images of the country shaped on the ashes of the old, perhaps less imaginative, flamboyant, and influential, but more firmly rooted in what was really there.

9

RISING FROM THE ASHES

*I*f you were returning to Athens in the early days after the Second World War, having spent your war years elsewhere—flying in by way of Africa, or across the Atlantic with fuel stops in Newfoundland, Shannon, and somewhere on the Continent—it would be difficult to make out exactly how the city had changed. There was still ample evidence of destruction around Piraeus harbor, and in certain sections of Athens you could come across what Seferis's journal described as "houses blown open like cracked walnuts" and many others shattered or scarred by street fighting. But by the summer of 1945 Athens was relatively calm, collected, and, with the scarcity of cars, quiet and unhurried in the downtown streets as well as in the Royal Garden and the wooded slopes of Lycabettus. During the day, business was more or less back to normal, though inflation made it necessary for you to bring a large bag full of the local currency to any serious transaction. Soon you would become aware of unfamiliar license plates with odd acronyms on the few recent-model cars and trucks on the road, the acronyms announcing the presence of foreign agencies that had arrived to distribute relief assistance or provide observation or exercise influence: UNRRA for United Nations Relief and Rehabilitation Administration, AMFOGE for American Mission for Observing the Greek Elections, and, most portentously, JUSMAG for Joint United States Mission for Aid to Greece, the "joint" presumably bringing together relief aid, military assistance, and intelligence gathering. These agencies signaled a gradual transition from British to American patronage, the insertion of a new "foreign finger" into Greek affairs, which earned the gratitude of some and the antipathy of others.

In the evenings, the Miami Night Club was open to entertain well-to-do Athenians and foreigners, including visiting American congressmen not in a mood for touring the countryside, and those in search of classical music could easily find tickets for a Beethoven symphony in the Herodus Atticus theater or take a ride in an open Jeep to a more casual midnight concert in the forest on Pendeli mountain. And the better restaurants, though surprisingly expensive, found the means, by way of domestic or foreign sources, to bring back most of their normal prewar fare. But the finest nighttime entertainment, anyway in the warmer months, was reserved for those lovers who could commandeer a car of whatever kind and vintage for a ride to the coast to find a rehabilitated taverna where they could feed their strength and spirit on the sea's aphrodisiac fruit—squid, octopus, clams, and any fresh fish garnished with parsley and olive oil—then make their way along the empty roads to Vouliagmeni or Varkiza or some other nearby stretch of deserted coast where they could head for the open beaches or climb over the low rocks protecting a crescent of private shore, strip for a naked swim, then lie down and love the remnant night away under the watchful constellations.

The war had thinned the forests around Athens and rutted most of the roads, but a climb up Lycabettus or Hymettus on a morning or afternoon free for that impulse showed the air to be again as pure as the prewar mythmakers had made it out to be, the light as cleanly luminous, the offshore islands as purple as they ever were and as close. What had changed dramatically lay beyond one's vision from any high point in the city: the burned-out villages in the Peloponnese to the south and on the mainland over the mountain ridges to the north; the bloated, skeletal children suffering from malnutrition in the more remote provinces; the concentration camp on the island of Makronisos to the east where many ardent members of the left were exiled for reeducation as the civil war began to disintegrate; and the various sections of the country where the Communist campaign of terror and government retaliations left villages abandoned to unattended animals and the fated elderly.

The processes of nature kept much beauty alive in Greece. With traffic diminished, industrial enterprise largely dormant, and the tourist trade still undeveloped, you could easily discover a bit of pristine mainland coast or an island cove that would give you as much clear emerald and aquamarine water close to shore and as much royal blue farther out as Durrell's islomanes might have cared to celebrate. And there were island villages once again radiant in the blazing light, having by that time whitewashed away all their bad history. You had to go where it wasn't easy to travel to see what even nature's brilliance couldn't blind you to: the remnants of man's evil spirit in time of war, whether in the heart of the enemy facing his victim or of brother facing his brother. Any road north or south of Athens would lead you at some point to a wounded village surrounded by ravished forests and barren fields, but getting there by car required special means so long as the civil war persisted, and after that was over, in 1949, the condition of the roads and the remains of destruction in many regions still made a village tour in the remoter areas an act of sacrifice that only the benevolent on a mercy mission or those in search of history were likely to undertake.

Salonika, the country's second city, then beyond the reach or concern of most Athenians, was one relatively cosmopolitan place where you came across undedicated memorials to the war's evil, both in the center of town and on its outskirts. The expanding Aristotelian University was at that time opening new ground where the Jewish cemetery used to be, the headstones dislodged to serve as lintels and stoops for cottages now spilling over the old city walls on the hillside that would eventually house a new university complex. Presumably the renovators and their patrons assumed that Salonika's once-vast community of Sephardic Jews, which had brought so much talent and color to the city during the centuries since the expulsion of their ancestors from Spain under Ferdinand and Isabella, would no longer be needing that portion of sacred territory in their home city, now that the Germans had succeeded in transporting and exterminating all but some two thousand of the fifty thousand Sephardim who had lived there in peace until the spring and summer of 1943. And a climb up the old potholed road leading to the Panorama suburb and the village that used to be called Arsakli would bring you past the villa that had been Kurt Waldheim's billet. Beyond that, after crossing a stretch of green meadow guarded by a crumbling bunker, you would come to the mountainside that used to cradle the village of Hortiati, now reduced to an untidy tableau of crude stone shapes outlined in charcoal. Eventually the village was rebuilt, concrete columns and red brick replacing the charred stone, and one day the high fields on the mountainside that were once thyme-rich pastureland for sheep and goats would be tightly fenced in to house the topless towers of a NATO tracking station.

The transformations of this dark history were not part of the landscape that Lawrence Durrell encountered on his return to Greece from Egypt in the summer of 1945. The island of Rhodes, in the Dodecanese, had been liberated from the Italian occupiers, but it was in fact not yet Greece, being under British authority until officially recognized as part of the Greek kingdom at the end of January 1948. Durrell was to serve as Public Information Officer attached to the British army there, with a staff of his own, a printing plant, and responsibility for editing a daily newspaper in Greek, Italian, and Turkish. After a while he wrote his editor at Faber and Faber, Anne Ridler, to say that his official duties were killing him and that he couldn't find time to do more than "lunch with Brigadiers in all their boredom." But there were other compensations. For a start, he was newly married to his second wife, Eve Cohen, whom he had described in a letter to Henry Miller a year earlier as Gypsy Cohen, a "strange, smashing, dark-eyed woman . . . with every response right: every gesture, and the interior style of a real person," and, in a second letter, as a "tormented jewish-greek" who "burns black and fierce under her Tunisian eyebrows; the flavor is straight Shakespeare's Cleopatra." The two of them, who had lived "a kind of refugee life" in Alexandria, settled on Rhodes in a villa called Cleobolus with a garden, the whole enveloped in bougainvillea, and in due course Durrell found enough time to write a portion of his book about Rhodes with the title *Reflections on a Marine Venus*.

The title of the opening chapter, "Of Paradise Terrestre," anticipates Durrell's response to the questions he tells us were on his mind as he approached the prospect of seeing Greece again. The letters he had received in recent months seemed to have an obituary flavor. "You will find it [Greece] completely changed," said one. "The old life has gone forever," said another. "Go to America," said a third. But, he tells his reader, tomorrow he will see for himself whether the old Greek ambiance has survived the war, whether that ambiance was still a reality based in the landscape and the people, or "whether we had simply invented it for ourselves in the old days, living comfortably on foreign exchange, patronizing reality with our fancies and making bad literature from them." Tomorrow he will know whether he must relegate his feelings about Greece "to the dusty corners of memory along with so many other mad vagaries of the heart."

Getting to that earthly paradise was not so easy (is it ever?). The voyage was storm-tossed and exhausting, many of the passengers "picturesquely" sick, the arrival in a blackness that swallowed up both the details of war and the harbor's anticipated beauty. But images of the new Eden that set the book's tone come before us with the first description of light after a long night's dying in the "once famous" Albergo della Rosa, the island's luxury seaside hotel built under Mussolini. Durrell wakes to feel "the warm early sun in my eyes, reflecting the running dazzle of water from the white roof of the room." Still half-drugged with sleep, he and his new friend Gideon burst into an Aegean Sea that was "clear and cold as wine." In front of them, across the narrow straits separating the island from Turkey, "the Anatolian mountains glowed, each one a precious stone." And though the water was icy, they stayed in a while, "speechless with gratitude— rubbed by the salt until our skins felt as cold and smooth as the pebbles which tesselated the shining floors of that magnificent beach." Later Durrell tells the reader that he had been trying for years to describe Aegean scenery to Eve Cohen but she had always suspected him of poetic license. When she finally joins him on the island, she exclaims, "But why didn't you tell me it was so marvelous." Having now convincingly rediscovered and effectively promoted remnants of the old paradise, Durrell sits down with Eve under the huge plane tree on the walls of the grand fort, and there the two of them "dawdle away our afternoons watching the windmills turning against the blue sky and listening to thin bored cries of the fruit-vendors in the market stretched below our feet."

Though Durrell's image of Rhodes in *Reflections* (as I shall call the book) includes the occasional reference to the "infernal wreckage of war"—the esplanade studded with pillboxes, German prisoners at work filling bomb craters in the asphalt, violet smoke hanging over Monte Smith from the disposal of enemy mines—it only sporadically projects the physical and psychic damage that were part of the reality and that undermined purely idyllic representations of the postwar Greek scene. In the typescript version of the book, which Anne Ridler drastically cut, there are more allusions to the aftermath of war, including references to mines that riddled the island and signs with skull and crossbones below the German legend *Achtung Minen*. But even in the uncut typescript the author explains—with some exaggeration—that he has decided to avoid "all" mention of the war despite "our knowing in our hearts how much it has aged and poisoned us." Anne Ridler clearly felt that a travel book about Rhodes for postwar readers should not be marred by too much remembrance of wartime reality, and though Durrell was too conscientious to avoid all mention of the subject, his first interest in writing about Rhodes was to record his rediscovery of a terrestial paradise there, however poisoned his heart may have been. More curious to anyone familiar with recent Greek history was his decision to keep the civil war, then violently in progress, from revealing its grim presence anywhere in the book. Durrell may have felt that exclusion was justified by the fact that the civil war did not extend to Rhodes either before or after his sojourn there, and he therefore found less clear evidence of its debilitating effect on the Greek psyche, but its influence must have been felt on Rhodes, and it was certainly pervasive wherever Durrell traveled beyond the Dodecanese islands. Any evocation of the "spirit of place" in the Aegean at that time that did not in some measure take the new war into account was less than faithful to that spirit.

As far as one can gather from his travel writing and his letters, Durrell's view of Greek politics was never very broad or deep, and though he celebrated the courage and vigor of the Greeks' resistance to the Italian invasion in 1941, he subsequently appears to have shared something of the superficial cynicism of those

Western observers who could not fathom or were uninterested in penetrating the complexities of a political landscape that often seemed alien to them in the conflicting passions it occasioned, especially in times of crisis. The year before Durrell left Alexandria for Rhodes he wrote to Henry Miller that he didn't see what sort of political future awaited Greece, but, he added, "It only affects me inasmuch as I hope to live there and recover from this wave of world neurosis." In March 1945, six months later, less than three months after the "December events," and just two weeks after the Varkiza agreement between EAM-ELAS and the government, he wrote again to Miller to offer a confused account of the political situation in Athens: "we [presumably the British] are defending the Acropolis caryatid by caryatid against the rest of Greece." The rest of Greece he identifies as the leftist EAM, no less "totalitarian than Metaxas was," but somehow containing "the best of the ancient Venezeli [supporters of the famous statesman Eleftherios Venizelos] like Katsimbalis and Theodore [Stephanides]." That identification with EAM would surely have startled the two members of the little band of friends who served in the war wearing the uniforms respectively of the Greek and the British armies! Then Durrell makes a curiously opaque generalization about "a final curtain" falling on the smallest country in Europe (presumably he was not counting neighboring Albania and Bulgaria, let alone Austria, Denmark, Switzerland, Portugal and a few even smaller countries): "withstanding Fascism in the field, nazidom at home, and now the reaction on the part of the people they love and admire most." He concludes that he plans to write a history of the last four years as soon as he is free of his current job—a project that was fortunately superseded in the first instance by his inventive evocation of Rhodes and in the second instance by the brilliant fictional account of his "last four years," *The Alexandria Quartet*, both much more suited to his creative energies.

Though the narrator of *Reflections*, shown to be living mostly in a bucolic setting at some distance from mainland Greece, reveals little awareness of conditions in the world beyond his island, we know from Durrell's letters to Miller that the author was in fact not so insulated. During his several trips to Athens from Rhodes in a futile search for what he hoped would be a more permanent job in Greece, Durrell became conscious of a difference in the mood and the resources of the city that in the prewar years had been the fast-pulsing heart of Greek intellectual and social pleasure. He tells his American friend that during a visit in February 1946 he finds Katsimbalis and Seferis unchanged, but the world around them "unbelievably sad, crowded, ill-housed, with money practically worthless and prices soaring." On second thought he senses with perspicacity that his two friends are in fact not quite the same: what they have been through has made them "gentle and friendly and sympathetic to each other as they have never been before." Even behind the "tremendous effervescence" of the Colossus, Durrell sees "a repose and resignation—as of someone who has faced death in his imagination for a long time, so that it has detached him from the ordinary life—which is only after all the joy of expectation." He asks Miller to send Katsimbalis a few pounds from time to time to help Greek poets because many of them are starving, "Sikelianos among them." And "little captain Antoniou" has also "been through it," though he continues to be "silent and smiling as ever." He concludes that Miller will have to give Athens a year or two "to settle down politically etc." before he can think of going there, even if the "intellectual hunger is terrific." And at the end of the month he writes Miller again to say that he should not be surprised if he doesn't hear from his Athenian friends: they are "simply hemmed in by their gloom."

The mood of Athens was apparently distant enough not to compromise the idyllic construct that dominated Durrell's book about Rhodes, a project that was at least a training exercise for his fictional re-creation of the Aegean Greece that appears in *The*

Alexandria Quartet. One aspect of the fictional mode of *Reflections* is the character called Gideon, the one-time "tramp in the Eastern Mediterranean" who had lived in Athens and Alexandria before the war and who plays a major role in the book as the narrator's alter ego. There is no substantial external evidence that Durrell actually had a monocled friend of Gideon's features and disposition among his known friends on the island, nor that anyone of that name was accidentally killed in crossing an unmarked minefield on Nisyros, as he has it in a note. But there is some internal evidence that Gideon was created to offer opinions and generate sentiments that Durrell shared to a large degree yet preferred, for one reason or another, to voice through this character rather than by way of his narrator.

Gideon in fact has several voices. Responding at one point (in what the narrator calls an excellent imitation of a New York accent) to a Greek American who made "the inevitable comparison between Detroit and this 'lousy country,'" Gideon sounds like Henry Miller: "You stinking empty-headed son-of-bitch, . . . why the hell do you come back here and poison the air of your mother-country with your cheap snarls and your passion for Coca Cola?" Then again, another friend suggests that Gideon perfectly fits his own definition of an Englishman, namely, "a soft-centred creature with a tough and horny shell, through which two sensitive antennae (humor and prejudice) explore the world around him." And yet again, in his passionate acknowledgment of Greek hospitality, Gideon sounds like some combination of both Miller and Durrell: "What a country . . . One only has to look hungry, to sit around for a while, and people just send you things."

Were the separation from the author more thorough and the characterization broader, Gideon would qualify for a place beside the more colorful minor figures in *The Alexandria Quartet.* This character's "fictional" presence and the frequent treatment of Rhodes's landscape on a level somewhat removed from its historical reality at the time again suggests that Durrell's work on this book, especially when the island was recollected in tranquillity from another country, was preparation for the fictional island landscape of *The Alexandria Quartet*; the later invention is central to those introductory and concluding portraits of the Aegean island to which the narrator, Darley, has "escaped" with Melissa's child in order to "heal himself" and to re-create an imaginary city across the sea called Alexandria out of the memories of his time there. If Durrell's imaginary Alexandria is "the capital of memory," as Darley calls it in *Clea*, then Durrell's imaginary island in *The Alexandria Quartet* is the place where memory finds its most fertile ground, a composite of those places where the Mediterranean sensibility has captured what Darley speaks of as the "heart's mind." The island has elements that can be traced not only to Rhodes but to Durrell's Corfu and to other sea-girt places, with or without their "Cycladean simplicities," that he visited at one time or another; its vineyards, olive groves, volcanic remnants, its familiar Greek flora and fauna, and its characteristic rituals inhabit perhaps more islands than anyone's memory could store.

Still, two moments in Durrell's Greek experience seem to have been most influential in shaping Darley's imagination during his island retreat, especially as it appears in *Clea*: his departure by caique from Kalamata for Crete and then Egypt in 1941, and his leaving Rhodes for England and then Argentina in 1947. The first departure early in the war is paralleled by Darley's account of his imaginary island's farewell hospitality toward an Englishman, who becomes a target for "the affection and gratitude of every Greek" now that the war has come "so softly towards us over the waters" and the young men of the island village have gone to Albania "to die among the snows." As Darley slips out of the bay heading toward Egypt in the caique sent by Nessim, the "warm incoherent goodbyes" that "poured out across the white beaches" toward the departing made him exclaim on the beauty of the Greek words of greeting and farewell, and he was soon possessed by exultation mixed with profound sadness. He decides that the war does not portend the end of the so-called civilized world but "simply the end of kindness and safety and moderate ways; the end of the artist's hopes, of nonchalance, of joy."

The date and mode of departure at this point in Darley's story are those of Durrell's Kalamata exodus, but the mood is also that of the author's departure from Rhodes, which he records with something of the same mix of emotions and sense of inevitable loss. Durrell's mission there ended shortly before Rhodes was finally handed back to Greece in early 1948, a transfer of authority that he tells the reader delights him, though his departure "means yet another separation from a country which I have come to recognize as my second home." But the regret has another dimension. His parting encomium to Greece, "born into the sexual intoxication of the light," is coupled with an encomium to Italy "of the domestic arts," where he sees a "passionate feeling for husbandry and family order" as exemplified by a vineyard built "with the fingers, pinch by pinch, into terraces of household wine." Both these countries belong to "the sacred territory" that Durrell is now leaving, as do husband and wife, myrtle and olive, and he thinks it unlucky that this truth "should not have been made plain."

By the end of *Reflections*, the narrator's vision has broadened to include Greece's Mediterranean neighbor, anticipating Darley's preparation for a second departure from Greece at the end of *Clea* (after a brief return at the war's end to help set up a relay station on his old retreat and to settle for the moment in a small house "in the heart of the vineyards"). Though Darley is again living in a "nearly ideal present," he foresees the change that will come with imported money, which will slowly alter the island's economy, displace labor at inflated prices, create needs that the inhabitants did not have before, and eventually destroy "the tightly woven fabric of this feudal village with its tense blood-relationships, its feuds and archaic festivals." The symmetrical

wholeness of the place "will dissolve under these alien pressures."
He now recognizes that the idyll cannot last, and in any case his
post will soon come to an end. He writes Clea that his mind has
been turning more and more toward the West, toward "the old
inheritance of Italy or France."

Durrell's departure from Greece in 1947 was a culmination
that he did not fully recognize at the time but that must have begun to work into his consciousness while he was finishing the
manuscript of *Reflections* in Belgrade, where he was serving as
press attaché at the British Embassy, five years later, and even
more insistently during the writing of *Clea* some eleven years
later, when he had settled in southern France with the writer
Claude Forde, soon to be his third wife. By that time he had been
back to Greece briefly in 1952, and had lived in Cyprus for three
years as both teacher of English and Director of Information Services for the British. During those years he had also kept up, by
correspondence and occasional meetings, with both his older
prewar friends—Seferis, Katsimbalis, Stephanides, Spencer—and
a younger group of British writers with whom he had become ac-
quainted during and after the war: among others, Patrick Leigh
Fermor, Xan Fielding, and Rex Warner. But his shifting political
outlook eventually led to a further separation from some of his
Greek friends, for he became ardently anti-Communist and con-
siderably more conservative, even if we temper his remark, in a
1949 letter to Theodore Stephanides, that what he was seeing in
Yugoslavia had turned him "firmly reactionary and a Tory." But
more important in the context of his association with Greece, he
began to reveal during his days on Cyprus an allegiance to British
policy regarding the island that he himself did not fully acknowl-
edge, especially when his duties as Director of Information Services came to include "cultural" and other less subtle forms of
British propaganda.

George Seferis was especially distressed by what he perceived
to be a crucial change in Durrell's political posture. He apparently

expected that in Cyprus his young friend would remain consistently partial to Greece's national interest and persistently ironic about his British compatriots, as he had been during his early days in Greece and even during his wartime service as press officer in Egypt. Seferis's journal entry for October 1, 1954—that is, while Durrell was in his second year on Cyprus—reports on a conversation with one M.C. (probably their mutual friend Maurice Cardiff), who tells him that Durrell had become, since his time in Yugoslavia, "very nationalist" and no longer capable of thinking for himself: "if they [i.e., the British] regard it as essential for Cyprus to be part of the Empire, so be it." Seferis then recalls the time when Durrell gave the five-finger sign of contempt to English generals in Cairo, and, before that, when he cursed England during his days as a pacifist.

Whatever the precise coloring of Durrell's pro-British sentiments while he was Director of Information Services on Cyprus—is it possible, after all, to think of him being less than pro-British once he accepted that office?—one of his biographers reports that by 1957, after his book on Cyprus, *Bitter Lemons*, appeared, Durrell felt that he had compromised himself too much ever to return to the island or to Greece. No source is given for these sentiments, and Durrell did in fact return to Greece several times during the 1960s, but he did so only for short visits; during one such visit in 1963 he told an interviewer that the problem with Greece was that you could find a perfect paradise there in April only to find it overrun by Scandinavian tourists in August. At one point, discovering that things in Greece were cheap and the tax on foreigners minimal, he and his new wife, Claude, had apparently considered the possibility of looking for a place to live in Greece, but on returning to France the prospect seemed less appealing, and France is where they settled thereafter once and for all.

Though Durrell met Seferis and Katsimbalis briefly at least twice during the 1960s and was visited by Katsimbalis once in

France, the Englishman's parting from Athens in March 1947 seems in retrospect to have the aura of a last supper for the little band of prewar friends, with Henry Miller attending in more than spirit. In July of that year, Durrell wrote to his American friend from Bournemouth, England, to describe this "little meeting" the evening before he flew off from Athens. Seferis, Katsimbalis, Ghika, and Durrell's new friend Rex Warner gathered in a "quiet booklined room" (Seferis's?) to listen to a record Miller had sent Durrell and to hear Miller's "burring" voice read out several "long ghostly sequences" from his *Tropic of Cancer*. The strangeness of hearing his friend's voice in this way took Durrell back to his days with Miller in Paris and Corfu. Seferis and Katsimbalis had tears in their eyes, he reports. When it came time to say goodbye to them, Durrell gave them the record, and they thanked him as if he had given them "a portion of you, a hand or an arm or a voice." Durrell then imagines Seferis "there alone now listening to [the record] and shaking his head with that sad smile as he repeats: 'Ah Miller, Miller, what a fellow.' "

That record was not the only parting gift. In collaboration with Bernard Spencer and Nanos Valaoritis, Durrell translated a selection of Seferis's poetry into English while he was on Rhodes, and this thin volume, *The King of Asine and Other Poems*, was completed as he left the island. (He gave it to John Lehman for publication in London the following year.) Rex Warner, then working for the British Council in Athens, wrote the introduction and eventually translated a larger selection. But Durrell's promotion of Seferis's work, first in the *Personal Landscape* issues during their Cairo years and subsequently in *The King of Asine and Other Poems*, brought Seferis his first substantial recognition abroad, even if this and later mutual gestures of affection failed in the end to insulate their friendship against the cooling influence of politics.

In August 1944 Durrell had written Henry Miller to say that he had a wonderful idea for a novel set in Alexandria, "the nexus for all news of Greece, side by side with a sort of spiritual butcher's shop with girls on slabs," but he wouldn't be able to make that "big effort" until he was free. A month later he tells Miller that the "action" of his long-standing work in progress, called "The Book of the Dead," has now shifted to Alexandria—presumably in keeping with his impulse to write a new novel set there—and that he has made the two central characters twins, but he hasn't got "enough force to work on it even if I had the leisure." By the time he reaches Athens in 1945, we learn from his friend Buffie Johnson that he walked the streets with George Katsimbalis and spoke of wanting to write a book set in Athens but that Katsimbalis told him it would be a mistake: if he did write such a book, he could never live there again, because Athens was too small a world, and his acquaintances, thinking themselves caricatured, would turn on him with vitriolic rage. This may have confirmed Durrell's earlier impulse to focus his "big effort" on Alexandria, a crucial relocation of his imaginary city. We have seen that some of the invention which went into Durrell's image of the Greek paradise in the postwar years, especially during his idyll on Rhodes, was transformed into a fictional mode by the time he came to write *The Alexandria Quartet*, finding its ultimate expression in Darley's Aegean island retreat, so essential to the rehabilitation of the narrator's memory. One is tempted to think that Durrell's two years in Greece after the war also showed him how he might use his knowledge of Athens and its cosmopolitan imagery in shaping his fictional Alexandria. If so, Durrell's long voyage of discovery that began in Corfu before the war and ended with his flight out of Athens in 1947 had finally taken a direction that would lead him to the Ithaka which both he and Henry Miller took for granted from the start of their friendship was somewhere out there on the English writer's horizon.

During the same postwar period, the several years after Seferis had returned from exile in Egypt and South Africa, the poet's long Odyssean voyage, which had begun in 1933 "on rotten brine-soaked timbers," also took a new direction that led to his own highly personal, purely Greek image of Ithaka. We saw in his 1942 "Stratis Thalassinos Among the Agapanthi" that his contemporary Odysseus, at that time in Transvaal, was surrounded by alien flora and a creed he couldn't understand, and longed for the language of his homeland flowers, the asphodels, violets, and hyacinths that might help him talk to the shades in Hades who would guide him to his island home. That *nostos*, the desired return to Ithaka, did not come easily to the poet's imagination, and when it did, the home island for the exercise of his creative spirit proved to be Poros, whose streets he and Miller and Katsimbalis had sailed through in a holiday mood during their prewar voyage into the Greek light. Then, he had thought of Poros as a kind of "cocotte's bedroom" for "eminent international lovers." But Seferis's return to Poros in the fall of 1946 came after eight or nine years of the kind of government service that had turned his nighttime dreams into "performances" of his public life and filled his daytime monologues with like "exclamations." This meant to Seferis, as he wrote in his journal, that he was carrying "a great deal of filth" inside him that had to go.

The beginning of his release from bad dreams and monologues came on October 2, 1946, when he took advantage of a two-month leave of absence granted him by the Ministry of Foreign Affairs to retreat to his sister-in-law's place on Poros, a Victorian villa in Pompeian red appropriately called Galini (Serenity). Here he hoped to revive his exhausted spirit and once again serve his first mistress, his muse. Within a few days of his arrival he begins to write notes for a poem and fragmentary lines that make him think he is "climbing up words as though a rope ladder." He returns to his critical commentary on Cavafy, a project he had started in Pretoria and then set aside, but he's not sure that he's in "Cavafy's climate," and he finds reading articles about him boring. Instead he reads the *Iliad*, and Matthew Arnold, and Eliot's *Four Quartets*. He swims and takes walks, heads for the open air to provide relief from the "hothouse atmosphere of Poros." More fragments of poetry follow, though the beauty outside the house interrupts his work, and he begins to think he had better close the shutters during the daytime and continue under electric light. Clouds, rain, winter approach "with infinite gentleness." By mid-October he reports, "I don't think of anything now."

Then a remarkable thing happens. At dawn on October 21, voices wake him calling out, "The sun! The sun." He opens the window to find the "sun's disk huge, still bit into by the horizon," its color as he had never before seen it: a touch lighter than blackberry juice. Several hours later, alone in the house, the sun now higher, he goes out onto the veranda facing the sea and encounters a scene at the edge of mystery:

> You couldn't distinguish the light from the silence, the silence and light from the serenity. Sometimes you could pick up a sound, a distant voice, a faint chirping. But these were somehow *closed in elsewhere*, like the beat of your heart that you felt for a moment and then forgot. The sea didn't have a surface; only, the hills opposite didn't end at the earth's margin but continued beyond and below, starting over again with a dimmer image of their shape that vanished gently into the depths of a void. A feeling that there is another face to life. (I write with difficulty, trying to avoid generic words, trying to *describe* this indescribable thing.) You discerned the sea's surface by looking into the distance to see the oars as they dipped into the water with a dry gleam, like a windowpane slashed by the sun . . . A feeling that if the slightest fissure were to open up in this closed-in vision, everything at the four points of the horizon would spill out and leave you naked and alone, begging alms, murmuring inexact words, without this extraordinary precision you had seen.

Seferis then returns to his room dizzy, "almost a visionary," and closes the shutters so as to let in only "the dim light of the north." He now records the following fragment of poetry:

> *Contours of mountains, contours of sounds.*
> *Smoke under the nostrils of a god.*
> *A tree's leaf that's only a leaf is not a leaf.*
> *And you are in a large house with many windows open*
> *and you run from room to room, not knowing from where*
> > *to look out first*
> *lest the pine-trees vanish . . .*

The next morning Seferis begins the greatest of his Odyssean re-creations, the long, three-part poem called "*Thrush*," and he completes it in just ten days.

The poem is colored throughout by the history and recent drama of his experience on Poros, but the full force of that experience is reserved for the brilliant ending. The opening section is subtitled "The house near the sea," that is, Galini, which Seferis will tell his friend Katsimbalis, in an open letter on the poem published several years later, "gave me, for the first time in years, the feeling of a substantial home rather than a temporary camp-site." The poem begins with a rumination on houses and their character that is subtly highlighted by images which suggest nostalgia for Seferis's lost childhood home in Smyrna, his experience of exile over the years, and his return finally to a house that has the feel of permanence:

> *The houses I had they took away from me. The times*
> *happened to be unpropitious: war, destruction, exile;*
> *sometimes the hunter hits the migratory birds,*
> *sometimes he doesn't hit them. Hunting*
> *was good in my time, many felt the pellet;*
> *the rest circle aimlessly or go mad in the shelters.*

Don't talk to me about the nightingale or the lark
or the little wagtail
inscribing figures with his tail in the light;
I don't know much about houses
I know they have their nature, nothing else.
New at first, like babies
who play in gardens with the tassels of the sun,
they embroider colored shutters and shining doors
over the day.
When the architect's finished, they change,
they frown or smile or even grow resentful
with those who stayed behind, with those who went away
with others who'd come back if they could
or others who disappeared, now that the world's become
an endless hotel.

I don't know much about houses,
I remember their joy and their sorrow
sometimes, when I stop to think . . .

In the poem's second part, "Sensual Elpenor," we witness an encounter between two figures who appear below the persona's window in the prewar "hothouse atmosphere" of Poros to engage in an erotic dialogue: modern versions of Circe and Elpenor, presumably members, along with Odysseus, of the poet's mythical "eminent international" set which comes for sensual pleasure to this luxurious and indolent equivalent of Circe's island. Seferis tells Katsimbalis that the broken erotic dialogue between Elpenor and Circe leads nowhere in part because Elpenor can't bring himself to be directly seductive, say by using Cavafy's open eroticism in his approach to her. Instead he persists in using lyrical images from Seferis's early verse, talk about bending statues that divide desire in two like a peach and so forth, which Circe can curtly dismiss. But the encounter fails mainly because Circe has eyes only for sailor Odysseus, who is down by the seashore, about to leave her and set out for his visit to the underworld—this just as a radio on the light-flooded beach brings news of imminent war.

The third and final section of the poem (subtitled in two parts: "The wreck 'Thrush'" and "The light") delivers us to the long-awaited *nostos* as the Odyssean figure returns to Poros after the war's end to discover a sunken ship called "*Thrush*" that carries the voices of the dead in its dark underworld, shades who will tell him what he needs to know in order to reach "the light" that will come to represent his Ithaka. From Homer he learns that the weak companions of his voyage were denied their homecoming because they committed the hubris of eating the cattle of the Sun and so can no longer face either the sun or man, the two defining elements of the Greek homeland. From the shade of Socrates he learns about justice by way of Socrates' apology before his critics and by the example of his death: this ancient teacher was a man who preferred to be an unjust victim rather than to do injustice to others. And from blind Oedipus, father of the fratricidal sons Eteocles and Polynices, he learns about compassion and reconciliation as this tragic figure of belated wisdom crosses "the invisible fields" to his wondrous death.

The persona's final lesson comes with "The light" that signals his homecoming. This light is both angelic and black, qualities that belong both to this world and to another, the apparently conflicting attributes unified in the visionary moment that concludes his poem, what Seferis told his French translator Robert Levesque was "an affirmation of a moment of dazzling and eternal life." It is the kind of visionary moment that the poet experienced on the veranda of the Villa Galini and that freed him to bring his Odyssean voyage to a lyrical culmination:

> Day, angelic and black;
> the brackish taste of woman that poisons the prisoner
> emerges from the wave a cool branch adorned with drops.
> Sing little Antigone, sing, O sing . . .

I'm not speaking to you about things past, I'm speaking
    about love;
adorn your hair with the sun's thorns,
dark girl;
the heart of the Scorpion has set,
the tyrant in man has fled,
and all the daughters of the sea, Nereids, Graeae,
hurry toward the shimmering of the rising godess:
whoever has never loved will love,
in the light;
                    and you find yourself
in a large house with many windows open
running from room to room, not knowing from where
    to look out first,
because the pine trees will vanish, and the mirrored
    mountains, and the chirping of birds
the sea will empty, shattered glass, from north and south
your eyes will empty of the light of day
the way the cicadas all together suddenly fall silent.

The concluding lines echo several that Seferis jotted down on October 21 when he returned to his room "almost a visionary" and closed the shutters against all but "the dim light of the north," yet his journal entry merely confirms what the poem itself conveys of this visionary moment through the allusions, the imagery, and the lyrical rhythm of its ending.

Not that it did so for all readers, including one of Seferis's faithful early critics, Andreas Karandonis, whose "difficulty" with the poem is mentioned at the start of Seferis's open letter on "*Thrush.*" A note to the second edition of that letter tells us that George Katsimbalis initially solicited it and then published it in the journal he edited after the war, the *Anglo-Hellenic Review*, in order to help the well-intentioned reader understand more easily a poem whose difficulties the author acknowledged. As readers in

Greece became more familiar with the modernist mode—especially that of T. S. Eliot, whom Seferis had first translated before the war and retranslated later—Seferis apparently decided the poem was more approachable, and his reluctance to give authority to any particular interpretation of it, including his own, then became acute: the second edition of the letter to Katsimbalis is only a fragment of the original. Yet one point he made in the original version of the letter, about his Homeric source, gives us a crucial clue to the significance of the poem's progress from sensual Elpenor's dialogue with Circe to the visionary moment that concludes the poem's Odyssean voyage: "Notice this: Circe of the fleshly sensations, of sensual pleasure, sends us to the other world, to the dead, so that they can show us the *nostos*. And the truth is, what we call eroticism heavily burdens—as many examples indicate—man's nostalgia and his effort to achieve a final liberation, what some call a return to a lost paradise and others union with God."

Given Seferis's imagery since his 1935 *Mythistorema*, with its beautiful islands "somewhere round about here where we grope" and its blossoming almond trees and gleaming marble "a little farther" ahead, he surely conceived the Odyssean *nostos* early on as a return to a lost paradise that was just out of reach. And it remained so during his wartime exile in Africa, where his Stratis Thalassinos found it impossible to talk to the dead and therefore couldn't "go forward any further." Now, by the end of "*Thrush*," it seems not only that his Odyssean persona has reached some version of the lost paradise but that the impulse which led Seferis there emerged from what his journal calls a "feeling that there is another face to life." This feeling ended up as "an affirmation of a moment of dazzling and eternal life."

Some nine months after the Poros experience, Seferis's journal records a second visionary moment that would seem to be further evidence of his new perspective. One day in July 1947, he feels a "need to see the sun," and when he goes out for a long walk things are revealed to him with such clarity that it is as if he has "the *serious* feeling of a sudden hallucination in the heart of day [his underlining]." Returning home, what he does in fact *see* (also his underlining) against the rock and marble of the Acropolis is the tall skeleton of a woman, "bones pure white, gazing at me with a proud air, like the ghost of some hero." She gazes at him from a world that is no longer today's but a future world "where nothing of what I know, things and people, had survived," and he feels the same love for this pure white skeleton in the sun that he now has "for life with all its beautiful and evil things." He concludes: "I have the impression that I saw a moment of eternity."

There is no doubt that Seferis reached a turning point during his days of leave on Poros, a cleansing of his spirit and a vision of possibilities that resulted in the kind of liberation which brought forth his most ambitious poem to that date and which satisfied his muse for another six or seven years. And his moment of illumination on the veranda of Galini, the house by the sea, along with the second moment some months later, no doubt encouraged him to develop the visionary dimension of his subsequent work, for example, what takes the form of an apparition (called an Assumption) in "Engomi," in his 1955 Cyprus volume, and the recurring association of "light" with "resurrection" in his 1966 *Three Secret Poems.*

In his open letter to Katsimbalis, Seferis tells his friend that he can see himself being accused of robbing the grave of Yannopoulos—the writer Katsimbalis portrayed for Henry Miller as so intoxicated by the Greek sky, mountains, sea, islands, and vegetables even that he killed himself—but, be that as it may, Seferis continues to believe that "there is a process of humanization in the Greek light." He might have added that the last section of "*Thrush*" also suggests that there is a process of transcendence in the Greek light, even if the process remains imprecise. It would be going too far to claim that Seferis's *nostos* in the third part of the poem returned his persona not only to a lost paradise but to something approaching a union with God in a Christian sense, for the poet's lyrical, allusive rendering of Odysseus' arrival at "The light" is beyond any precise prose exegesis using religious terms. (The allusions are anyway eclectic, more pagan than Christian.) And at the very end the poet has avoided describing what he himself called "the indescribable," offering us not a representation of his vision of "another face to life," eternal or otherwise, but images of things of this world that are meant to evoke the appropriate feel of a transcendent moment—things that will pass out of sight and hearing when the vision is gone.

Or so it seems. As Seferis himself says to Katsimbalis, "no one explains the light: one sees it." And in his poetry, at least in the original, one also hears it. But the poet's prose commentary helps. With that and our own response to his lyrical representation of the persona's homecoming, we leave the poem sensing that it has an otherworldly dimension new to Seferis's work. In the end it affirms agape over eros, and it points toward a possibility that Seferis himself called "eternal life." We also leave the poem knowing that his modern Odysseus has arrived, primarily by way of Homer, Socrates, and the ancient tragedians, at a new moral perspective and an access to reconciliation. The vision of home in the Greek light, which Seferis's persona had little hope of seeing while groping for those islands just out of reach some thirteen years earlier or while silenced by the agapanthi of Transvaal during the war, was finally realized.

If the publication of "*Thrush*" in March 1947 signaled both an end of Seferis's Odyssean voyage and the beginning of a new illumination in his work, the mood of postwar reconciliation beyond his poetry was not long-lived. A journal entry in December 1946 records that he is leaving Poros "toward the unknown," as he left Crete in 1941, now "with certain 'ideas' about the *light*" that he considers the most important thing "I've 'discovered' " since the ship of his return entered Greek waters, but by February in the new year he feels himself on an Argonaut expedition caught between many clashing rocks, pelted by stones, on his feet again half-dead yet going on, "a mindless visionary in the golden light of the sea." The publication of "*Thrush*" brings no relief from what he feels to be the dark reality of his life in Athens. In April his journal reports, "The situation around me is unhealthy, damned, I'd say, in this swamp of souls and bodies to which Greece has sunk." The following month we learn that his public life "is an internecine jungle: with fraud, with slander, with cowardice, with shamelessness." And a month after that: "From the middle of May until now I've been swimming in public sewers." Then, in need of the sun, he goes out to encounter the skeletal apparition that leads him to the vision of a future world where nothing that he knows has survived, and beyond that, to a moment of eternity. But the known present cannot be so easily transcended: ten days after this otherworldly experience a journal entry takes up the theme of "parting" in a way that foreshadows not only the poet's return to a kind of peacetime exile but also the final dissolution of the little band of friends who together had once worked to create their individual images of an earthly paradise which, more often than not, Greek gods had presided over.

The relevant entry, dated July 23, 1947, introduces the theme by quoting a line from Cavafy: after a conference at the Ministry of Coordination, Seferis hears "musical instruments of the mysterious procession," and he then reports, "The hour has come." The music of this invisible procession heralds the departure of the god who presides over Antony's last days and abandons him before the battle of Actium: Dionysus in Plutarch, Hercules in Shakespeare, the city of Alexandria in Cavafy's poem "The God Abandons Antony." In that poem, Antony is urged to face the departure of divine Alexandria, home of his delectation, with courage and with no illusions, as is fitting in one who proved worthy of such a city. In his journal Seferis develops this theme with reference to Henry Miller's departure from Athens in the winter of 1939: "I remembered . . . how difficult it was for him, until he made his decision: 'Now I don't care any longer,' he said, 'I've felt the finger of Fate.' " And Seferis goes on to report what a friend had said when bidding him goodbye the previous evening: "When a country hinders you from thinking logically, you must leave it behind." Seferis concludes the entry with a laconic gesture of agreement: "With people, with cities, that's how it is."

Clearly Seferis was anticipating his own departure from Athens six months hence, on assignment to the embassy in Ankara, Turkey. Not only was he accepting, as Miller did, what Fate decreed, but in keeping with Cavafy's admonition he was avoiding any illusions about what happened: since leaving Poros his everyday life had prevented him from thinking properly, and the time had arrived for him to move into the future with courage. When he did so early in 1948 (after an unexplained operation in the Evangelismos hospital), his journal reports that the thought of Ankara had worried him but that during the trip to his new assignment he became unburdened. Now he thinks he prefers anything to the confinement of Athens—"the mental confinement, I mean." What he means specifically is the "enslavement" of his life at the ministry, he goes on to say, and, in literature, both the threat that you will be charged with the ideas of others if you speak your mind fully and the threat to the Greek language from fanaticism. He concludes, "One must get out."

What Seferis did not know at the time was that his departure from Athens would be the beginning of a fourteen-year period abroad—Ankara, London, Beirut, New York, London again—with only a short return to the homeland in 1956–57. For him, as for his friend Lawrence Durrell, the fate that he invoked in the summer of 1947 led to a long separation from the country called Greece, source of his richest imaginary landscape. The separation for both Seferis and Durrell was not so final as Henry Miller's, but it allowed both of them, as it had allowed Miller, to move on to new sources for an imaginary landscape in another country. The poems in Seferis's next volume, published almost a decade later, are set largely in Cyprus. Durrell's most important subsequent work of fiction, published a little more than a decade later, is set mostly in Egypt, with gestures toward an Aegean landscape. And Henry Miller, having bought and settled into a house in Big Sur in 1947, takes that for the setting of his next image of paradise in *Big Sur and the Oranges of Hieronymus Bosch*, published exactly a decade later. For each of these, Greece had served at a crucial time to liberate the imagination and to provide the richest ground for a country of metaphor and myth. By the end of 1947, it had completed its best work for the two foreign visitors, and in the case of Seferis, it again had to wait some years for the sailor's homecoming.

Two weeks after Durrell sent Miller his report on the nostalgic last evening in Athens in March 1947, with their Athenian friends listening to the record of Miller reading, Miller wrote to thank him for the return gift of an "incomparable" recording of voices out of the past, which Durrell had apparently sent him in the meanwhile. The voices are not identified, but they fully roused Miller's nostalgia and his longing for a reunion. He tells Durrell that he would "come a-running if he could" but that "it seems each one of us is being made to play his own part, go his own way, just at the moment," though he feels that "the time for reunions is soon." At the end of his letter he returns to those voices to say that, hearing them, he couldn't believe that eight years had gone by since the two of them last met. And he adds, "I remember vividly how I parted from you—in the rain up there in the mountains. Or how I parted from Katsimbalis. Partings, partings. Enough of them. More reunions, I say."

There were to be several reunions with Durrell and one with Katsimbalis, but not for some time, and none on Greek soil. Had Miller actually come a-running soon after he said he wanted to in

1947, he would have found the mood of Athens very much changed and his friends scattered. Durrell was in England, on his way to Argentina. Seferis was off to Turkey and then London. Stephanides was in England working in a hospital. Antoniou was at sea again on the cruise ships *Achilles* and *Agamemnon*. Ghika was now a professor of drawing at the Athens Polytechnic Institute. Only Katsimbalis was where he always was: editing others, then eating and talking the night away in some Athenian taverna—his roaring voice still capable of filling the four horizons, according to Durrell—but he was thinner, more contemplative, less flamboyant than the Colossus Miller had portrayed. The American sensed this postwar change in the posture and circumstances of his Greek friends. He had written Durrell early in 1947 to say that he couldn't muster the courage to write Katsimbalis and Seferis: "I allowed too long a silence to intervene. Besides, what can I say to people who are desperate?" It may well be that, despite his nostalgia, what kept Miller from ever returning to Greece was an astute if pained recognition that the country he had left could never again be the country that had so stimulated his imagination, as he had predicted would be the case early in the war. Now, in 1947, he must have seen with full clarity that the mythmaking Greek journey could no longer be what it had once been to him in either freewheeling pleasure or inspiration, and that the little band of friends could never be a band again.

Still, the invention they inspired had an abundant legacy. Writing to his editor Anne Ridler from Rhodes, Durrell declared, "I'm afraid that we've had a bad influence, Henry's and I's [*sic*] books about Greece. It is becoming a cult"—and he adds with sublime exaggeration: "In the last few weeks the number of poets who are compiling anthologies called SALUTE TO GREECE has risen." His claim then engenders a mock solicitation from a made-up poet for a contribution to "a strong powerful anthology dedicated to Greece," Durrell's work to appear beside contributions by "Sheila Sniggs, Roly Besom, and John Baller," and anticipated contributions by T. S. Eliot, Henry Miller, and Max Beerbohm. The solicitation concludes: "While we cannot pay . . ."

There is an element of truth inside the mockery of this immodest self-appraisal, even if it was a bit premature. In due course *The Colossus of Maroussi*, *Prospero's Cell*, and *Reflections on a Marine Venus*—the first of these in particular—projected an image of Greece that was, however heightened by imaginative rhetoric, very contagious. Many English-speaking travelers in the postwar years—in fact, most subsequent English and American writers—who took the Greek journey, or who wanted to, were drawn there by the country Miller and Durrell had created and by the liberated sensibility they had caused it to project. And those who took the trouble to search out the work of their Greek companions—the poets Katsimbalis promoted, his friend Seferis first of all—discovered further riches that our two early voyagers were among the first to bring to light and celebrate.

The generation of writers who immediately followed Miller and Durrell to Greece was much in their debt for opening up new ways of seeing the country and a new style for rendering what was seen, but the approach of this younger generation was more firmly grounded in Greece's historical reality, and their imaginative projection of it, while generally less expansive, was also less colored by rhetorical flourishing. The Peloponnese in the books written by Kevin Andrews and Patrick Leigh Fermor is rooted in the contemporary history of the place, in the warfare that has scarred its villages, in the idiosyncrasies of language and custom and ritual that have created the particular character of its people. Philip Sherrard's various portraits of Greece highlight the religious and poetic traditions that still define the country's living culture, and his perspective provides full warning of the damage to the Greek landscape from contemporary progress even while it illuminates the enduring beauty of the natural world. All of these American and British writers who came to Greece during the war or immediately after were more than visitors, short or long term.

They married the country for better or for worse, lived with it through times of romance and disillusionment and rejuvenation, and remained faithful to their belief in the vitality of its gifts into the last decade of this century. Their story is another story, in part mine as well, and that being so, this seems to me the right moment to end this story, before I'm tempted to start another in the inimitable first-person mode of my elders.

BIBLIOGRAPHICAL NOTE

The English versions of Greek poetry quoted in this book, unless otherwise indicated, come from the following collections:

D. I. Antoniou, in *Six Poets of Modern Greece*. Chosen, translated, and introduced by Edmund Keeley and Philip Sherrard. New York: Alfred A. Knopf, 1961.

C. P. Cavafy. *Collected Poems*. Translated by Edmund Keeley and Philip Sherrard, edited by George Savidis. Rev. ed. Princeton, N.J.: Princeton University Press, 1992.

Odysseus Elytis. *The Axion Esti*. Translated and annotated by Edmund Keeley and George Savidis. 2nd printing, English only. Pittsburgh: University of Pittsburgh Press, 1979.

Odysseus Elytis, in *Voices of Modern Greece*. Translated and edited by Edmund Keeley and Philip Sherrard. Princeton, N.J.: Princeton University Press, 1981.

Yannis Ritsos. *Repetitions, Testimonies, Parentheses*. Translated by Edmund Keeley. Princeton, N.J.: Princeton University Press, 1991.

George Seferis. *Collected Poems*. Translated, edited, and introduced by Edmund Keeley and Philip Sherrard. Rev. ed. Princeton, N.J.: Princeton University Press, 1995. The spelling of quotations from this volume has been Americanized.

Angelos Sikelianos. *Selected Poems*. Translated and introduced by Edmund Keeley and Philip Sherrard. 2nd bilingual ed. Athens and London: Denise Harvey (Publisher), 1996.

NOTES

In the notes that follow, a source is cited in full the first time only, thereafter appearing as a short title. Sources for the English versions of poems by Antoniou, Cavafy, Elytis, Ritsos, Seferis, and Sikelianos are cited in full in the Bibliographical Note.

1. THE FIRST EDEN

PAGE

3 "holding their breath": *The Durrell-Miller Letters 1935–1980*, edited by Ian S. MacNiven (New York, 1988), 123.

"War is not just war": *Hamlet*, Vol. 2 (New York, 1941), 387.

4 "like that! . . . the paradise of the over-driven scribes": *Letters*, 119.

"the dim alarm": Ibid., 126.

5 "where man is nil": Ibid., 125.

"Return to Corfu": Ibid., 127.

"passionate about his own country": Henry Miller, *The Colossus of Maroussi* (New York, 1958), 46.

"had begun to ripen": Ibid., 47.

6 "how much I envied your patriotism": Letter to Seferis, February 16, 1971. This letter, and other previously unpublished letters from Miller to Seferis

quoted below, are in the George Seferis Collection, Manuscript Division, Department of Rare Books and Special Collections, Princeton University Library.

"Situation in Europe": George Seferis, *Meres* [*Days*], 3 (Athens, 1984), 112. The quotations from Seferis's journal here and elsewhere (that is, in vols. 3–6) are translated by me. The passage from Homer, translated by Robert Fagles, appears in *The Odyssey*, Book 9, ll. 125–29 (Penguin Books, 1997), 215.

"we are living in a time": *Meres*, 3, 114.

7 "bright articles about politics": Ibid., 112.

"quazi-fascist rhetoric": Richard Clogg, *A Concise History of Greece* (Cambridge, England, 1992), 119.

8 "we have to face the fact": *Meres*, 3, 119.

"in this fog": Ibid., 126.

"the first Anglo-Saxon writers": Ibid., 131.

"with deep feeling . . . a human phenomenon": *Colossus*, 239.

9 "Katsimbalis, who is brilliant": Ioanna Tsatsos, *My Brother George Seferis*, translated by Jean Demos (Minneapolis, 1982), 206.

"That, that—you know what": In conversation with the author.

10 "the most learned man": *Colossus*, 17.

"queenliness": Ibid., 48.

16 "That man walks along weeping": "Narration," in *Logbook I*, George Seferis, *Collected Poems*, 126.

18 "*hypocrite lecteur!*": Baudelaire, Preface to *Les Fleurs du mal* (via T. S. Eliot, *The Waste Land*).

"Spring shakes the windows": Bernard Spencer, "A Spring Wind," *Collected Poems* (Oxford, 1981), 48.

20 "laying it on": *Colossus*, 4.

"Miller, you will like Greece": Ibid., 14.

"contradictoriness, confusion . . . easy to reach": Ibid., 6.

"like an animal": Ibid., 8.

21 "It remains in my memory": Ibid., 11.

"Seeing lovers sitting": Ibid.

"the naked strength of the people": Ibid., 11–12.

22 "every Greek dreams": Ibid., 7.

"with all their machine-made luxuries": Ibid., 6.

"the more nostalgic we grow . . . timeless, tireless routine": *Greece*, text by Henry Miller, drawings by Anne Poor (New York, 1964), 21.

23 most likely all these simple folk": Ibid., 30.
   "we are offering them": Ibid., 48.
24 "columns whose burden": George Seferis, *Collected Poems*, 41.
25 "Out of the sea . . . moving their heavy burdens": *Colossus*, 13.
   "might still behave like human beings": Ibid.
   "completely detached from Europe": Ibid., 14.
   "with the full consciousness": Ibid., 14–15.
26 "God's magic": Ibid., 15.

2. ISLAND OF THE ALMOST BLEST

27 in the hamlet of Kalami: See Ian MacNiven, *Lawrence Durrell: A Biography* (London, 1998), 126.
28 "goodish beginning": *Letters*, 82.
   "lame and halting": Lawrence Durrell, Preface, *The Black Book* (New York, 1960), 13.
   "spiritual and sexual etiolation": Ibid., 14.
   "You enter Greece": Lawrence Durrell, *Prospero's Cell* (London, 1962), 11.
   "To know [Greece] thoroughly": *Greece*, 45.
29 the dominant post-Byronic mode: See David Roessel's dissertation "In Byron's Shadow: Modern Greece in English and American Literature from 1831–1914," submitted to the Department of English, Princeton University, January 1997.
   "About 3 this morning": *Edward Lear: The Corfu Years*, edited and introduced by Philip Sherrard (Athens, 1988), 39–41.
30 "I am almost thanking God": Ibid., 21.
   "sitting on the yellow shore": *The Travels of Edward Lear*, Introduction by Fani-Maria Tsigakou (London, 1983), 11.
31 "an English gentleman": *The Corfu Years*, 31.
   "was to demean itself": Ibid., 16.
32 "the island is, if possible, lovelier": Ibid., 141.
   "a weary day": Ibid., 144.
   "shrieky shrieky music": Ibid., 151.
   "There was an Old Man": *Travels*, 15.
   "there is just now perfect quiet": *The Corfu Years*, 160.
33 "accursed picnic parties": Ibid.
   "moony miracles": Ibid., 162.
34 "so immersed and desolated": Ibid., Appendix 2, 237.

35 even if the dates are not historically accurate: See MacNiven, *Lawrence Durrell*, 293.

"the waking world": *Prospero's Cell*, 11.

"old fisherman's house": Ibid., 12.

36 "a heroic blue arc": Ibid., 13.

"The hill runs clear up": Ibid., 12.

"seem of almost mythological quality . . . a firmness and modesty": Ibid., 14.

"some new world Armenian newspapers": Ibid.

"The gold and moving blue": Ibid., 20.

37 "possessor of the dryest": Ibid., 15.

"reincarnation of the comic professor": Ibid.

38 An early photograph: *Nea Estia* (October 1980), 1455.

"sufficient for *field* work": Gerald Durrell, *My Family and Other Animals* (Penguin Books, 1977), 79.

39 "*well developed*": Ibid., 259.

"Really, Theodore . . . If it were anywhere": Ibid., 259–60.

40 "Eden": *Prospero's Cell*, 19.

"fresh springs": Shakespeare, *The Tempest*, I, 2.

"possessor of a literary mind": *Prospero's Cell*, 78.

"the gravity and charm": Ibid., 77.

"not the *interpretation*": Ibid.

"remarkable flights": Ibid.

"chain of reasoning": Ibid., 78.

41 "dark viscous raisin jam": Ibid.

"wouldst give me": *The Tempest*, I, 2.

"a south-west blow on ye": Ibid.

"almost too obvious an anagram": *Prospero's Cell*, 79.

"And thy broom-groves": *The Tempest*, IV, 1.

"were *out of the country*": *Prospero's Cell*, 80.

"skeptical good humour": Ibid., 81.

"drenched in the silver": Ibid., 60.

42 "peculiar sentimentalities": Ibid., 62.

"like earnest mastodons": Ibid., 59.

"head thrown back": Ibid., 62.

"build in the gleaming sand": Ibid., 118.

"the wide-eyed fisher-boys": Ibid., 119.

43 *La Semaine Egyptienne*: Cairo (October 21–22, 28, 1941), 42–43. In this connection, Seferis commented wryly to Henry Miller in a 1941 Christmas letter from Pretoria, South Africa, "I have the feeling, as Tonio [Antoniou]

used to say, that I am throwing a bottle into the sea . . . This bottle makes me think of Larry, who instead of posting his letters to me, he publishes them in a Cairo reviews [sic]." Durrell published large segments of this letter, very slightly revised, in the "Epilogue in Alexandria" section of *Prospero's Cell*, the source of the quotations offered here.

"Greece as a living body . . . conforming so marvellously": *Prospero's Cell*, 131.

"Summer": Lawrence Durrell, *Collected Poems* (London, 1960), 187.

44 "baptized [themselves] anew in the raw": *Colossus*, 16.

"a desultory air": Ibid.

"hallucinating descriptions . . . an enthusiastic letter": Ibid., 17.

"completely blotted out . . . remarkable colloquy": Ibid., 18.

45 "where we bit one another": Ibid., 19.

"strange sultry day . . . wading through phantom seas": Ibid., 19–21.

46 "all men ever born": "Song of Myself," 5.

"heavenly fellowship": "Sunday Morning," VII.

47 "In this mountain pass": *Colossus*, 21–22.

"like a song": Ibid., 22.

"shameful scramble": Ibid., 23.

48 "poetic idea comes and goes insistently": "Dareios," C. P. Cavafy, *Collected Poems*, 108.

"on either side of us . . . neither can be enjoyed": *Colossus*, 24.

49 "wonderful period of solitude": Ibid., 40.

"thoroughly and completely lazy": Ibid., 42.

"You know there is a war . . . to become something other than they are": Ibid., 42–43.

"impulsively": Ibid., 43.

3. THE MYTHMAKERS

50 "intelligent and far-seeing": *Colossus*, 25.

51 "far more clearheaded": Ibid., 26.

"classic Belle Epoque aesthete": *Nea Estia* (October 1980), 1331.

52 "great carnivorous gulps": *Colossus*, 29.

"a commemorative . . . This is how I started": *Nea Estia*, 1355.

53 "he writes it, reads it aloud": *Colossus*, 28.

54 "a great element of the tragic": Ibid.

"trickles in the corner of his eyes": "Narration," in *Logbook I*, George Seferis, *Collected Poems*, 126 (see pages 16–17).

55 "always talked against a landscape . . . thyme, sage, tufa": *Colossus*, 30–31.

"a spread eagle performance . . . had ceased to be of human size": Ibid., 39–40.

"a power and a magic": Ibid., 31.

56 "succulent repast": Ibid., 33.

"stalwart friends": Ibid., 35.

"sorry lot": Ibid., 36.

"The Greek has no walls": Ibid., 36–37.

"For stubbornness, courage": Ibid., 37.

57 Xan Fielding: See MacNiven, *Lawrence Durrell*, 219.

"had made a translation": *Colossus*, 37.

"book-learning": Ibid., 42.

"the man who can make": Ibid., 34.

"writing his poems as he walks": Ibid.

58 "Obstacle to what?": The poem's title is this opening line. See *Six Poets of Modern Greece*, 141.

59 "left us useless": Ibid., 142.

"seafaring friend": All these quotations regarding Antoniou, translated by me, are from Seferis's essay of that title, in *Dokimes* [*Essays*], Vol. I (Athens, 1974), 47–49.

60 "wild boar": *Colossus*, 47.

61 "warmth and tenderness . . . it is impressively vast": Ibid., 48–49.

"Our country": *Mythistorema*, No. 10. George Seferis, *Collected Poems*, 14.

62 Seferis's essay on Eliot appears as "Letter to a Foreign Friend" in *On the Greek Style: Selected Essays in Poetry and Hellenism*, translated by Rex Warner and Th. D. Frangopoulos (Boston, 1966), 165–81.

63 "the spirit of eternality . . . special peculiarity": *Colossus*, 46.

"I mean taking the Greek lands": George Seferis, *Modern Greek Poetry: Voice and Myth* (Princeton, 1983), 207 (first published in *The Paris Review*, no. 50, Fall 1970).

"He could look at a headland": *Colossus*, 47.

64 "by the following dawn": George Seferis, *Collected Poems*, 120–21.

"a very great work": Undated, in Durrell's hand, Gennadius archive ("Dear George—yr little piece of autobiography . . .").

The drafts of the poem, with commentary, appear in Yiorgis Yatro-manolakis's book *O Vasilias tis Asinis: I Anaskafi enos Poiimatos* [*The King of Asini: the Excavation of a Poem*] (Athens, 1986).

66 "All morning long": George Seferis, *Collected Poems*, 134.

67 "the power for carving": Ibid., 133.

69 "his way of looking forwards": *Colossus*, 47.
70 "I'm not a writer . . . greater than your Walt Whitman": Ibid., 66–67.
   "there's a difference . . . the true Greek": Ibid., 68.
71 the earth black: Pericles Yannopoulos, *I Elliniki Grammi* [*The Greek Line*] (Athens, 1965), 86.
73 "Autumn, what can I say": Kostas Karyotakis, *Other Worlds Than This*, translated by Rachel Hadas (New Brunswick, N.J., 1994), 145.
74 "Ah, Preveza": "Preveza," in Ibid., 151–52.
75 "terrain of Paradise": From "Otan katevoume . . ." ("When we go down"). My translation.
   In a talk on the poetry: *Dokimes*, Vol. I, 167. My translation.
76 "the true face of Greece": *Odysseus Elytis: Analogies of Light*, edited by Ivar Ivask (Norman, Oklahoma, 1981), 7.
   "the teethmarks of the tropics": George Seferis, *Collected Poems*, 130.
77 "the encircling movement of embrace": *Colossus*, 47.

4. VOYAGING INTO THE LIGHT

78 "down the dank / moldering paths": *The Odyssey*, Book 24, ll. 11 ff., translated by Robert Fagles, 468–69.
80 "vigil . . . / Of feeling life": *Hell* (*L'Inferno*), xxvi, ll. 115 ff., translated by Dorothy L. Sayers (Penguin Books, 1949), 236.
   "Enough of this place": *Ulysses*, Modern Library ed. (1946), 113.
   "other side of the sun": "*Thrush*," III, l. 15, George Seferis, *Collected Poems*, 167.
   "the heart of the Scorpion has set": Ibid., "The light," ll. 44 ff., George Seferis, *Collected Poems*, 169.
81 "as fresh and clean . . . jubilant": *Colossus*, 52.
82 "voyage into the light . . . the sun is man": Ibid., 57.
83 "in a frenzy of self-surrender": Ibid., 53.
   "joy too deep": Ibid.
   "cocotte's bedroom . . . place for eminent": *Meres* [*Days*], 5 (Athens, 1977), 47.
   "the look of a worm": *Angloelliniki Epitheorisi* [*Anglo-Hellenic Review*] (July–August 1950), 503. The translations from this journal here and below are by me.
   "—'Athens. The public has heard' ": "*Thrush*," II, "The radio," l. 25, George Seferis, *Collected Poems*, 166.

84 "In point of truth": *Colossus*, 54.

"war, destruction, exile": *"Thrush*," I, "The house near the sea," l. 2, George Seferis, *Collected Poems*, 161.

85 "the whole human race": *Colossus*, 55.

"like a huge loaf . . . along a path": Ibid., 55–56.

"very epitome of that flawless anarchy": Ibid., 55.

As one critic succinctly remarked: Dora Iliopoulou-Rogan, "Foreword" to Ekdosis Adam, *Ghika* (Athens, 1991), 19.

86 "silent symphonies . . . At the midday hour": "Reflections on Hydra," in *An Investigation of Nationality*, translated by John Leatham (Athens: Efthini, 1985), 17.

free spirit: "Thravsmata" ["Fragments"], *Lexi* 95 (1990), translated by John Leatham.

87 "the monks in Tibet": *Colossus*, 58.

"birth-place . . . the cultural link": "First Impressions of Greece," *Sextet* (Santa Barbara, 1977), 58–60.

88 "dissolves everything in gold dust . . . who is called": Ibid., 60.

"of divine origin": *Colossus*, 58.

89 "(The story of the banker": "First Impressions," 60.

"waiting to fall on us": *Colossus*, 62.

"a mythological animal": "First Impressions," 61.

90 "marks an important step . . . vitally important": Ibid., 63.

"now in exile": Ibid., 62.

"to be discreet . . . an extemporaneous fellow": *Colossus*, 65–66.

91 "fucked her way to fame": "First Impressions," 63.

"fat fellow . . . Funny, you like it here": *Colossus*, 64–65.

92 "a fat sow . . . a discarded tin can": "First Impressions," 62–63.

"most everything else": *Colossus*, 65.

"meaningless babble . . . Smoke a Murad!": "First Impressions," 64.

93 "an absurd simulacrum": From John Fowles's introduction to his collection *The Greek Experience*, edited by Circe Kefalea (published in Athens by Olkos in 1996, in a translation by Circe Kefalea; the English version, still largely unpublished, includes *Behind the Magus* [London: Colophon Press, 1994]).

"rather like village schoolmasters . . . a jewel, a paradise": *Behind the Magus*, 14.

94 "floating under Venus . . . isolated, framed": *The Magus: A Revised Version* (Boston, 1977), 50–51.

"ultimate Mediterranean light . . . so beautiful, so all-present": Ibid., 49.

95 "naked eyeball of God": *The Greek Islands* (New York, 1978), 18.
"who like life easy . . . just escapes being": Ibid., 271–72.

97 "What are they after, our souls": *Mythistorema*, 8, George Seferis, *Collected Poems*, 12.

5. OF GODS, DEMIGODS, AND DEMONS

99 "bathed naked": Lawrence Durrell, *Spirit of Place*, edited by Alan G. Thomas (London, 1988), 66.

100 *"We've got a language*: *Colossus*, 67.

101 "to milk life": Angelos Sikelianos, *Selected Poems*, 99.

102 "a deep breath I drew": Ibid., 29.

103 "The sun set over Acrocorinth": Ibid., 15.

106 "Drinking the sun of Corinth": *Voices of Modern Greece*, 151.

107 "dismal and deserted": *Colossus*, 75.

108 "long and devious route": Ibid., 79.
"the road to Epidaurus": Ibid., 76.
"could not have known": Ibid., 79–80.
"There will be no peace": Ibid., 79.
"Neither God nor the Devil": Ibid., 83.
"the intangible residue": Ibid., 84.

110 "My child": Sophocles, *Oedipus at Colonus*, ll. 1–2, in *Three Theban Plays*, translated by Robert Fagles (Penguin Books, 1984), 283.
"Here, stranger": ll. 763 ff., ibid., 326.

111 "something godlike": Euripides, *Helen*, l. 560, in *The Bacchae and Other Plays*, translated by Philip Vellacott (Penguin Books, 1973), 152.

112 "At Troy, nothing": George Seferis, *Collected Poems*, 178–79.

113 "artistic to the core . . . the grandest and emptiest city": *Colossus*, 86–89.

114 "Where are the buffalo": "First Impressions," 66.
"hippopotamic . . . until the gods": *Colossus*, 90.
"the first man I admired": *Modern Greek Poetry: Voice and Myth*, 200.

115 "played the mole . . . renunciator": *Colossus*, 91–92.
"take flight": Ibid., 93.

116 "a more powerful spirit": "First Impressions," 83.
"spills out into the open . . . *when we have ceased*": *Colossus*, 93–94.

117 "a flimsy little English car . . . the cold sweat": Ibid., 211–13.
"still going through the motion": Ibid., 215.

118 "To Argos," *Collected Poems*, 88–89.

120 "The Isles of Greece": *Don Juan*, Canto 3, ll. 86 ff., *The Poetical Works of Lord Byron* (London, 1945), 695.

121 Poets and travelers in the post-Byronic tradition: See David Roessel's dissertation "In Byron's Shadow: Modern Greece in English and American Literature from 1831–1914."

122 "vulgar, pushing": *Colossus*, 217.
"never in my life . . . perversely gay": Ibid., 222.
"the most easy-going": Ibid., 220.
"What would I do with an Englishman": Ibid., 218.

123 "sour, moth-eaten, bilious": Ibid., 220–21.
"melancholy Christmas carols": Ibid., 220.
"back to jail": Ibid., 224.
"antithetical anomalies": Ibid., 222.
"bovine righteousness . . . its unthisness": Ibid., 221–22.

124 "oft-kissed far-roving body": Nikos Kazantzakis, "Pilgrimage Through Greece," *Greece*, edited by Artemis Leontis (San Francisco, 1997), 34.
"freed men from the empty": *Plutarch's Lives*, translated by Bernadotte Perrin (London, 1928), Vol. I, 251–53.
" 'A long time now' ": Angelos Sikelianos, *Selected Poems*, 9.

6. GARDEN OF EARTHLY DELIGHTS

129 "men of inconstancy": *Angloelliniki Epitheorisi* (July–August 1950), 501.

132 "Had we too the good will": Yannis Ritsos, *Repetitions, Testimonies, Parentheses*, 31.
"What were they supposed to do?": Ibid., 32.

133 "like a young man": C. P. Cavafy, *Collected Poems*, 72.

134 "That we've broken their statues": Ibid., 34.
"small corner": From "The City," ibid., 28.
"range of their daily pleasures": Ibid., 144.

135 "understanding": The poem's title is "Understanding"; ibid., 86.

136 As Seferis has suggested: See "Letter to a Foreign Friend," in *On the Greek Style*, 171.
"glaring white town . . . piping hot": *Mani: Travels in the Southern Peloponnese* (London, 1984), 31–32.

137 "a whole world . . . close beside us": "Letter on 'The *Thrush*,' " in *On the Greek Style*, 103–4.

138 "shabby": *Colossus*, 113.
"almost a ringer": Ibid.

"drawn to the spot . . . painted in raw": Ibid., 120.

"down to earth . . . worldly in the best sense": Ibid., 121–22.

139 "an equal role": Ibid., 121.

"most gracious and lovely . . . of royal descent": Ibid., 106.

"even the most beautiful . . . sheds a distinct fragrance": Ibid., 108.

"a thousand and two things . . . A ridiculous situation": George Theotokas, *Tetradia Imerologiou* [*Diary Notebooks*] (Athens, 1980), 116.

140 "peasant woman . . . not wanted": *Colossus*, 109–11.

141 "starved dream of love . . . almost the symbol": Ibid., 111–12.

142 "were always predominant . . . train to walk upright": "First Impressions," 86.

143 "she can do just as great deeds": *Spirit of Place*, 370.

she may seem "enslaved . . . the queen bee": Ibid., 375.

"violent coherence . . . poetry and vehemence": Ibid., 370.

"sacredness of emotion . . . the uncritical enjoyment": Ibid., 373.

"a certain innocence": Ibid., 370.

"She can let her sensuality": Ibid., 377.

"it lacks . . . defeats words": Ibid., 376.

145 "quick bad lands . . . From this sublime": *Colossus*, 157–62.

147 "dried up prune": Ibid., 137.

"the last Paradise on earth": Ibid., 144.

"sorely-laden donkey": Ibid., 136.

148 "barbarious": Ibid., 144.

"she will quiver like a snake": Ibid., 141.

"the Shangri-la of the cinema . . . its character, its charm": "First Impressions," 70–71.

149 "this stupendous gift": *Colossus*, 165.

"heady, molten wine": Ibid., 163.

"lousy—without taste": "First Impressions," 70.

"especially because you are . . . give without motive": Ibid., 75.

"magnificent homage . . . an equally florid": *Colossus*, 167.

150 "always just enough progress": Ibid., 170.

"thousands of innocent men": Ibid., 172.

"Such is America today": Ibid., 173.

151 "crazy with boredom": Ibid., 187.

"the full devastating beauty . . . In the belly": Ibid., 189–90.

152 "a tropical Iceland . . . a state of dazed, drunken": Ibid., 191–92.

"Tell the king": Quoted in George Seferis, *Delphi*, translated by Philip Sherrard (Munich, 1963), 12.

"a long glimpse . . . we move in clock time": *Colossus*, 195–96.

153 "again we find ourselves . . . we must call things eternal": *Delphi*, 13.
154 "all the signs of divinity": *Colossus*, 203.
   "chastened . . . to the final expression": Ibid., 205–6.
155 "living openly . . . living thus, as a river": Ibid., 207.
   "weird spectacle": Ibid., 208.
   "the little band of friends": Ibid., 210.
   "sparkles like a chandelier . . . the ideal meeting place": Ibid., 209–10.
156 "I love those men . . . the mother of nations": Ibid., 210–11.
   "a teeming mist . . . There will be no resuming": Ibid., 224–26.
157 "man-sized world": Ibid., 235.
   human phenomenon: Ibid., 239.
158 "Houses, an embassy": James Merrill, *Selected Poems, 1946–1985* (New York, 1994), 132.

7. SAILING OUT OF PARADISE

160 "luxurious appearance": *Colossus*, 233.
   "in another world . . . clean, vacuous": Ibid.
161 "praying that by some miracle": *The Air-Conditioned Nightmare* (New York, 1945), 12.
   "the only one we will ever know . . . make it a Paradise": Ibid., 22–23.
162 "unorganized lunatic asylum": Ibid., 53.
   "roseate, insidious opulence": Ibid., 96.
   "mad, completely mad": Ibid., 240.
163 "Glorious gentle France!": Ibid., 75.
   "but not of it": This letter, and other previously unpublished letters from Miller to Seferis, and from Seferis to Miller, quoted below, are in the George Seferis Collection, Manuscript Division, Department of Rare Books and Special Collections, Princeton University Library.
   Claude Bragdon: Claude Fayette Bragdon (1866–1946), architect, writer, theatrical designer and producer, Theosophist, yoga practitioner. The chapter to which Miller refers is the brief essay "The Delphic Movement (Angelo Sikelianos)" in Bragdon's 1929 collection of essays and reminiscences, *Merely Players*. It is among the earliest of the very few commentaries on Sikelianos to appear in the United States before Miller's evocation of the poet, via George Katsimbalis, in the *Colossus*.
170 "Powell's book on Jeffers": Lawrence Clark Powell, *Robinson Jeffers: The Man and His Work* (Los Angeles, 1934).
172 "small blue bud of flame . . . more unreal than ever": *Letters*, 134.

173 "to round off": *Colossus*, 243.
     "called": *Letters*, 135.
     "the system closing in . . . an utterance": Ibid., 136.
     "without the offensive spirit . . . but it's like the meeting": Ibid., 138.
174 "ridden off gigantically . . . away with the fleet": Ibid., 144.
175 "except bad poems . . . all blacked out": Ibid., 148.
176 "An Anthology of Exile": (Editions Poetry London, 1945).
178 "literary inflation": *Climax in Crete*, Foreword by Lawrence Durrell (London, 1946), 5.
179 "was cracking": Ibid., 14.
180 "who might be treated": Ibid., 18.
     "a most terrific screaming sound": Ibid., 21.
     "a tremendous clatter": Ibid., 22.
181 "On May the 14th": Ibid., 53.
     "Hodja claimed": Ibid., 88.
     "to make the war seem misty . . . The youth who never has aspired": Ibid., 42–43.
182 "into a sea of blood . . . as distant": Ibid., 56–57.
     "old baboon": Ibid., 82.
183 "I won't give up": Ibid., 119.
     "all the humane feelings": Ibid., 149.
     "war does *not* bring out": Ibid., 151.
184 "staunch and willing comrade": Ibid., 163.
     "a rather rude joke": Ibid., 165.
     "Information has recently": Ibid., 166.
185 "blew up": Ibid., 18.
     "with no sign of the defeated": The journal entries by Seferis referred to on this page and through page 189 are from *Meres* [*Days*], 4 (Athens, 1993), 66–140, covering April 23–September 27, 1941.
189 "the beautiful island bleeding": George Seferis, *Collected Poems*, 139.
190 "who is he who commands": "The Figure of Fate," Ibid., 142.
     "the pouch of the wind": Ibid., 144, 145.
192 "On the blackened ridge": Ibid., 282, end note for p. 145.
     "cooling [his] heels": Miller to Durrell, December 28, 1941, *Letters*, 152.

8. EDEN BURNING

193 "it must be frightful": Miller to Seferis, January 29, 1942.
194 By December the shortage: The principal source for the historical details

that follow is Mark Mazower, *Inside Hitler's Greece: The Experience of Occupation, 1941–1944* (New Haven and London, 1993), 32–41.

their ration cards used: Ibid., 38.

hauled away by municipal carts: Ibid.

the official price of bread: Ibid., 65.

195 "Once at sunset": Angelos Sikelianos: *Selected Poems*, 137–41.

197 "5 November 1941": *Fylla Katochis* [*Pages from the Occupation*] (Athens, 1987). Most further references to this source are identified by the date of the entry. The translation is by me.

198 "because, whether by deception": Ibid., 15.

"a man of profound spirit . . . to calm the demon": Ibid., 16–17.

199 ". . . they came out early": Odysseus Elytis, *The Axion Esti*, 34.

200 "Herr Professor": *Fylla Katochis*, 170.

201 "Will I see him again? . . . He always strengthened": Ibid., 103.

"When the two of us . . . All of us pay": Ibid., 127.

202 "after your brother": Miller to Seferis, January 22, 1950.

"A few hours ago": Ioanna Tsatsos, *My Brother George Seferis*, 239.

"by doing interesting things": Ibid., 241.

"little house": *Meres*, 5, 199.

". . . I remember still": George Seferis, *Collected Poems*, 188–89.

204 "like a drowning man . . . the tears running down": Durrell to Miller, c. mid-February 1946, *Letters*, 193.

205 "It has been almost two years": Seferis archive, Gennadius Library, Athens. My translation.

206 "But I love Seferis": Reported to me by a friend.

207 "the forces of evil . . . one ordered universe": From a commentary given to me by the poet.

"In the griever's courtyard": *Voices of Modern Greece*, 177–78.

208 "Enough if a sharp sickle": Ibid.

209 "the somewhat arbitrary movement": From a commentary given to me by the poet.

"How very much I loved you . . . For years and years": *Voices of Modern Greece*, 180–81.

210 "I hide behind simple things": From "The Meaning of Simplicity," Yannis Ritsos, *Repetitions, Testimonies, Parentheses*, 125.

211 "Women are very distant": Ibid., 138.

"The afternoon": Ibid., 135.

213 "The woman stood up": Ibid., 137.

"where the use of terror": Mark Mazower, *Inside Hitler's Greece*, 226.

214 Ioanna Tsatsos's diary: See *Fylla Katochis*, "9 September 1944," 177.

German First Mountain Division: *Inside Hitler's Greece*, 176.

village of Komeno: Ibid., 192 ff.

215 Distomo and Hortiati: Ibid., 212 ff.

"It was as if": *Fylla Katochis*, 161.

216 enormous commotion: *The Waldheim Report*, International Commission of Historians (Copenhagen, 1993), 185.

Asked many years later about the incident: Ibid., 199.

217 protest demonstration in Syntagma Square: *Inside Hitler's Greece*, 352–53.

218 "with images of the horror . . . *over there*": *Meres*, 4, 360–61.

". . . We come from the sands": George Seferis, *Collected Poems*, 155–57.

221 "My premonitions and the nightmares": *Meres*, 4, 371.

"A desire for the first time": Ibid., 369.

9. RISING FROM THE ASHES

223 "houses blown open": *Meres*, 5, 11.

227 "lunch with Brigadiers": Lawrence Durrell, *Spirit of Place*, 85.

"strange, smashing, dark-eyed woman": *Letters*, 169.

"tormented jewish-greek": Ibid., 171–72.

"a kind of refugee life": Ibid., 169.

"You will find it . . . to the dusty corners": *Reflections on a Marine Venus*, introduction by David Roessel (New York, 1996), 17–18.

228 "picturesquely": Ibid., 20.

"once famous . . . speechless with gratitude": Ibid., 23–24.

"But why didn't you tell me . . . dawdle away": Ibid., 41.

"infernal wreckage of war": Ibid., 26.

229 there are more allusions to the aftermath of war: See David Roessel, "Cut in Half as It Was: Editorial Excisions and the Original Shape of *Reflections on a Marine Venus*" (unpublished paper delivered at the British School in Athens, May 1997).

"our knowing in our hearts": Ibid.

230 "It only affects me": *Letters*, 175.

"we [presumably the British] . . . last four years": Ibid., 180.

231 "unbelievably sad . . . intellectual hunger": Ibid., 193–94.

"simply hemmed in by their gloom": Ibid., 196.

232 "tramp in the Eastern Mediterranean": *Reflections*, 25.

"the inevitable comparison . . . You stinking empty-headed": Ibid., 124.

"a soft-centred creature": Ibid., 127.

"What a country": Ibid., 173.

233 "escaped": *Justine* (Penguin Books, 1991), 13.

"the capital of memory . . . heart's mind": *Clea* (Penguin Books, 1991), 11.

"Cycladean simplicities": Ibid., 20.

"the affection and gratitude . . . simply the end": Ibid., 21–22.

234 "means yet another separation": *Reflections*, 180.

"born into the sexual intoxication . . . should not have been made plain": Ibid., 183.

"in the heart . . . the old inheritance": *Clea*, 273–76.

235 "firmly reactionary": *Spirit of Place*, 101.

236 "very nationalist . . . if they [i.e., the British]": *Meres* [Days], 6 (Athens, 1986), 147.

one of his biographers: Gordon Bowker, *Through the Dark Labyrinth: A Biography of Lawrence Durrell* (New York, 1997), 254.

he told an interviewer: Ibid., 307.

on returning to France: Ibid., 308.

237 "little meeting . . . there alone now": *Letters*, 211.

"the nexus for all news of Greece": Ibid., 174.

238 "enough force to work": Ibid., 176.

his friend Buffie Johnson: "Personal Reminiscences of Lawrence Durrell," *Deus Loci*, Vol. V, No. 1 (Fall 1981), 71.

"on rotten brine-soaked timbers": *Mythistorema*, No. 8. George Seferis, *Collected Poems*, 12.

239 "cocotte's bedroom": *Meres*, 5, 47.

"performances . . . a great deal of filth": Ibid., 52.

"climbing up words . . . hothouse atmosphere": Ibid., 56–57.

240 "with infinite gentleness": Ibid., 60.

"I don't think of anything now": Ibid., 65.

"The sun! The sun . . . Contours of mountains": Ibid., 66–68.

241 "gave me, for the first time": *Angloelliniki Epitheorisi* (July–August 1950), 501.

"The houses I had": George Seferis, *Collected Poems*, 161.

243 "the invisible fields": Ibid., 169.

"an affirmation of a moment": "Seferis," *Permanence de la Grèce* (Paris, 1948), 337.

"Day, angelic and black": George Seferis, *Collected Poems*, 169–70.

244 "difficulty": *Angloelliniki Epitheorisi* (July–August 1950), 501.

note to the second edition: *Dokimes* [Essays] (Athens, 1962), 365.

245 "Notice this": *Angloelliniki Epitheorisi* (July–August 1950), 504.

"somewhere round about here": *Mythistorema*, No. 8. George Seferis, *Collected Poems*, 12.

"a little farther": *Mythistorema*, No. 23. Ibid., 27.

Stratis Thalassinos: "Stratis Thalassinos Among the Agapanthi," ibid., 144.

"need to see the sun . . . I have the impression": *Meres*, 5, 104–5.

246 "there is a process of humanization": *Angloelliniki Epitheorisi* (July–August 1950), 505.

247 "no one explains the light": Ibid.

"toward the unknown . . . I've 'discovered' ": *Meres*, 5, 83.

248 "a mindless visionary": Ibid., 92.

"The situation around me": Ibid., 95.

"is an internecine jungle": Ibid., 100.

"From the middle of May": Ibid.

"musical instruments . . . With people, with cities": Ibid., 106.

249 "the mental confinement . . . One must get out": Ibid., 120.

250 "incomparable . . . I remember vividly": *Letters*, 216–17.

251 "I allowed too long a silence": Ibid., 202.

"I'm afraid that we've had a bad influence . . . While we cannot pay": *Spirit of Place*, 84–85.

PERMISSIONS

*

The author gratefully acknowledges the following sources:

C. P. Cavafy: From C. P. Cavafy: *Collected Poems*, revised ed., trans. by Edmund Keeley and Philip Sherrard. Copyright © 1992 by Edmund Keeley and Philip Sherrard. Reprinted by permission of Princeton University Press.

Lawrence Durrell: From *The Black Book, Prospero's Cell, The Greek Islands, Collected Poems, Reflections on a Marine Venus, Spirit of Place, The Alexandria Quartet,* and letters to George Seferis. Reproduced with permission of Curtis Brown Ltd, London, on behalf of the Estate of Lawrence Durrell. Copyright © the Estate of Lawrence Durrell.

Lawrence Durrell and Henry Miller: From *The Durrell-Miller Letters 1935–1980*. Copyright © 1963 by Lawrence Durrell and Henry Miller. Reprinted by permission of New Directions Publishing Corp. and Faber and Faber Ltd.

Odysseus Elytis: From "The Great Sally" in *The Axion Esti*, trans. by Edmund Keeley and George Savidis. Copyright © 1974 by Edmund Keeley and George Savidis. Reprinted by permission of University of Pittsburgh Press. In *Voices of Modern Greece*, trans. by Edmund Keeley and Philip Sherrard. Copyright © 1981 by Edmund Keeley and Philip Sherrard. Reprinted by permission of Princeton University Press.

INDEX

feris on, 239–41, 246, 247; Seferis's view of, 83–84, 239

Poseidon, 142

Prospero (character in *The Tempest*), 41

Prospero's Cell (Durrell), 28, 35, 37, 40, 43, 252

Psara, 191–92, 193, 194

Pythagoras, 47

Rallis, Ioannis, 217

Reflections on a Marine Venus (Durrell), 95, 227–29, 230, 231–33, 234–35, 252

Renoir, Pierre-Auguste, 140, 141

Repetitions, Testimonies, Parentheses (Ritsos), 132–33

Rhodes: home to Durrell after Second World War, 226–29; as subject of Durrell's *Reflections on a Marine Venus*, 227–29, 230, 231–33

Ridler, Anne, 99, 227, 229, 251

Ritsos, Yannis, 130–33, 209–13; "Afternoon," 211–12, 213; "Eurylochus," 131–33; "Miniature," 212–13; *Parentheses, 1946–1947*, 210–13; *Repetitions, Testimonies, Parentheses*, 132–33; *Romiosyni*, 210; "Women," 211

Romiosyni (Ritsos), 210

Russell, Pee Wee, 148

Russell and Volkening (agents), 165

"Sacred Way" (Sikelianos), 101–2

Salonika, 99, 215; postwar, 226

Schubert, Sergeant Fritz, 215, 216

Sciron, 100

Second World War: Athens during, 172, 178–79, 186–87, 193–94, 196–201, 216; France in, Miller's response to, 162–63, 164; Greece in, 10, 17, 50–51, 163, 165–66, 167, 169, 175, 179, 193–94, 196–201, 207, 213–18; Greek government-in-exile during, 186–87, 187–88; Greek poetry during, 206–13; Greek resistance to occupation in, 10, 163, 214; imminence of, 123, 149, 150; Italy in, 166, 170, 213, 226, 229; Nazi massacres in Greece during, 213–16; outbreak of, 48, 50–51; U.S.A. in, 169

Seferis, Angelos, 201–2, 221

Seferis, George: on Antoniou, 59–60; and brother Angelos's death, 202; as civil servant, 7, 216–17; correspondence with Durrell, 168, 174, 175–76; correspondence with Katsimbalis, 52–53, 129, 241, 242, 244, 245, 246, 247; correspondence with Miller, 163–71, 185–86; 202; on Crete during Second World War, 176, 185–87; death of, 204, 206; and Delphi, 153–54; and Durrell, 8, 235, 236, 237; in Egypt, 201, 203; and Elytis, 75; in exile during Second World War, 69, 167, 169–70, 185–92, 201; Fowles's views compared to, 94; funeral of, 204, 206; and Greek history, 63; as Greek national poet, 204–6; on Helen of Troy myth, 111–12; as jazz enthusiast, 148; and *kaimo tis Romiosinis*, 17, 54, 59; on Karyotakis, 75–76; and Katsimbalis, 8–9, 10, 11, 168–69; love of Greece, 5–6, 69;

Seferis, George (*cont.*)

and Miller, 5–6, 8, 10–11, 44, 56, 57, 60–61, 63, 69, 76, 87–89, 114, 160, 161, 221; as myth-maker, 61–69, 76–77; as Nobel Prize winner, 5, 62–63, 204; and Odysseus myth, 83–84, 129–30, 190–92, 238–39, 242, 243, 245, 247; on Orthodox Christianity, 136; *Paris Review* interview of, 63, 114; as part of group of Greek writers, 10, 49, 56, 221, 237, 251; as poet, 61–69, 128, 129–30; and political stance vs. dictatorship, 205–6; on Poros, 83–84, 239–41, 246, 247; returns to Greece after Second World War, 221, 238–39; Ritsos contrasted to, 130, 131; after Second World War, 216–17, 221, 223, 247–50, 251; during Second World War, 173, 176, 180, 185–92, 201, 218; in South Africa, 167, 168, 169–70, 189, 239; and Tsatsos, 90; vision in Athens, 246; vision of sunrise on Poros, 240, 246; visit to Ephesus and Asia Minor, 202–3; voyage to Greek islands with Miller and Katsimbalis, 81–82, 83–85, 89; "Waste Land feeling" and, 129; works: "At Troy, nothing . . . ," 112, 113; "Days of June '41," 189; "Engomi," 246; "Helen," 111–13; "In the Manner of G.S.," 6; *I Sterna* (*The Cistern*), 9; journal, 6–7, 8, 17, 64, 221, 223, 236, 240, 244, 247–48, 248–49; *The King of Asine and Other Poems*, 64, 237; "The King of Asini," 8, 64–69; "The Last Day," 64; "Last Stop," 218–21; "Les Anges Sont Blancs," 76–77; *Logbook I*, 16–18, 68; "Memory II: Ephesus," 202–3; *Mythistorema*, 61–62, 76, 97–98, 129, 245; "Narration," 16–18; "The Sentence to Oblivion," 68; "Stratis Thalassinos Among the Agapanthi," 190–92, 239; *Strophi* (*Turning Point*), 8; "Syngrou Avenue," 24; *Three Secret Poems*, 246; "Thrush," 69, 80, 83, 129, 241–45, 246–47, 248

Seferis, Ioanna, *see* Tsatsos, Ioanna

Seferis, Maro, 87, 168, 185, 187, 188

Seferis, Roxani, 201

"Sentence to Oblivion, The" (Seferis), 68

Shakespeare, William, 4, 40, 41

Sherrard, Philip, 31, 34, 56, 152, 252

Sikelianos, Angelos, 10, 70, 88, 128, 129; at Palamas's funeral, 203; as poet, 100–4; after Second World War, 231; works: "Agraphon," 194–96; "On Acrocorinth," 103–4; "Pan," 102–3; "The Sacred Way," 101–2; "Sparta," 124; "The sun set over Acrocorinth," 103–4

Smyrna, 150, 202, 241

Socrates, 243, 247

Solomos, Dionysios, 5, 171, 191–92, 194, 203

Sophocles: *Oedipus at Colonus*, 110–11

Sparta, 122–23, 166

"Sparta" (Sikelianos), 124

Spencer, Bernard, 18–19, 176, 235, 237; "A Spring Wind," 18–19

Spetses, 97; Durrell's view of, 95;